PAUL, LEAST OF THE APOSTLES

The Story of the Most Unlikely Witness to Christ

By Alain Decaux

Translated by Celia Sirois

Pauline
BOOKS & MEDIA
Boston

Library of Congress Cataloging-in-Publication Data

Decaux, Alain, 1925–
    [Avorton de Dieu. English]
    Paul, least of the Apostles : the story of the most unlikely witness to Christ / Alain
Decaux ; translated by Celia Sirois. — 1st English language ed.
        p. cm.
    Includes bibliographical references and indexes.
    ISBN 0-8198-5958-3
    1. Paul, the Apostle, Saint. 2. Christian saints—Turkey—Tarsus—Biography. I. Title.
BS2506.3.D4313 2006
225.9'2—dc22
    [B]
                                            2005032626

Cover design: Rosana Usselmann

Cover art: Fifteenth-century Deesis, Church of St. George, Leningrad Museum, Russia.
Archives of Paoline Edizioni, Rome, Italy.

Location photos:
    Todd Bolen / BiblePlaces.com: Tarsus, Antioch in Pisidia, Philippi, Corinth, theater in
Ephesus, marketplace in Ephesus, Colossae, Miletus.
    Jack Hazut / jhm@isrealimage.com: Damascus Gate in Jerusalem, Old City of
Jerusalem, and Cesaria.
    Mary Emmanuel Alves, FSP: Ruins of ancient Rome, Mamertime prison, and interior
of Mamertime prison.

Art pieces:
    "San Paolo nell'arte contemporanea," Edizioni San Paolo, Cinisello Balsamo (MI), and
the Archives of Paoline Edizioni, Rome, Italy.

Scripture quotations are from the *New Revised Standard version of the Bible,* copyright
© 1989 the National Council of the Churches of Christ in the USA. Used by permission.
All rights reserved.

The Martyrdom of St. Paul from New Testament Apocrypha edited by Wilhelm
Schneemelcher and Edgar Hennecke. © 1990 Westminster John Knox Press. Used by
permission of Westminster John Knox Press.

Original edition published in French under the title *L´avorton de Dieu—Une vie de Saint
Paul.*

Copyright © 2003, Desclée de Brouwer/PERRIN

First English language edition, 2006

Published by Pauline Books & Media, 50 Saint Paul's Avenue, Boston, MA 02130-3491.
www.pauline.org.

Printed in the U.S.A.

Pauline Books & Media is the publishing house of the Daughters of St. Paul, an interna-
tional congregation of women religious serving the Church with the communications
media.

1 2 3 4 5 6 7 8 9   11 10 09 08 07 06

To Bernard Decaux, my brother

CONTENTS

1

NO MEAN CITY

This story begins with a murder, a lynching of the kind the world has too often seen. To be specific, this murder was a stoning. Authorized legally as well as religiously, the execution was not the work of monsters but of ordinary men filled with a hatred that unleashed all their baser instincts. Each one armed himself with stones to hurl with increasing speed and strength at the living target; this killing was a game of skill.

The year was A.D. 34; the place, outside the city of Jerusalem. The man whom the crowd pelted with stones did not look for a way to protect himself. Kneeling motionless, he prayed: "Lord Jesus, receive my spirit" (Acts 7:59).

The blows increased. Bruises and blood marbled his body. Bones broke. The executioners threw down their outer garments at the feet of a young man who undoubtedly consented to the stoning (Acts 8:1)[1]—by action or by word?

One stone struck the victim head-on. He found the strength to whisper, "Lord, do not hold this sin against them" (Acts 7:60).

The man fell and died. His name was Stephen. The small Christian community of Jerusalem had chosen him to be one of their seven administrators when, falsely accused of speaking "blasphemous words against Moses and God" (Acts 6:11), he was handed over to the Sanhedrin. Not content to affirm his faith, he proclaimed it boldly, causing the whole assembly to cry out: "Stone him!"

The young man at whose feet the mob laid their cloaks was named Saul. He was from Tarsus, in Cilicia.

I have been drawn to Paul of Tarsus for more than forty years, ever since one of my friends said to me, "Did you know that Saint Paul never knew Jesus?" Since that time, I have wondered about Paul. I have "met" him in the places where he lived, where he walked, and where he stopped; where he proclaimed Christ to Jews, evangelized pagans, and wrote letters that have become foundational sources of Christianity. I have "seen" him the object of hatred, imprisoned, scourged many times, stoned once yet still surviving. I have visited Ephesus before Tarsus, Thessalonika before Jerusalem, Rome before Corinth. From this convoluted trajectory a figure of immeasurable greatness emerged before my eyes. I waited twenty years to dedicate a book to him. And I ask myself: was it to avoid confronting this overpowering personality that I chose instead to tell Bible stories to children?

The man was larger than life. Fool for Christ: *apostolus furiosus.* His burning faith disturbed people and his many contradictions disrupted things. Merciless persecutor of Christians—his methods anticipated those of twentieth-century police states—and yet he recognized the Son of God when, on the road to Damascus, Jesus spoke to him directly. Self-proclaimed apostle. Mystic and militant. Neurotic. Suffering a thousand deaths when his convictions were questioned, but refusing to renounce even one. He alone seemed to understand that the future of Christianity lay in the Gentile mission. Master letter-writer with a genius for conversion. Architect of Christianity—its inventor, according to Reimarus in the eighteenth century; its founder, according to Nietzsche in the nineteenth—he imposed his vision of Christ and, well before the Gospels were written, he forged the principles that would guide the Church.

In the book of Paul's life each new fact contradicts the one before it. He seems to have enjoyed erasing his own footprints. He exhausts his biographers and sometimes exasperates them. Yet they forgive him because he is unique.

Tarsus stretched along the foothills of the Taurus Mountains in southern Turkey, that great chain that juts out over the Mediterranean

Sea by several hundred miles. A half-century before the birth of Saul—Paul's original name—elephants, lions, leopards, ostriches, hyena, onagers (wild asses), bears, wild boars, and panthers lived in these mountains. On September 5, 51 B.C. the aedile* Caelius, needing wild animals for a public spectacle he was planning, wrote to Cicero, then governor of Cilicia: "Since Pasticus sent Cuirio ten panthers, it would be a disgrace if you did not send me many more." One wonders if Cicero did.

The animal life in this region has grown rare, but at the beginning of the first century, when Saul lived in this world, it was far from extinct. And everywhere that these wild animals were suppressed wild men emerged to take their place.

At the time Saul was born, Octavian, the grandnephew and adopted son of Caesar, was finally coming to the end of a bitter fourteen-year war against Antony, Cassius, and Brutus. According to the Roman historian Dio Cassius, Octavian fought this war "with more vigor than any man, with more wisdom than a man of many years." Since he was already emperor, the senate bestowed on him the sacred name Augustus and the title *Princeps senatus,* which would be renewed five times, penultimately in 3 and finally in 13. Between these two dates Saul's birth increased by one the population of Cilicia, the province over which the Roman Empire imposed the crushing weight of its power.

IN A.D. 51 THIS SAME SAUL, now known as Paul, declared: "I am a Jew, from Tarsus in Cilicia, a citizen of an important city" (Acts 21:39). He doesn't mention the date of his birth. The lifelong baggage that we carry—surname, first name, age, birthplace—was totally unfamiliar to the people of the first century. Lacking more precise markers, most scholars locate Saul's birth sometime between A.D. 6 and 10 Some, and I count myself among them, choose the middle ground of A.D. 8. This makes Paul ten years younger than the Christ who will consume his life. Jesus wrote nothing but said a great deal. Paul spoke less but wrote a great deal—not enough that we might know his family or his childhood, but just enough so that we might later follow his steps and, even better, try to understand him. Add to this the great good fortune of his encounter with Luke, "the beloved physician" (Col 4:14), who, moved by admiration, became Paul's chronicler. The writings of Paul and Luke combined restore this

---

* A Roman official in charge of public games (Ed.).

illustrious person to us to an extent practically unequaled in ancient history.[2] Paul's thought is much better known to us today than that of Tiberius, his contemporary. The biographer delights in this advantage.

Tarsus, no "mean city"? As an affluent port city, it deserved infinitely more than this false modesty. Consider the map of modern-day Turkey. To the east and to the bottom of the Mediterranean, the coast descends perpendicularly toward the south as though wanting to close off the great river that it helped to form. Tarsus lies before this angle and to the right, stretching toward Syria and Lebanon. With some audacity, the German Dieter Hildebrandt, an early Pauline scholar, wrote: "The place is well chosen." Anticipating the reader's astonishment, he went on to explain: "The place as it is situated gives the impression that a genius of religious history, without much reflection, pointed his pencil on one of the ancient maps of the world and missed, by just a few millimeters, the point where East meets West in a hidden union." A striking image!

The oldest description of Tarsus dates from the first century. Strabo described it as "situated in a plain," not far from the sea: "The Cydnos River flowed through the middle of the city, along the young men's gymnasium. As the river's source was not far from the city, and it traversed a steep gorge just before reaching it, the water was cold and swift. As a result it was a great help to the animals and to the people suffering from rheumatism."

Founded by the Hittites around 1400 B.C., Tarsus was later conquered, ravaged, and occupied by many peoples, among them Assyrians, Macedonians, Seleucids, and Armenians. It saw Cyrus, king of Persia, and Alexander the Great. Galloping toward Asia and glory, Alexander bathed in the icy water of the Cydnos and almost died of it. Annexing Tarsus in 64 B.C., Rome made it the capital of the province of Cilicia. It pleased Pompey, Caesar, and Cicero. In 41 B.C. a young queen, endowed with a nose that would enter history, disembarked from her trireme [an ancient warship] "adorned with gold and royal purple," to conquer Antony.

Even now Cleopatra is honored in Tarsus, a city of 185,000 inhabitants that is filled with contrasts: ancient shops crushed between modern structures; overloaded donkeys indifferent to the diesel fumes of trucks; scooter salesmen adjoining kneeling rug repairers; centuries-old mosques lost among one-way streets. In the middle of the main road, I saw flying from the top of a mast the Turkish flag—red with a white star and crescent. It marked the monumental entrance at which, it is said, the last Egyptian queen was welcomed. Archaeologists believe that it was in fact constructed sometime after the royal visit. No matter. Leaving Paul for a moment, I stopped to dream of this rare woman, beloved of Caesar and of Antony.

Suddenly, at the threshold of the old city—with its strident music and the smell of spices—I spied a notice: *Saint Paul's Wall Excavation.* Kept out by a chain link fence—paid admission only—I noticed a long trench at the bottom of which were walls in fairly good condition. How astonishing it would be to discover Paul's house! Experts agree that these walls are Roman, but they describe them as nothing more than a spot where drinking water was protected by masonry.

I was persuaded to look elsewhere. Searching the soil a few years ago, Turkish archaeologists uncovered a Roman road still intact. It stretches about 650 feet before plunging under ground not yet excavated. I could not resist; I went down and walked on the stones, convinced that the mystic traveler—as our guide of the same name liked to call him—had one day used this road to launch on foot his conquest of souls.

All that remains of the Cydnos River is a stream of greenish water that, having changed its course, meanders lazily toward the sea. Without it, would Tarsus even have existed? It joined the city to the Mediterranean and made it a port laden with the wealth of three continents. Heavy sailing ships crossed the river, some gliding to the open waters, others arriving from Alexandria, Ephesus, Corinth, Rome, and Spain.

Winter is mild, but summer soon brings the "dog days" of oppressive heat. From the river's edge I look for the child Saul. I imagine him approaching a pile of iron extracted from the mines of the Taurus; bales of wool from the sheep of the plains of Cilicia; rolls of cloth—wool and linen; cords of wood for construction floating down the river from the mountains of Taurus; rows of jars filled to overflowing, some with the excellent wine of Cilicia, others, carefully wrapped, with aromatic spices and perfumes.

Here is a paradox: this city, which seemed only to exist for commerce, concealed an intense intellectual life. Once again Strabo attests: "The inhabitants of Tarsus are so passionate about philosophy [and] have such encyclopedic minds that little by little their city eclipses Athens, Alexandria, and all the other cities you can name for giving birth to certain sects or philosophical schools." The people of Tarsus were proud of their city and yet they left it voluntarily. "Those who are of this country do not remain there but go elsewhere to complete their education. Once they have completed [it], they install themselves elsewhere; few come back to their homeland. In the other cities we have mentioned, with the exception of Alexandria, it is quite the opposite." Will the call of the "great beyond" win over the love of one's city?

I picture the young Saul stretching his neck to see the philosopher Athenodorus, meditating along the river. Formerly Octavian's tutor—and having arrived at the threshold of old age—he was installed at the head of the local government in order to free the city from the pillaging of a certain Boethius, "wicked priest, wicked citizen." Expelled from Tarsus with his accomplices, this Boethius had the city covered with inscriptions defaming Athenodorus. One that remains says: "Action belongs to young men, counsel to mature men, and gas to old men." A Greek philosopher in charge; what more could a city want, even if it is Roman?

Tarsus justifies a hundred times over the praise that Xenophon bestowed upon it: "a city great and happy." Nations, religions, languages—all live together within it, without conflict.

"Circumcised on the eighth day, a member of the people of Israel, of the tribe of Benjamin, a Hebrew born of Hebrews; as to the law, a Pharisee" (Phil 3:5): thus would Paul proudly present himself to his contemporaries. If there can be no doubt that his parents were themselves pharisaical Jews, the question remains: when did they arrive in Tarsus? Saint Jerome, having information from Origen—a theologian born in the first century and unrivalled master of the catechetical school of Alexandria—believed that "the parents of Paul were originally from Gischala, in the province of Judea." He summed up: "When the whole province was devastated by the Roman armies and the Jews dispersed throughout the world, they were transported to Tarsus, a city of Cilicia." He even suggested that Saul, born in Judea, was just a baby when he arrived in Tarsus.

"I am a Roman citizen!" Throughout his life Paul claimed this honor that was his through his father. At the time there were no more than four or five million Roman citizens in the Empire, making up ten percent of the total population. There is no doubt that some Jews were citizens. Caesar granted the right to Antipater, who transmitted it to Herod the Great, his son. Flavius Josephus, a Pharisee like Saul, though settled in Rome, received the same honor from Vespasian. It is believed that Tiberius Alexander, a Jew from Alexandria and nephew of the famous

Philo, held his Roman citizenship from his father. He used it to advantage to gain a position in the imperial administration. Initiated into the equestrian order, he became prefect of Egypt in 66 and was among the highest ranks of those who would carry Vespasian into power. Florus, a Roman governor of Judea, was censored for having had Jews of the equestrian order scourged and crucified, confirming the presence of Roman citizens among the elite Jews of Jerusalem. In Ephesus, Delos, and Sardis, Jews who were Roman citizens were dispensed from military service which, according to the school of M. de La Palice, proves that they existed.

In his *Antiquities of the Jews,* the subtle Flavius Josephus, historian of the Jewish people, demonstrated that in countries the Romans colonized and controlled, his coreligionists represented a useful and effective link with those peoples less inclined to adapt to the laws and customs of their conquerors. There is no doubt that this accommodation sometimes created crises of conscience for "romanized" Jews. Flavius Josephus himself admits to having been torn for a long time between the two. That is, until the day when he made himself the intermediary between Rome and Judea by proclaiming himself—we are never so well served as by ourselves—the "savior" of his people. Remember that the Romans perceived the Jews to be a coherent group—the "Jewish nation"—favored to the extent that they turned toward Rome.

To the Jews as to others, Roman citizenship could be granted individually or collectively. It was transferable. It only required that the father, at the birth of his son, make a declaration to the appropriate authority, and the child became a Roman citizen from that day. Citizenship was proven by witnesses. It was recommended that one have a copy made of the declaration of citizenship from birth. But carrying this document—inscribed on tablets bound with a heavy thong—was not practical. The Letters or Acts never mention such a document.

Was Paul's father the first of his family to have received Roman citizenship? It seems unlikely. One questions whether such a coveted honor would have been given to Jews newly emigrated from Palestine. More likely, as Jean-Robert Armogathe would have it, the honor itself demonstrates that Paul's family had lived in Tarsus for many generations. Paul's parents did not come from Gischala. Paul was born in Tarsus, as Luke affirms. And Michel Trimaille concludes, "It is hard to see why Luke would have invented Paul's birthplace." So much for Origen and Saint Jerome.

Citizenship was most often won by seizing the opportune time. Thus in the bloody conflict that pitted Octavian and Antony against Brutus and Cassius, Tarsus sided with the first two, which brought upon the city the wrath of Cassius—and what wrath! According to the Greek historian Appian, the city was made to pay the "exorbitant sum" of 1,500 talents (one talent = 66 lbs. of silver). This meant not only selling the goods of the city, but—it takes one's breath away—selling into slavery a large part of the population as well. Finding Tarsus depleted and devastated, Antony dispensed the city from making any contribution to the war.[3] Then, having triumphed over Antony at Actium, Octavian held it even more dear; he lavished gifts upon the city.

In the midst of the frequent tumult noted by Dio Cassius, it would have been enough for just one Jew from Tarsus, already distinguished by his wealth, to support the winning party to justify such favors as citizenship.

Henceforth all responsible administrators, at whatever level they might be, were required to respect a Roman citizen. On more than one occasion this would affect Paul's life.

THE FAMILY WAS—apparently without effort—established in this Diaspora, which for many years had scattered Jews far from Palestine: in Asia, in Europe, and in Africa. The Greek word *Diaspora* means dispersion. Not all Jews whom Nebuchadnezzar deported in 586 B.C. took advantage of the edict of Cyrus (538 B.C.) allowing them to return to their homeland. Some did not want to leave the flourishing businesses they had established in Persia. By hellenizing the Middle East, Alexander and his successors encouraged relocation to Greek-speaking regions. According to Philo, one million Jews lived in Egypt, and Alexandria had become the largest Jewish city in the world. Others established themselves in Greece, Rome, and elsewhere.

The first mention of a Jewish community on the shores of the Tiber is from 139 B.C.: the magistrate Cornelius Hispanus denounced those rites and cults liable "to infect Roman morality." In 59 B.C. Cicero criticized this "barbaric superstition" and, according to the prefect Flaccus, was astonished at the large number of Jews who participated in it. "You know what a large crowd they are, how many in their group and what influence they have in their gatherings."[4] At the beginning of the first century, about fifty-five million people lived in the Empire. One million in the East were Jews, with another million elsewhere in the known world. Under the rule of Augustus, Strabo again underscored that at the

time of Scylla (ca. 85 B.C.) this people had already "invaded all the cities."
He added that "it would be hard to find a place where these people had
not been received and become rulers." Toward the end of the first century, Flavius Josephus affirmed with pride: "There is no people in the world
that does not possess some element of our race." Caesar declared himself
the friend of the Jews. Augustus and Tiberius were quick to punish those
who molested them. In the first century, the Jews enjoyed in the Roman
Empire a jurisdiction of their own—however limited—where their
dietary laws were kept. They were exempt from serving in the army so as
not to have to break the Sabbath. In Rome uniquely they were allowed to
observe their rituals with certain stipulations. The Romans were willing
to recognize in the sacrifices they offered in honor of YHWH the equivalent of the homage offered to the emperor-god. Even better: an annual
tax for the Jerusalem Temple was collected throughout the Diaspora, and
laws from the time of Augustus permitted Jews to receive and to deliver
this contribution. There was something for everyone.

The big question was that of the relationship between Israel and the
Diaspora. The question was raised in antiquity—certain older Jews
looked down on the expatriates—and it continues to be raised today. In
answer, Schalom Ben-Chorin, a learned Jew of the twentieth century,
draws a parallel between Jesus and Paul. He sees in Jesus "a typical representative of Palestinian Judaism"; we would say today that he is a *Sabra*.
He spoke only Hebrew or Aramaic, his culture was rooted in the Hebrew
Bible, and he spoke only to Jews. This was not the case with Paul, who
admitted to having made himself a Jew with the Jews and Greek with the
Greeks, becoming "all things to all people" (1 Cor 9:19–23). Such behavior leads Ben-Chorin to discern in him "the attitude characteristic of a
Diaspora Jew, of *the hyphenated Jew,* the citizen of two worlds [or perhaps
it would be more exact to say 'of three worlds'], the Jewish world, the
Hellenistic world, and the Roman world."

Having discovered Jesus, Paul would have to wage an ongoing battle
to maintain his Jewishness at the heart of Christianity.

WHAT CAN WE SAY of the Jews of Tarsus at the start of this era? Great
in number, they were not marginalized; no text mentions a Jewish quarter. They willingly acceded to the administration of the city that welcomed them without reservation. They practiced their religion freely in a
city of many cults, among which the first was the official cult of Rome;

from the second year of his reign, the emperor Augustus was made god. In this Roman city of Greek culture, the temples dedicated to the gods of Olympus occupied the first position, but the "mystery religions" also had their place. Born in Anatolia with Cybele, in Thrace with Dionysius, in Egypt with Isis and Osiris, in Syria with Adonis, and in Iran with Mithras, they stimulated the senses with "emotive symbols, intoxicating songs, and joyous festive dances."[5] The zealous worshipers of Mithras immersed themselves in the blood of a bull still living; those of Adonis permitted voluptuous embraces in his temple. A Jew of the Diaspora would be open to the subtleties of Greek philosophy but would look with disapproval, if not with sheer horror, at the spectacle of unbridled licentiousness that was pagan worship. We find an explicit trace of this sentiment, which stayed with Saul all his life, in the letter he will later write to the fledgling Christian community of Rome:

> They became futile in their thinking, and their senseless minds were darkened. Claiming to be wise, they became fools; and they exchanged the glory of the immortal God for images resembling a mortal human being or birds or four-footed animals or reptiles. Therefore, God gave them up in the lusts of their hearts to impurity, to the degrading of their bodies among themselves (Rom 1:21–24).

Enlightening.

Of Jesus' childhood we know at least that he "increased in wisdom and in years" and that he "was obedient to [his parents]" (Lk 2:52, 51). Of Saul's, we know nothing. Perhaps the life of one Jewish child of that time was like that of all other children. We can picture Saul, frail and crying, emerging from the womb of his mother, who sat in the birthing chair and was assisted by skilled women. Congratulations abounded: *Praise God!* A boy, which meant that the Most High had blessed this house. We can wager that at the birth of the baby's little sister, the expressions of joy were greatly muted.[6] We read in the Talmud: "Girls are false treasure! And they have to be watched all the time!"

The Scriptures trace back to Abraham the practice of circumcision of a boy eight days after his birth: "You shall circumcise the flesh of your foreskins, and it shall be a sign of the covenant between me and you. Throughout your generations every male among you shall be circumcised when he is eight days old, including the slave born in your house and the one bought with your money from any foreigner who is not of your offspring" (Gen 17:11–12). In each community in the first century, a specialist—the *mohel*—performed the rite according to a precise method: "Make the incision, tear the membrane, suck the blood, and place on the wound a dressing of oil, wine, and cumin."

His first name received on the day of circumcision—*Shaoul*—recalled the first King of Israel, incontestably the greatest man of the tribe of Benjamin. Saul, *Saoulos* in Greek, would only become Paul much later. From the time the little boy began speaking, his father began to teach him the Ten Commandments. The head of the family draped himself in a white prayer shawl with a blue border: the *tallith*. (The white and blue are the colors of the State of Israel today.) Daily the little one had to repeat the same verses: "Blessed are you, Adonai, God of Abraham and God of Isaac and God of Jacob, great God, maker of heaven and of earth, our shield and the shield of our fathers, our strength from generation to generation." Every day, the same words, the same form, the same rhythm, the same beauty. The child was immersed in the presence of YHWH.

AT FIVE YEARS OLD Saul discovered school—a great novelty. I envision him toddling in a tunic that hits his knees, while his forelocks dance at his temples (an obligation originating in a text from the Pentateuch: "You shall not round off the hair on your temples"—Lev 19:27). No desks; the students wrote on their knees. Each Jewish school possessed the text of the Torah inscribed on parchment scroll. Rocking front to back, the children recited pages of it in loud voices that sometimes became clamorous. Such memorization would give them, for the rest of their lives, perfect recall of those laws it would be a grave fault to forget.

Did Paul attend a Greek school? Tradition would not have encouraged his family to send him to one. He studied in a Jewish school, but in Greek. In Palestine, from the fourth century B.C., Aramaic had become the *lingua franca* to the neglect of Hebrew. In the Diaspora, instruction offered in the synagogues was in Greek. The sacred texts were learned in Greek, which did not preclude a first reading in Hebrew. Paul discovered the Bible in the version known as "the Septuagint," a Greek version composed in Alexandria in the third century B.C. Everything points to the fact that his religious culture was derived from this version.

Exegetes—and nothing escapes them—have discerned in it Paul's understanding of the word "sin," as well as expressions such as "divine inheritance" and "earthly journey." The first Christian theological concepts about the one God, about his speech—*logos,* the Word—and about the movement toward one universal Church "took root in the language of the Septuagint."[7]

Another feature that would weigh heavily on Paul's future choices was his membership as a Pharisee. *Pharisee, son of Pharisees.* To understand the Judaism of the first century, it is necessary once again to return to Flavius Josephus. From the time of Jonathan (ca. 160), he distinguished certain "philosophies" or sects "who differed in their opinions on human affairs. They are known as the Pharisees, the Sadducees, and the Essenes." The Sadducees prided themselves on their descent from the priestly family of Aaron. A sort of aristocracy attached to the Temple, they were close to Roman power and the majority of high priests belonged to their party. "The Pharisees," as Flavius Josephus goes on to say, "have imposed on the people, as though coming from the tradition of the fathers, prescriptions not written in the Law of Moses and therefore rejected by the Sadducees, who say that only what is written is legally binding, which excludes the tradition of the fathers." It is obvious that Flavius Josephus had no esteem for the Sadducees, "who have only convinced the wealthy and found no followers among the common people." This was not the case with the Pharisees, quite the contrary. "They have much influence among the crowds who readily believe them, even when they speak against the king and the high priest." Reading Flavius Josephus—without whom we would not understand the great diversity of the society in which Paul lived—leaves no doubt that the Essenes were his favorite sect. He granted them more space than he gave to the other two groups combined.

To this day we remain astonished by the obligation that devolved upon the Pharisees to keep 613 commandments. But this is no reason to misconstrue their constant claim at that time: they considered the Law to be an instrument rather than an imposition, and insisted that it must not remain the prerogative of the priests only; each person must strive for holiness. The Pharisees sought to free themselves from the priestly establishment, from the hellenized Herodian kings, and from the Sadducean priests bundled up in their complacency. They wanted to be "just, pure," learned in the Law. They remained close to the common people, opened schools, welcomed the sick and the poor. Unlike the Sadducees, who denied the immortality of the soul, they believed in the resurrection of the dead. Would Christians be so different?

RETURNING TO WHAT WE KNOW of Saul as an adult, it is tempting to attribute to him from youth a difficult character, to see in him a tendency to rebellion. That would only be so to the extent that a young "grumbler" was not quickly reduced to silence by the absolute authority of the head of the Jewish family and the corporal punishments he might inflict. If we are inclined to think of him as pious, it is because he was a Pharisee. It is also because a Jew—young or old—situated his day entirely under the sign of prayer.

From the rising of the sun, Saul turned in the direction—every Jew knows it—of the Jerusalem Temple and offered the first prayer of the day: "Hear, O Israel: the LORD is our God, the LORD alone" (Deut 6:4). At least three times a day—morning, afternoon, and evening—he thanked God for the blessings granted to him. Each day he strove to offer as many "blessings" as he could. Certainly it is impossible to know if Saul as a child was willing—or not—to enter into this ritual. But it is unthinkable that he would not go to the synagogue each week with his parents.

Can we stop short of attributing to Saul those impulses that abruptly launch one, heart racing and breathless, toward this God whose sovereign presence makes itself suddenly felt?

Traditionally, wealthy Diaspora Jews had their children educated in several languages. Saul already spoke two from infancy: Hebrew, learned of necessity, and Greek, the mother tongue, well named as it was learned at the mother's knee. The Greek spoken in most parts of the Empire was *koine* ("common"): the Greek everyone understood. The Acts of the Apostles also indicates that Paul knew Aramaic as well, though he himself in his letters used only a word or two from this language—*abba* or *maranatha*—which belonged to the earliest Christian tradition. He wrote nothing in Latin; remember that he lived in a city where all officialdom was Roman: power, army, police. Therefore, everyone must have had to at least manage in the official language of government, which was Greek. The revenge of Socrates' homeland on its Roman conquerors!

The Letters of Paul—the Epistles—are all written in Greek. He had read the great writers because he cited them: the Athenian poet Menander, the Cretan poet Epimenides, the stoic Arathos. The purists have scrutinized these texts under a magnifying glass, discerning in them familiarities, neologisms—often those of Cicero—but none of the affectation one would expect of a second language learned with effort. Paul's Greek flowed naturally.

WE KNOW NOTHING of his home—it was probably one of those cubic houses surrounded by gardens, so common in the East. We are free to imagine the kitchen aromas that would greet a Jewish child as he returned from school: warm bread from the oven, the staple of Jews in Palestine and in the Diaspora,[8] and grilled fish. Over a wood fire, a lamb being turned on the spit. A slave plucking a pigeon for the evening meal. Vegetables cooking in olive oil: cucumbers, beans, lentils. How could Paul not have relished such culinary delights, such as grasshoppers, of which, according to a treatise of the time, there were 800 edible species, and which were eaten cooked in salt and water as shrimp are today? All of these dishes were seasoned—with capers, cumin, saffron, coriander, mint, anise—to set one's mouth deliciously on fire.

Saul could not feign ignorance of those foods that were forbidden: pork unclean, rabbit not allowed, other animals only tolerated if they had been bled. His parents must have explained to him that "the life of all flesh is in the blood." It would be perilous to ingest an animal's life.

In his letters, Paul alludes to the trade that, no less than his apostolate, he will never cease practicing: *skenopoios*. The word can mean "tentmaker" or "leather worker." The Pharisaic tradition prescribed that a father teach his son a trade.[9] From whom would Paul have learned his but from his father? The biographer must see him spending time each day in the workshop learning from his fellow workers the secrets of their trade and—why not?—of their art. He must also imagine a watchful father overseeing this training from a distance. Saul's father was like one of those famous Jews of the Diaspora of whom there were many examples around the Mediterranean. The prosperity of Tarsus was built on the textile industry. In addition to embroidered cloth and fine linens, rough woven horsehair was one of the specialties of Cilicia.[10] Above all, ancient society had a pressing need for tents. They were required in all circumstances of life: as shelter for an individual and as coverings for chariots and ships, and even as huge canopies like the pavilions of our day that can accommodate up to 400 people. The market was immense. Tent workers were legion and, according to Dio Cassius, their large numbers led to contradictory debates: "One says that they are becoming too numerous and that they cause trouble and disorder. More recently they are treated like an integral part of the state and they are respected."

During his missionary journeys, Paul would often come into contact with textile workers and merchants: Lydia, the dealer in purple in Philippi; the weavers in Corinth; the dyers or traders of wool in Ephesus. When Paul began to evangelize Lycaonia, he used—as a kind of reflex— the route traditionally traveled by the merchants of Tarsus going to buy the wool of the goats of Taurus.

It is impossible to dismiss the image of the young Saul roaming with curiosity in the shop where his father's men busily worked. The material had a peculiar smell, especially when it was made of goats' hair. Saul would never forget it. They cut, they sewed, they assembled. If they were working with leather, it too had its own odor. As anyone who has visited the East knows, it is unthinkable for manual laborers to work in silence. Exclamations of all kinds abounded, along with replies that led to laughter and songs intoned at the top of one's voice in honor of the sun, the wind, the sea, and—of course—love.

When the tents were carried to the ships that would transport them, Saul no doubt ran behind the wagons—what child wouldn't?—and helped the young men pile the bundles onto the wharves.

Was Saul a brilliant student? Surely he was. Had he not been, his father would not have gathered the family to tell them that his son, having learned all the religion Tarsus could teach him, would now pursue his studies in Jerusalem, Judaism's "city on a hill."

I picture this Jewish family listening in silence to the pronouncement of its head. No one moved, not even Saul's mother, despite the tears she was unable to hold back. The choice of Jerusalem was not surprising, but at the same time it made a certain impression; a young man who went up to the city of David was not only a student but a pilgrim. *'Aliya* was the Hebrew word for this ascent.

How old was Saul at this point? Luke has him attesting that he arrived in Jerusalem "from my youth" (Acts 26:4). How old is that? Tradition gives some sense when it defines the stages of the rabbinate: a young Jew passed that of the Bible at five years old; at ten years, that of the Mishnah; at thirteen, the practice of the commandments; at fifteen, the Talmud; and at eighteen, the wedding.

Are we to imagine Saul was married at the time he left to study in Jerusalem? Logic brings us back to the question of his "youth," and I would tend to place his age closer to fifteen. Consequently, I'd suggest the year 23 as the probable date of his departure from Tarsus.

Nine years had passed since the death of the emperor Augustus and the start of Tiberius' reign. That year, a certain Jesus—*Yeshu'a*—was a woodworker in Nazareth, a village so obscure no one of that time ever mentioned its existence. He must have been about twenty-seven years old.

From the moment the young Saul was launched toward his destiny, one would imagine that he was possessed by an ardent flame and pushed by a mysterious force. Enough dreaming. We know for certain nothing of what he was, nothing of his experience. Nothing of what he thought at that time.

2

THE CORNERSTONE

To his left, the Taurus Mountains. To his right, the sea. As long as he was making his way to Adana, it seemed to Saul that he was still in Cilicia, still at home.

He set off on a Sunday morning, a precaution no Jew would fail to take, permitting him to travel six whole days before stopping for the Sabbath. Already his knapsack was cutting into his shoulder; it takes just a half day's walk before all travelers start to reproach themselves for having overpacked. In addition to the necessary clothing, it is certain that he had also included the playthings to which so many fifteen-year-old boys are attached. Was he traveling in winter? He wrapped himself in a mantle, his *chalouk,* a simple piece of material with a hole for the head. This woolen tunic fell well below the knees but didn't touch the ground. Not to be encumbered, he pulled it up and tucked it in his belt. Was he traveling in summer? He rolled up his mantle and stuffed it into his bag. Did he regret not having taken one of the ships that regularly left Tarsus bound for Caesarea Maritima? Probably not. I cannot imagine that his father would have dreamt of providing him such comfort: *'Aliyah* * obliged one.

WHEREVER ONE TRAVELED at this time, constant dangers loomed: bogs in which wagons broke down, flooded roads, slippery mud that

---

* *'Aliyah* is a Hebrew word meaning "to go live in Israel." The sense here is that going up to Israel brought with it certain obligations that the young Saul would now have to observe (Ed.).

17

sometimes swallowed travelers, falls in chasms, unmarked routes, inept guides, the threat of brigands and wild beasts, "deadly waters," pain caused by mosquitoes that one swatted before their bites could cause contagious disease (Pliny tried to defend himself from these by fumigation.) Add to this the language barrier and crowded lodgings at stopping places where people took advantage of travelers. These dirty inns were so disgusting or uncomfortable as to make one want to quickly escape. Saul discovered all this without pleasure.

Leaving Adana for Antioch, he crossed the colossal bridge—1,017 feet long—which the Romans built on each of the two branches at the mouth of the Sarus River. Two thousand years later, fourteen of the original twenty-four arches still stand.

Did he know the history of the places he passed through? Surely not. For him history was summarized in the Bible. The first Jew was Abraham. Saul knew his life by heart but could not date it, and he did not give that a thought. When he entered Syria, how would he have known that the kings of Ebla had made it an empire twenty centuries earlier, the oldest in Asia? Saul knew from the Bible that the Assyrians had definitively subjugated the region, destroying the cities and deporting the population. The name of Alexander would mean something to him, because Tarsus honored this Greek conqueror. He firmly believed that there had been many Jewish kings because the Bible named them.

Since the Bible did not mention other recent kings, he would have known only the name of Herod I, which resounded even to Cilicia and whom some people called "the Great." This Herod had received his crown from the Romans. At his death twenty years earlier, his kingdom had been divided among his three sons. But each of them only obtained it, at the pleasure of Rome, through bribes. From that time the Romans ruled as masters in Jerusalem. A procurator—or prefect—exercised power in the emperor's name. Would Saul know the name of Pompey? Perhaps, because all that was wrong came from there. In 63 B.C. Caesar's rival, having made an end of the pirates that infested the Mediterranean, attacked the kings who ruled over Asia Minor and defeated them. He had made Syria a Roman province. When he took Palestine, he found a country torn by civil war where many princes vied for power. This worked to the advantage of the Roman, who laid siege to Jerusalem, secured it, entered the Temple, and sacrilegiously violated the sanctuary. This story must have been recounted to Saul, but at fifteen years old, did he remember?

EVERY TRAVELER LOOKED to mingle with others with whom he was glad to share a stretch of the road for a time. One always learned something from those accustomed to covering the distance. They gave practical advice on road conditions, ambushes to avoid, and the dangers from which one must protect oneself.

Then suddenly a dazzling sight arose before Saul: Antioch! So proud was he of his native city, the adolescent could never have imagined that one like this existed. Imagine it stretching between the Orontes River and the slopes of Silpios: crossed from one end to the other by an avenue almost two and a half miles long, and bordered by porticoes with numerous streets winding among the hills, dales, ravines, torrents, high rocks, waterfalls, caves, and gardens. Flavius Josephus trenchantly said that Antioch, a Greek metropolis located in the East, was the third city of the world after Rome and Alexandria. I picture Saul ecstatic before the theater carved into the rock of Silpios, before the circus—650 feet long—the immense forum, and the imperial palace, built on an island of the Orontes River.

Five hundred thousand inhabitants! Saul lost himself in the chaos of people always rushing and—at least in appearance—happy to be alive. The rhetorician Libanios would show Antioch to be the City of Light *par excellence:* "The sun is replaced during the night by other lights. Night and day do not differ at home except for the means of lighting. Zealous workers do not notice the difference and continue cheerfully to hammer; and anyone who wishes can sing and dance all night since Hephaestus and Aphrodite share the hours."

Continuing onward, Saul needed to choose between two paths: to continue east to rejoin the Transjordanian trail—the beginning of a future Roman road—or to head south. I wager he preferred the south. Parallel to the Mediterranean ran a path blazed by the Egyptians around 2000 B.C. Originally conceived for transport on the backs of asses or mules, it was later used by heavy wooden wagons drawn by onagers [wild asses]. When camels were imported from Mongolia, caravans also used the path. Needless to say, pedestrians too found it useful. The path's name—the *Way of the Sea*—could stir the dreams of a young boy.

Leaving Antioch, Saul already knew that he should patiently wait for a convoy or a caravan. Traveling any other way would be foolish; brigands would prey on travelers to despoil them, and, in order to silence their cries, would even strangle them. Gangs of professional beggars, deserting soldiers, and fleeing slaves stole so much that Flavius Josephus wrote drolly, "If they cannot pilfer from others, they pilfer from each other." On this path the caravans permanently busied themselves without interruption in both senses. To have the right to join them, it was enough to pay the leader. Saul did so.

He had two antidotes to the monotony and boredom that threatened the journey: first, the young Pharisee could not transgress the obligations of prayer learned in childhood. They required that one take refuge in the thought of the Creator of all. Second, curiosity consumed him at fifteen years old, and the wonders that greeted him from one stage of his journey to the other provided quite a diversion.

Saul's bag grew heavier; his legs weighed more and more painfully. Then, four or five days' walk from Antioch, he caught sight of Laodicea (modern Latakia), famous for the fertility of its cultivated lands. A few days more and the path passed along the Adonis River, which, in the rainy season, coursed with a strange bright-red color from the iron ore in its bed. Further on, the mountain plunged perpendicularly into the sea and the caravan had to pass through a tunnel. Dug long before the Romans, this tunnel had demanded superhuman labor. Seneca detested these undergrounds, which were relatively numerous at the time: "Nothing is longer than this prison, nothing more obscure than these torches whose effect is not to help us see in the dark, but only to make themselves seen." Like him, Saul must have complained of the dust: "It flies up in a whirlwind and falls back on those who stirred it up."[1] Here was Byblos and its Phoenician port, largely open to the sea. Here was Berytus (Beirut), whose climate the emperor Augustus had so loved that he had given it the name of his dear daughter, Julia Augusta Felix. Here was Tyre the illustrious, watered by the rivers of Anti-Lebanon. All imports and exports met there: silver, iron, wheat from Syria, horses from Armenia, tin from Cornwall, lead from Spain, copper from Cilicia—a marvelous array of choices that, alas, concerned Saul not at all. At Caesarea Maritima, built by King Herod the Great, one left the Mediterranean to go east toward Jerusalem. They still had thirty-seven miles to travel, a two-day walk. When Paul came to the end, he would have covered a distance of 466 miles, from Tarsus to Jerusalem.

In the twenty-first century, no region of the world is as present to our minds as this one. The Arabs and Israelis who tear each other apart and kill each other lead us directly back to the Old and New Testaments. The names of Jerusalem, Gaza, and Hebron are familiar to our children. The confrontations of today stake out the course of King David as well as that of Jesus. I think of Paul Dreyfus, the great reporter who covered the Six-Day War. While on assignment for his newspaper, trying to count the cars destroyed and the airplanes downed, he felt drawn toward a past where people had confronted as much violence as we do today. From that time, he committed himself to finding "witnesses" who had disappeared two thousand years ago. Among these, Paul of Tarsus struck him more forcefully than all the others because he too had wandered between two camps. While the bullets whistled all around him, Dreyfus decided to devote his life to retracing Paul's itinerary. I owe him a great deal.

THE YOUNG SAUL is there, before our very eyes. We see him leave the *Way of the Sea* to go down into the plains of Sharon where the wheat, the olive trees with heavy branches, and the vineyards on display all screamed opulence. He stood on the side of the first hills, these mountains of Judea covered with oak trees and terebinths, with junipers and cypress trees. Little by little the slopes grew bare and rock prevailed. Saul forgot his tiredness as the end of his journey drew near. At the same time he was surprised; in Tarsus he had sung the glory of Jerusalem, never dreaming that the city of David would be situated in the middle of the mountain.

Around one bend, behold, "perched between heaven and earth," the holy city.

Who can forget one's first sight of Jerusalem? Mine, so long dreamt about, was anything but usual. A few days before Christmas 1965, after having flown over the sands of Jordan, a plane exhausted by the years landed at the airport in Amman. A small group of French men and women disembarked, resolved to brave anything in order to attend midnight Mass at the basilica in Bethlehem. A few Jordanian soldiers dressed in uniforms of very British cut pushed us, more or less cordially, into the bus. The road needed much repair. Gripping the elbow rests, we fixed our gaze on the windshield hoping, at every turn, that the longed-for walls would rise before us. It was still daytime. Most of us had never seen Jerusalem.

We entered the city without even knowing it. Night had fallen all at once. City lighting was poor. Not a crescent of the moon, not a single star allowed us to discern even the outline of a church, the shadow of a synagogue, or anything resembling a minaret. Arising suddenly in the glare of the headlights, we noticed only a patrol of the Arab legion marching in locked step. We were made to disembark and, having claimed our baggage, were pushed into a building where light finally awaited us. Opening the door, the religious women greeted us with that smiling astonishment usually reserved for family members returning from a long adventure.

We were in a school whose students, because of vacation, had deserted their rooms. At the first glimmer of daylight, I was standing before the open window, looking at a Jerusalem street for the first time. It happened to be in the Arab section of this city cut in two since the day the Israeli army had admitted that they would never make an end of the soldiers of Glubb Pacha. The armistice of April 3, 1949 had caused to rise up in the middle of the city a wall almost impossible to climb, doubly barbed with mines, with zigzagging passageways and armed guards stationed at long intervals. To see the Israeli side—and I was determined to do so—I had to climb a hill from where I could observe intense activity from the other side. The noise of workshops and the din of cars and horns brought me back to proper silence.

I loved that silence. Sustained by the spectacle of crenellated walls built by Crusaders and Mamluks, I found myself again in the city where Joseph and Mary brought the infant Jesus to be presented to the Lord; the city where this same Jesus, his mission accomplished, died nailed to a cross. Early in the morning, I found myself practically alone in an alley that had not changed for two thousand years. Occasionally, our Jordanian guides commented as we wished on the texts of the Bible and the Gospels. Archaeologists had not yet demonstrated that the *Via dolorosa* was not the *Via dolorosa*. Muslim shopkeepers sold rosaries and "crosses of Jesus" with great conviction. In the basement of a convent—the city is full of them—we were shown the tiled floor of the courtyard where Jesus awaited his ineluctable fate, while the Roman soldiers who guarded him played dice. This was "proven" to me by pointing to the lines of a chessboard inscribed in the stone of the pavement.

The esplanade of mosques! The Mount of Olives! I have forgotten nothing. In Bethlehem, we did have our midnight Mass. Attracted as much by curiosity as by piety, the crowd was crushed into the church's nave. At the elevation of the host, the soldiers of King Hussein presented arms. Of all that unorthodox gathering, they seemed to us the most devout.

HOW TO IMAGINE SAUL before the walls of Jerusalem? Immersed as he was in the Law, steeped in the history of Israel, of its prophets, kings, and heroes, one would desire to see him burst into sobs and fall to his knees. But such a vision risks a certain romanticism, and Paul of Tarsus was never sentimental. Of the city of David, the rabbis, filled with pride, never tired of repeating: "The one who has never seen Jerusalem has never seen a beautiful city." Cicero's contemptuous remark—Jerusalem is nothing but a "dump"—was not supported by his contemporaries. Apart from the supply of water that the city cruelly lacked, Herod the Great endowed it with the Fortress Antonia which, with its massive towers, dominated the esplanade of the Temple; with the royal palace around which the homes of the rich and of royal retainers were clustered in the upper city; and with the towers of Mariamne, Hippicus, and Pharael. This impregnable city, including the three-mile wall that encircled it, was entirely built of the same egg shell stones quarried from the surrounding hills.

Which of the fortified gates did Saul enter? Was it perhaps the eastern one, also called the Gate of the Gardens? If that were the case, having passed through it, he would have fumbled into a tight network of small streets, of alleys so narrow that two saddled asses could not pass each other through it. No symmetry or perspective, the houses were totally mismatched; if those of the rich had the benefit of tiled roofs, those of the poor—infinitely more numerous—had to content themselves with roofs made of reeds wrapped in clay. Synagogues were everywhere. Saul would need time to count them all: 480, one for every fifty-two inhabitants. But none of that would mean anything once he had discovered the Temple.

Would we have remembered Herod's Jerusalem had he not sworn—a grandiose claim—to erect *his* masterpiece there? In 20 B.C., when he laid the first stone of the Temple, this bloodthirsty king earned the epithet "the Great." When Saul entered it the work was not yet done. For more than forty-three years, under the supervision of one thousand priests, ten thousand workmen labored in the Pharaoh-like project. What marvels were within the walls—1,611 feet long by 1,017 feet wide—erected on the site of the Temple of Solomon! Enormous walls, planted in the earth of the same hill, support the whole structure.[2] Everyone who passed through any one of the eight monumental gates was met by the vision of a sort of gigantic espalier.* The courts were connected one following the other: the court of the Gentiles—the non-Jews—where they could gain access and where the population of the city met, strolled, held forth, and traded; the court of the women; the court of the men; and the court of the priests. Beyond lay the altar of holocausts; and further, the sanctuary and—crowning glory—the Holy of Holies, in which the high priest alone had the right to enter.

Wood, stone, marble, precious metals—all came together to dazzle. From the rising to the setting of the sun, thousands of people milled about: pious Jews eager to pray or curious folk impatient to discover. At the time of the great religious feasts—especially those of Passover and of Tabernacles—crowds of pilgrims from everywhere in the whole Diaspora made their way to this place, defying our ability to comprehend how it could hold so many people. Flavius Josephus affirms that in one year alone 250,600 lambs were slaughtered, which, assuming one lamb for every ten pilgrims—even if he exaggerated—comes to two million Jews. All mingled, rubbed elbows, and jostled one another, juxtaposing costume and color: the modest dress of Palestinian Jews and the motley dress of the Diaspora; red and black *akals,* and white, yellow, or multicolored veils.

IN THIS CITY, which must have caused the adolescent some anxiety because it was unfamiliar to him—remember what it was like to be fifteen years old—was anyone waiting for him? It is hard to imagine that Saul's father, a tentmaker, would have let his natural offspring go without providing shelter for him. Saul's sister lived in Jerusalem. We know that she had a son who, when the time came, would fly to the rescue of his uncle then in danger. Who can doubt that she welcomed her brother at least until the time when he would take up residence at the home of his teacher, who was expecting him? Not without emotion, Saul—having become Paul—would later recall these years of apprenticeship: Here in this city, "at the feet of Gamaliel," he was "educated strictly according to our ancestral law" (Acts 22:3).

Gamaliel, one of the most respected members of the rabbinate of his time, was a Pharisee. The author of the Acts of the Apostles saw him as "a teacher of the law, respected by all the people" (Acts 5:34)—so much so that

---

* A plant trained to grow flat against a wall or fence (Ed.).

Jewish tradition referred to him by the term *rabban,* suggesting a stronger sense than *rabbin* or *rabbi.*[3] His grandfather, Hillel the Elder, was recognized for having founded in Jerusalem an academy whose liberalism was famous. Gamaliel's letters, which circulated even as far as Cilicia, spread a mode of thinking that often connected Jewish law and Greek philosophy, a combination less surprising than it may seem. At the time of the Maccabees, Jews were already claiming a relationship with Sparta. The Herodian kings made of Jerusalem a city open, for the most part, to Hellenism. In the Temple, directions were given in three languages: Hebrew, Greek, and Latin. In several synagogues of Jerusalem, people prayed in Latin or Greek.

It is necessary to pause at the image of Saul seated "at the feet of" his master. Did Gamaliel, in the manner of philosophical schools, stroll with his students in other places, in the Temple for example? Not likely. A Jewish teacher received his students in his home, thus creating a lasting bond with them. From the first day, Gamaliel would not have failed to formulate the rule that would become a law for his disciples: "Get yourself a teacher and thus avoid doubt." At his side Saul learned to handle with equal ease Greek, Hebrew, and Aramaic. He would know enough law to appear to his contemporaries as a jurist in the making. To this would be added some knowledge of medicine; in the course of his journeys, we will see him tending the sick. But the essential remained an exhaustive knowledge of the Bible.

The Letters show a Paul literally steeped in the Sacred Scriptures. Familiar with apocalyptic literature, he will often cite its primordial themes.[4] When he proclaimed that the Resurrection must be the center of the faith, he would only be sharing the belief of the Pharisees in a judgment after death that punished the wicked with "eternal prison" and empowered the righteous to live again. At the time of Gamaliel, it was widely believed that there were creatures, like demons and angels, that served as intermediaries between God and men, a conviction shared in the East by most intellectuals who had been hellenized.[5]

It was forbidden to doubt a single word of one's teacher. Gamaliel's word *was* the Truth and the Truth was not debatable. "The disciple must be like a newly renovated cistern that does not allow even the smallest drop of water to escape."[6]

PAUL WOULD WRITE, "[I] advanced in Judaism beyond many among my people of the same age, for I was far more zealous for the traditions of my ancestors" (Gal 1:14): a memory not modest but convincing. Paul's studies were long, some would say too long. Hearing Paul speak at the end of his career, the procurator of Judea, Porcius Festus, "raising his voice," will cry out: "You are out of your mind, Paul! Too much learning is driving you insane!" (Acts 26:24)

Paul studied in a city that was occupied but in no way compliant. The Jewish people tolerated Rome's presence less and less. Shortly after young Saul's arrival, under the mandate of Pontius Pilate—between 26 and 36—and continuing into the reign of Tiberius, popular movements were harshly repressed. No more speaking, no more dreaming of driving out the Romans. A Samaritan roused the crowds to arms by invoking Moses the Liberator; Judas of Gamala coordinated the subversive activities of the Zealots. Resisting in advance, some unknown persons prophesied, presenting themselves as entrusted with supernatural powers and calling people to revolt. The charismatic was in vogue: some declared themselves favored by extraordinary spiritual gifts (prophecy, visions, tongues[7]) granted by the spirit of God. The ordinary Jew no longer knew to which prophet to dedicate himself. Penitential sects were born under the inspiration of the disciples of the late John the Baptist, decapitated in 28. In their retreat to the Dead Sea, the Essenes strove to attain the absolute.

Never had Elijah been so often evoked; after all, must not his return precede the coming of the Messiah, who was awaited with an increasingly feverish impatience? Messiah comes from the Hebrew *Maschiah* (in Aramaic, *Meschiha*) and means "anointed, marked with royal oil, consecrated by the Lord." The word is ancient. According to Isaiah, the Messiah "shall strike the earth with the rod of his mouth, and with the breath of his lips.... Righteousness shall be the belt around his waist, and faithfulness the belt around his loins" (Isa 11:4b–5). Without doubt, the Messiah would liberate Israel from the yoke of the Romans who enslaved her. The Psalms said: "Now I know that the LORD will help his anointed [*Maschiah*]; he will answer him from his holy heaven with mighty victories by his right hand" (Ps 20:6). Or again, "O that deliverance for Israel would come from Zion! When God restores the fortunes of his people, Jacob will rejoice; Israel will be glad" (Ps 53:6). In the streets of the city of David, every galloping of the Roman cavalry—red chlamydes* floating from their armor—caused a new cry, a new anger to burst forth.

---

* A short mantle, fastened at the shoulder (Ed.).

At Gamaliel's did the student Saul hear talk of this Jesus of Nazareth who, in Galilee at this time, was scouring the plains and mountains calling the Jews to draw near to God and better keep his Law?

Consider the chronology. In all probability Saul arrived in Jerusalem in the year 20. A plausible calendar suggests that Jesus was baptized by John the Baptist and immediately began to preach in the fall of 27. That year Saul was nineteen years old. It would be surprising if he had heard about the unique individual whose fame had barely spread beyond the vicinity of the Sea of Tiberias. At Passover of the year 28, Jesus—now as prophet of the Kingdom—arrived in Jerusalem for the first time. He caused scandal by driving the merchants from the Temple. His words convinced a certain number of the faithful but remained a non-event. Did they reach the ears of Saul, secluded in the home of his teacher as if in another world? Certainly one may consider that Gamaliel, very close to the priestly aristocracy, was informed about the anger of the money changers and the sellers of sacrificial animals, and that he discussed this strange incident with his students. But to believe he actually did such requires a great deal of good will.

At Passover of the year 30, Jesus returned to Jerusalem. This time he disturbed enough people for the hierarchy to be concerned. It all ended on Golgotha.[8] On that day, at noontime, the condemned was nailed to a cross that, as a sign of derision, was topped with a notice bearing the words: *Jesus of Nazareth, the King of the Jews* (Jn 19:19). The execution took place in Jerusalem outside the Gate of Ephraim, at the foot of the hill of Gareb. At three o'clock in the afternoon, a legionnaire pierced his right side with a lance and the condemned man died. His friends obtained from the Roman *praefectus* Pontius Pilate permission to remove the dead body. Before nightfall—as Sabbath law required—the stone, in the shape of a wheel, was rolled before the tomb.

The affair caused little rumor. Certainly, this Jesus had faithful followers, disciples, not to say partisans—without them, would he have been condemned?—but in a city of 25,000 inhabitants, they were hardly more than a few hundred.

The evangelist Luke affirms that on the road Jesus followed, there gathered "a great number of the people" (23:27): in the first place, those people motivated by an unhealthy curiosity who always hurried to executions; also those who, a few hours before, had cried out to Pilate: "Crucify him!"; and finally, beyond despair and lost in the chaos, his friends, his disciples, and no doubt a few of the Twelve who would be called apostles.

At the word that Jesus had died, some of the faithful were unable to overcome their fear and went into hiding. Most foundered, seized by their horror of the cross—torment of slaves—and devastated by the death of him whose least word sang in their memory. Three days of tears, of dreadful doubt, and suddenly, transmitted from mouth to ear, unbelievable news: *Christ is risen.*

And the disciples too were reborn.

AT TWENTY-TWO YEARS OLD, Saul was always studying. This time probability would suggest he did know about the execution of the Nazarene. If he did, was he moved by it? No more than he would have been by the fate of any other false messiah. Given their number, it would be a waste of time. The vast majority of people in Jerusalem would have reacted as he did.

It would take a while for Saul to learn that the high priest before whom Jesus was led had asked him if he was truly "the Christ, the Son of the Blessed One." He had answered, "I am; and 'you will see the Son of Man seated at the right hand of the Power' and 'coming with the clouds of heaven'" (Mk 14:62).

As soon as a false messiah was unmasked, he was executed and his small group of followers dispersed. This was not the case here.

How many were they, these "Christians" of Jerusalem?

Very few, no doubt. The number given in Acts of 5,000 who were converted after Pentecost is not plausible. One must consider that "the number of those who rallied was more modest and that the small community grew gradually."[9] Faith in the Resurrection of Jesus appeared as the prerogative of his closest disciples, of women, of members of his family, and of a few others only. They wanted to continue the work of the Risen One. They gathered to speak about Jesus, giving themselves the name "brothers." They were mostly Galileans who had come to Jerusalem as followers of Jesus. Why, despite the dangers and probably the concern about money, were they determined to remain there? Was it because they were convinced that Jesus would come again in glory to the place where he had been crucified?

Of this small community we only know that most of them sold their goods and held everything in common. The Apostle Peter, in his first epistle, urges them to have "sympathy, love for one another, a tender heart, and a humble mind" (1 Pet 3:8). Luke describes them taking their meals "with glad and generous hearts." They went to the Temple every day (Acts 2:46). Why not? They were Jews, and Jesus had said: "Do not think that I have come to abolish the law or the prophets; I have come not to abolish but to fulfill" (Mt 5:17).

At Gamaliel's the breath of the God of the Bible dwelt in Saul. We begin to see him devoured by certitude, assured that there is no salvation except by obedience to Jewish Law, and ready to manifest a righteous anger toward those who violate it.

But the small community of those faithful to Jesus was growing. It was in the process of giving itself the structure of an organization. Jesus solemnly confided a mission to Peter, an ex-fisherman from the Lake of Tiberias, who had abandoned his nets to respond to Jesus' call. The mission—*Peter, you are the Rock*—was to assure the permanence of the message Jesus had preached in the course of his public life. John remained "the disciple Jesus loved." With the assent of all, these two men had taken the reins.

Together they would bring attention to the community, abandoning the discretion that the faithful had until then preferred. The event took place in the Temple where the two apostles went daily. That day, having thrown the *tallis** over their shoulders, they walked in through the Beautiful Gate. Near the entrance, a professional beggar, crippled from birth and well known to those who regularly attended, pleaded for money. Peter stopped and faced him: "I have no silver or gold, but what I have I give you; in the name of Jesus Christ of Nazareth, stand up and walk" (Acts 3:6).

How many times had he heard his Master issue the very same order? And now, as then, the man stood. The Jewish crowd saw him "walking and leaping and praising God" (Acts 3:8) up to Solomon's Portico and the court of the Gentiles, where 162 columns were aligned. Scandal. The leader of the Temple and several priests came running. They seized Peter and John. Unable to judge them immediately—night was falling—they threw them into the very heart of the Temple, in a place reserved for this purpose. The next morning the two men were taken from there to be dragged before the supreme Jewish authority, the Sanhedrin. The high priest Annas presided over the assembly of priests, elders, and scribes. They pushed to the fore the startled cripple who had been made whole.

Seated in that solemn place, arranged in a semicircle, were many of those—beginning with Caiaphas—who had condemned Jesus. They

---

* The Jewish prayer shawl (Ed.).

interrogated the suspects about what had happened the day before. "By what power or by what name did you do this?" (Acts 4:7)

Peter's answer, as we can readily see, was endowed with the firmness and breadth of shoulders acquired by rowing his boat and pulling in his nets: "Let it be known to all of you, and to all the people of Israel, that this man is standing before you in good health by the name of Jesus Christ of Nazareth, whom you crucified, whom God raised from the dead. This Jesus is: 'the stone that was rejected by you, the builders; it has become the cornerstone.'"

Luke testifies: "Now when they saw the boldness of Peter and John and realized that they were uneducated and ordinary men, they were amazed" (Acts 4:10–11, 13).

Would such audacity elicit a heavy condemnation? No way. In these difficult times, the Sanhedrin decided that the affair was not important enough to risk provoking the kind of disturbance the Romans abhorred. They contented themselves with releasing Peter and John with a warning not "to speak or teach at all in the name of Jesus" (Acts 4:18).

The apostles' answer bit like a lash: "Whether it is right in God's sight to listen to you rather than God, you must judge."

No one opened his mouth to reply. Withdrawing, the two men warned: "We cannot keep from speaking about what we have seen and heard" (Acts 4:19, 20).

The turning point that just took place marks a critical event in the history of Christianity. Until then, Jesus' faithful followers continued to practice the Jewish religion, finding nothing in it contradictory to their own new faith. Suddenly they found themselves in conflict with those for whom Jesus was nothing but an agitator justly condemned. The Jews responded to the disquieting increase in the number of Christians[10] by tightening their own authority. Convicted of transgressing the prohibition against publicly preaching the teachings of Jesus, Peter and John would again be arrested.

This time they risked a long prison sentence.[11] On their behalf, a man arose: Gamaliel. He spoke out, believe it or not. "Fellow Israelites, consider carefully what you propose to do to these men.... I tell you, keep away from these men and let them alone; because if this plan or this undertaking is of human origin, it will fail; but if it is of God, you will not be able to overthrow them—in that case you may even be found fighting against God!" (Acts 5:35, 38–39)

Peter and John would only be flogged.

WE ARE NO LONGER surprised in the twenty-first century to see young people study ten years or more. Let us grant Saul ten years. No one in the first century would find ten years too much, despite a life expectancy that was barely twenty-five. At the top of the list of those who have investigated these things is André Chouraqui, an Israeli of French origin who has great authority in such matters. Not only has he translated the Old Testament, he has also taken on the New, which he claims has "married two worlds in one unique synthesis, one Hebrew and the other Greek," in pages on which Chouraqui confers "an exceptional beauty." He must be read. "Beginning with the Greek text, knowing the techniques of translation of the Hebrew into Greek and the Hebraic resonance in the *Koine,* I tried with each word, each verse, to touch the Semitic essence, then to return to the Greek which was necessary to rediscover, enriched by a new substance before passing to the French." According to André Chouraqui, "Schaoul of Tarsus, Paul, Jewish Apostle to the Gentiles, was without doubt the most influential Jewish genius of his time."

All the facts of Paul's life confirm that "he never broke with his roots or customs, biblical and talmudic, which he knew better than another great Jew of his time, Philo of Alexandria." Chouraqui scrutinizes the Pauline writings with the knowledge that imbues all of his works on the Bible; he points out the close parallels between Paul's deductions and rabbinic exegesis. This was already underscored a few years earlier by F. Amiot, a professor at the Seminary of Saint-Sulpice, when he saw Paul break up "subtle arguments in rabbinic manner." Not content to see in Paul "a Jew formed in rabbinic discipline," André Chouraqui leads us directly to a conclusion that goes beyond hypothesis: Paul would have been himself a rabbi. He would have functioned as such in the 30s, in one of the synagogues of Jerusalem. Monsignor Giuseppe Ricciotti, tracing the psychological portrait of Paul according to the Catholic context of today, does not seem to doubt this when he writes: "With the rabbi Saul, the great idea is the Law and the Jewish tradition."

What could he resemble, this adult now in the prime of his age? He certainly had a real physical vigor, proven by the exhausting and unceasing walks he would undertake over so many years. He had the strength to endure shipwrecks—he survived three of them—to the point that during one of these he was able to stay afloat for a day and a night before being fished out of the water.

When we read him, when we hear him—for we hear him by reading him—we discern in Paul's words such power that we at once accord to him the breath of Demosthenes at the height of his eloquence and the commanding presence of Moses commanding the waters to withdraw.

The Acts of Paul, redacted anonymously around 150, bring us down to earth: "And he saw Paul coming, a man of small stature, with a bald head and crooked legs, ...with eyebrows meeting and a nose somewhat hooked."[12] One cannot help but be struck by the tradition, almost unshakable since the first eastern sketches of Pauline imagery: thin, bald, bearded. Again we must ask ourselves what value we can give to this text so soon relegated to the rank of apocrypha. It had totally disappeared when, in 1896, a bundle of papyri surfaced in the sands of Egypt. Throughout the twentieth century, the discovery of other manuscripts— of various origins and epochs—permitted the reconstruction of a notable part of the text and the discovery of its complete title: *The Acts of Paul According to the Apostle.* The objective of the work seems to have been to narrate the missionary life of the apostle without reprising the version given in the Acts of the Apostles redacted by Luke, the indisputable witness of Paul's life. When we think of the reproaches so often reiterated with regard to the man of Tarsus, we cannot but be surprised that *The Acts of Paul* are feminist, a peculiarity that led Tertullian to denounce the author: "If certain people cite *The Acts of Paul,* which bear this title wrongly, to defend the right of women to teach and to baptize, let them know this: it is a presbyter[13] of Asia who forged this work as though he were completing the authority of Paul by his own; convicted and having admitted to acting thus for love of Paul, he left his post."

The admissions of the guilty party seem not to have convinced everyone. Willy Rordorf, a recognized expert in apocrypha, has inventoried "the frequent but exact allusions to *The Acts of Paul,* found in as many authors from the East as from the West." They were still used in the sixth century. In the tenth century, the rhetorician Nicetas of Paphlagonia used them constantly. All of these signs lead us to admit that the physical description of Paul corresponds to an image deeply rooted among the first generations of Christians over a vast area.

It is helpful to isolate one phrase from *The Acts of Paul* to complete the alleged portrait of the apostle: "For now he appeared like a man, and now he had the face of an angel"[14]—hence, a certain mobility of expression. Must we see here the continuation of the commonplace in antiquity that readily contrasted physical ugliness and spiritual beauty? Very homely, Socrates still mesmerized young men. An analysis drawn from the texts, the work of Jean-Robert Armogathe, underlines the role of Paul's hands and the force of Paul's look. The hands: "The gesture of the accomplice as he guards the garments of Stephen's executioners; the gesture of the apostle who adds to the end of his epistles 'large letters'[15]; the gesture of the martyr whose hands are bound with chains." In Pisidian Antioch as in Jerusalem, the movement of his hands tried to appease the hostility of the crowd. Paul's look? In several instances Luke insists on its intensity: "The verb used, *atenizein,* is a rare word, almost peculiar to the Acts; it signifies: 'to fix one's gaze intently.'" It was thus that Paul would look at the members of the Sanhedrin, and at many others.

We need to raise a question that may seem unusual: Was Paul married? We already know that a young Jew was dedicated from the age of thirteen to observing the commandments, at fifteen to the Talmud, and that at eighteen *the wedding* awaited him. This tradition dates from times past.

The issue arose not only for religious reasons but also because of a physiological fact: beyond eighteen years of age, one risked seeing the young man lose himself in dangerous adventures. Marriage protected him. Moreover, the Torah formally invited the Jew to establish a family. It is hard to imagine Saul dispensing himself from this obligation. The problem is that in his letters he makes no mention of a marriage, and neither does Luke in the Acts of the Apostles. In the First Letter to the Corinthians, Paul presents himself as not needing a wife and wishes—so much for married folk—that everyone might be as he is, adding, "To the unmarried and to the widows I say that it is well for them to remain unmarried as I am" (7:8). The Greek word *agamos,* which is translated here as unmarried, means not married—in other words, without husband or wife—and also designates those who have never taken a wife, the widowed, and separated spouses. The reader hesitates. If married, did Paul—at an unknown time—lose his wife? It should be mentioned that the historians and exegetes who believe in this marriage are a minority, but their argument is solid.

THE CHRISTIANS DECIDEDLY began to make too much noise. The appearance of certain "influences" confused a situation that until now had been perfectly clear, and made it more complex. The young community now included Jews from the Diaspora, who were multilingual and open to wider horizons. This could only highlight the difference with native Jews who were more turned in on themselves, speaking Aramaic at home and reading the Hebrew Bible in the synagogue. When these natives denounced the former as *Hellenists*, one sensed irritation mingling with irony. By the same token, the other group would hear themselves called *Hebrews*. Such is the power and danger of words.

From the first incident born of this situation, Luke has recollected this echo: "When the disciples were increasing in number, the Hellenists complained against the Hebrews because their widows were being neglected in the daily distribution of food" (Acts 6:1). At issue here were the meals taken in common in memory of the one Jesus had shared with his disciples on the night before he died.

In the ordering of community life, such treatment could not be considered trivial. The apostles took the affair seriously; there must not be one person who felt frustrated or humiliated. They, the Twelve, could not—nor did they want to—tear themselves at every instant from their already heavy spiritual and administrative responsibilities.

> And the Twelve called together the whole community of the disciples and said, "It is not right that we should neglect the word of God in order to wait on tables. Therefore, friends, select from among yourselves seven men of good standing, full of the Spirit and of wisdom, whom we may appoint to this task, while we, for our part, will devote ourselves to prayer and to serving the word."

The whole assembly accepted this proposal: "They chose Stephen, a man full of faith and the Holy Spirit, together with Philip, Prochorus, Nicanor, Timon, Parmenas, and Nicolaus, a proselyte of Antioch. They had these men stand before the apostles, who prayed and laid hands on them" (Acts 6:2–6).

It is impossible to be mistaken; these seven names are of Greek origin, the last being that of a Greek convert. The good will that the Twelve manifested hinged on a paradox: to demonstrate equality between Christians, they created at the heart of the first Church a state within a state; since the Hellenists complained, let them settle things among themselves! On the strength of the consecration conveyed by the laying on of hands, those who would be called *deacons*[16] would, well beyond serving at table, take on a potentially independent mission. Flavius

Josephus would identify the followers of Jesus as a "Hellenist sect." And Stephen would be more talked about than any of the others.

He rises before us: young, burning with impatience, radiant, not swerving from any audacity, "full of grace and power." Perhaps he came from Alexandria because, for one thing, his style was like Philo's, venerated by the Jewish population of an enormous city. Posterity has seen in Stephen the promoter of a revolutionary choice: the Jewish Law must not prevail over the teaching of Jesus.

In the double fidelity in which the Hebrew Christians persisted, Stephen believed he saw the heritage of Christ wear thin. He wanted to trample underfoot "the ruse linked to the disclosure of the truth." He was not content merely to defend this truth; he cried it from the housetops. In the line of charismatics, he is depicted doing "great wonders and signs among the people" (Acts 6:8).

Stephen's shattering independence did not delay in worrying the Hebrew Christians and, even more, the hierarchy of the Temple. Until then the sect that identified with the Galilean carpenter had caused little trouble. All it took was to flog two of its agitators, and they had not been heard from again. But this Stephen!

Here Saul of Tarsus rejoins us, nourished in Hellenism *but* attached to the Law with every fiber of his being. It is perfectly logical that he rose—with many others—against Stephen, Hellenist *but* heretic.

Stephen was denounced for having blasphemed against this holy place—the Temple—and against the Law. The people, the elders, and the scribes were roused. Stephen was seized and dragged before the Sanhedrin. Saul of Tarsus slipped into that crowd.

The agitated crowd accused: "We have heard him speak blasphemous words against Moses and God" (Acts 6:11). Disconcerted, the high priest—was it the eternal Caiaphas, who would only leave his seat in 36?—asked, "Is this true?"

Stephen skirted nothing—quite the contrary. "Brothers and fathers, listen to me. The God of glory appeared to our ancestor Abraham when he was in Mesopotamia, before he lived in Haran, and said to him, *'Leave your country and your relatives and go to the land that I will show you.'*"

After such an introduction, no one could have been surprised by what followed: Isaac, Jacob, the twelve patriarchs, Joseph in Egypt, Moses and the daughter of Pharaoh, the flight from Egypt, the Golden Calf, the Ten Commandments, the settlement in the holy land, the tribes, the kings,

David, Solomon and his Temple. Did this litany go on for two or three hours? One question grew as the speaker expressed himself: Where was this man going? They didn't have to wait long. Stephen presented Moses as a model that his brother Jews had misunderstood: "He supposed that his kinsfolk would understand that God through him was rescuing them, but they did not understand.... It was this Moses whom they rejected when they said, *'Who made you a ruler and a judge?'* and whom God now sent as both ruler and liberator through the angel who appeared to him in the bush. He led them out."

Stephen hammered on: "This is the Moses who said to the Israelites, *'God will raise up a prophet for you from your own people.'*"

And the Jews did not listen to Moses, the greatest Jew in history. That became as clear as the water in the pool of Siloam. The prophet whom Moses announced had come, he was the Messiah; the judges of the Sanhedrin had rejected him as well. As Stephen arrived at this point, we can be sure that a cry of rage arose. It was sounded anew when Stephen, evoking the building of the Temple of Solomon, saw in it a sign of the blindness of the Jews, proof of their misunderstanding of the divine will. God did not need a house built by human hands. He made that clear through the voices of the prophets: *"Heaven is my throne, and the earth is my footstool. What kind of house will you build for me?"* (Isa 66:1; also Acts 7:49).

Stephen was out of control:

"You stiff-necked people, uncircumcised in heart and ears, you are forever opposing the Holy Spirit, just as your ancestors used to do. Which of the prophets did your ancestors not persecute? They killed those who foretold the coming of the Righteous One, and now you have become his betrayers and murderers. You are the ones that received the law as ordained by angels, and yet you have not kept it."

Looking intently up to heaven, Stephen rose above the insults fired from all sides. "Look," he said, "'I see the heavens opened and the Son of Man standing at the right hand of God!'"

Among those whom Luke depicts grinding their teeth at Stephen, in the midst of the hateful frenzy that rejected the image of Jesus "standing at the right hand of God," what was Saul of Tarsus doing? He would never have imagined that one would dare rise to such a blasphemy. The greatness of God was incommensurable, to the point that a Jew was not even entitled to write his name. To remove any desire, even unconscious, of speaking it, it was designated by unpronounceable consonants. The unbearable idea of this carpenter being raised to the right hand of the Almighty chilled the blood of the man from Tarsus.

When the infamous Stephen was brought to them, the members of the Sanhedrin thought they would have to judge him. But here, before their very eyes, they threw themselves on him, seized him, and took him away! "They dragged him out of the city and began to stone him" (Acts 7:2–3, 25, 35–36, 37, 51–53, 56, 58).

The fifth book of the Pentateuch prescribes:

> If there is found among you, in one of your towns that the LORD, your God, is giving you, a man or a woman who does what is evil in the sight of the LORD your God, and transgresses his covenant, by going to serve other gods and worshiping them—whether the sun or the moon or any of the host of heaven, which I have forbidden—and if it is reported to you or you hear of it, and you make a thorough inquiry, and the charge is proved true that such an abhorrent thing has occurred in Israel, then you shall bring out to your gates that man or that woman who has committed this crime and you shall stone the man or woman to death (Deut 17:2–5).

The careful investigation prescribed by the Law was not carried out in this case. The *fact* was established. Saul of Tarsus would follow the executioners even to Stephen's death.

3

THE ROAD TO
DAMASCUS

In the streets of Jerusalem, people fled while others pursued and captured them. Curses, insults, and threats mingled with cries of terror and sorrow. This human hunt was a hunt for Christians, who were thrown into prisons. No quarter was spared. The pogrom of Jews by Jews went on for a long time, day and night. All the details can be deduced from the writings of the instigator himself.

He could be seen running through the city with appalling fury. He stirred up, drew in, risked his own skin. For those who wanted to know who this young unknown was—they put him at twenty-five years old—the answer would not wait: he was a young man from Tarsus named Saul.

Indeed he had arrived. The anger that had erupted in him on hearing Stephen's speech had not abated—far from it. The encouragement Saul had given to the stoning by his presence there had been followed by an unrestrained hatred. These Christians, having remained so long unnoticed, had become the enemies to defeat. In a letter addressed to a Christian community in central Anatolia twenty years later, he would write: "You have heard, no doubt, of my earlier life in Judaism. I was violently persecuting the church of God and was trying to destroy it" (Gal 1:13).

The persecution arose the very day Stephen was stoned: "That day a severe persecution began against the church in Jerusalem" (Acts 8:1). Paul would remain obsessed with it all his life. He would come back to it five times in his letters: three times in the one addressed to the Galatians, once in the First Letter to the Corinthians and once more in the Letter to the Philippians. The words he later used not only described verbal abuse but, without ambiguity, physical violence as well. It is necessary to consult Luke, the great witness; Paul had had arrested, or arrested himself, men and women. These unfortunate people thrown into prison were "a great number." From Luke we learn that Paul multiplied operations while the high priest encouraged them. Luke depicts Paul exceedingly mad with rage and "breathing threats and murder against the disciples of the Lord" (Acts 9:1).

Luke too confirms that Paul used the word murder in a discourse to the people of Jerusalem: "[I was] zealous for God, just as all of you are today. I persecuted this Way up to the point of death by binding both men and women and putting them in prison" (Acts 22:3–4).

To the point of death?

In his Letter to the Galatians, Paul does not conceal in any way that he wanted to *destroy* the Church of God, in other words, the Christians (Gal 1:13). "I was formerly a blasphemer, a persecutor, and a man of violence" (1 Tim 1:13), he would write. It is impossible, therefore, to dismiss the image of Saul incapable of self-control, terrorizing the small streets of Jerusalem and even the synagogues. That the thirty-nine lashes (the *makkot arbaim*)—clearly part of the discipline of the synagogues—was imposed on these Christians becomes a bitter logic.

Such relentlessness on the part of a future saint has appeared so strange that certain people have wondered if he was not rediscovering an "ancient malaise" in the exercise of his religion. In other words, they think that Paul was already estranged from Judaism. This is absurd. Having come from Tarsus to Jerusalem to better understand his religion and no doubt to teach it some day, the lessons he received from Gamaliel permitted him to achieve his goal. After the business with Stephen, Saul will describe himself as "zealous for the traditions of my ancestors" (Gal 1:14). That means for Judaism and nothing else.

One question irresistibly comes to mind regarding these Christians whom Paul arrested. Did he brutalize them, torture them, see them led to death without a hearing? It is impossible that these people did not try to explain themselves, to attempt to make him understand the sense of faith that he denied them having. Was his heart so hard that he remained unmoved by the pleas of men, by the tears of women? No less than he, these Christians had recourse to Jewish Law. They repeated that the prophets had announced Jesus the Jew, and that he came on earth only to redeem the sins of humanity, to make peace reign among them, and to sow love throughout all nations. Did they not at last succeed in penetrating his armor? Even as we relive the main event of this story, such questions remain uppermost in our minds.

WHILE "PIOUS MEN" quietly buried Stephen's remains, the Christians of Jerusalem, spared once again, did what they could to avoid persecution. The Jewish authorities never thought to have the gates of the city guarded; hurrying out, the Christians scattered throughout Judea and even Samaria. They had to have been truly terrified to move to a province that was the object of such loathing among Jews. Did not the rabbis swear that the water of this country was "more impure than the blood of pork"? The Gospel retains a trace of this hatred when it evokes the scandal raised by the unexpected exchange between Jesus and the Samaritan woman at the well (Jn 4:1–42).

The Christians who had sought shelter "went from place to place, proclaiming the word" (Acts 8:4). The case of the Hellenist Philip, one of the Seven, is striking. As soon as he arrived in Samaria, he began to proclaim Christ. Soon the whole region was talking about the miracles he performed and which Acts enumerates: unclean spirits coming out of the bodies of those afflicted, crippled people finding the ability to walk again. "So there was great joy in that city"[1] (Acts 8:5–8).

The rumor spread to Jerusalem where the apostles wanted to stay. Obviously, they refused to abandon the structure —still so fragile—born of the words of Jesus. Besides, the Sanhedrin had not bothered them: at no time had the apostles shown themselves to be on the side of Stephen, and their regular presence in the Temple confirmed their attachment to the Hebrew faith.

As soon as Philip's successes were reported to Peter and John, they understood that their "brother" needed reinforcement. Leaving the church of Jerusalem in the hands of other apostles, the two men decided to join him.

Faced with the prayers of the Samaritans begging to let them be baptized, the apostles found themselves on the horns of a dilemma, the first of many that awaited them. The Samaritans were Jews officially separated from the faith. Peter and John must consider them not only unclean but heretical. Did the apostles have the right to break with the condemnation pronounced long before their encounter? They seem not to have hesitated: "Then Peter and John laid their hands on them, and they received the holy Spirit" (Acts 8:17).

"I WAS SO FURIOUSLY enraged at them, I pursued them even to foreign cities" (Acts 26:11). In his letters, Paul speaks twice about Damascus, the illustrious city: at the beginning of the Letter to the Galatians and at the end of the Second Letter to the Corinthians. We know that a Christian community—still fragile—was already planted there. Faith in Christ made its way to Syria relatively early. The new faith must have recruited from among the many Jews long established in the city: a Jewish bazaar has been found dating from the ninth century B.C. Flavius Josephus affirms that at the beginning of the first century, Damascus numbered 50,000 Jews, which is considerable.

When Saul decided to go there, the tight Christian community was for the most part—we think—composed of Hellenists converted by people close to Stephen.[2] In the grip of his hatred, would Saul have gone to Caiaphas to ask for "letters to the synagogues at Damascus" declaring that "if he found any who belonged to the Way,[3] men or women, he might bring them bound to Jerusalem" (Acts 9:1–2)? Luke is mistaken in this: the Sanhedrin did not exercise the least authority over the synagogues of Damascus. The most we can say is that Saul armed himself with a warning meant to alert the Jews of Syria to the danger represented by their rebellion.

Summer burned the sparse grass. Under the pitiless sun, the son of Tarsus took to the road anew. Even though the region had been a Roman province for sixty-two years, it was not safe. The Herodian kings and the Nabateans, unceasingly in conflict, prevented Rome from establishing here a security worthy of its glory. Seeking to control all the caravan traffic between Arabia and the Syrian coast, the Nabateans continually marked out points, the principal one being occupation of the mountains that dominate Damascus. It was an excellent base of departure from which to undertake raids on the city. From the year 30, war had gone on in the country. As of 33–34, Damascus rejected the authority of Rome.

To cross a region in full warfare, Saul of necessity must have traveled in a group. He joined one of the many caravans. The distance from Jerusalem to Damascus is 174 miles. By going quickly—and they did move quickly—by getting up early—and they did get up early—such a journey required seven or eight days. The caravans took a shortcut by climbing the Jordan Valley.

Before Saul's eyes, the Sea of Galilee displayed its splendors. The man from Tarsus passed through Tiberias and Capernaum without suspecting anything of the one who, a few years earlier, had proposed unforgettable parables to the bewildered crowd gathered there. Saul climbed the heights of the Golan and, at an altitude of almost 2,300 feet, advanced to a pebbly steppe. He breathed the bitter wind, which—and this was its only advantage—tempered the heat of the sun a bit. On the left of the caravaneers unfolded the enormous barrier of Anti-Lebanon. Visible from everywhere at 9,232 feet, with its snow-covered summit—even in summer—was Hermon, the holy mountain.

The end was not too far now. The landscape seemed to reverse itself. Plane trees in full bloom, palm trees bristling, the strong perfume of roses and jasmine, orchards among which water flowed from irrigation ditches—how to cheer a traveler saturated with aridity! They were nearing Damascus.

SUDDENLY, THE UNSPEAKABLE happened. A violent light enveloped Saul. Those with him saw him stagger and then fall in the dust of the road.

They ran toward him, surrounding him. Slowly he opened his eyes, but they met only the night. Saul was blind.

Forget about Rubens, Caravaggio, and Michelangelo, who show Saul falling off a horse; being neither a Roman officer nor in the retinue of the client king Herod Antipas, he could only have traveled on foot.

On several occasions he later expressed himself about what really happened to him, in terms for which every word requires meditation. To his eyes there was no ambiguity: he met Jesus. To the Galatians he wrote, "[The one] who had set me apart before I was born and called me through his grace, was pleased *to reveal his Son to me,* so that I might proclaim him among the Gentiles..." (1:15–16). To the Corinthians: "Have I not *seen Jesus our Lord?*" And again: "Last of all...he *appeared* also to me" (1 Cor 9:1, 15:8).

What was revealed to him was so precise, the remembrance of it would remain imprinted on his memory. The encounter would remain so totally palpable to him that he would liken it to that with which the

Twelve were favored after the Resurrection of Jesus. Later, wanting to be considered equal to Peter, John, Andrew, Matthew, Bartholomew, Thomas, and the others, he would designate himself as an apostle, a word that means "sent," with a boldness that is typical of him. Yet, the role of the Twelve was defined the day that Judas was replaced; the apostles had to be able to testify that the risen Jesus was, "in his body and his person," the same one "with whom they had lived" (cf. Acts 1:21–22). Let us open the Book of Revelation: Christianity rests on twelve foundation stones, each one bearing the name of one of the twelve apostles of the Lamb (cf. 21:14). No one anticipated a thirteenth. Not once in Acts does Luke give Paul the name of apostle. This did not prevent Paul, in the addresses of his letters, from returning again and again to this "title." To the Romans: "...a servant of Jesus Christ, called to be an apostle.... Jesus Christ our Lord, through whom we have received grace and apostleship" (1:1, 4–5). To the Corinthians: "...called to be an apostle of Christ Jesus by the will of God" (1 Cor 1:1). To the Galatians: "...an apostle—sent neither by human commission nor from human authorities, but through Jesus Christ and God the Father" (1:1).

He says—and will insist—that his vocation was born here: "So if anyone is in Christ, there is a new creation: everything old has passed away; see, everything has become new" (2 Cor 5:17).

On the circumstances of the encounter, Saul brought to bear no precision, no details that would seem anecdotal. Nothing would ever pass his lips that would be unworthy of such a privilege. Luke is careful—and had the good fortune as a biographer—to follow his master's example. Acts cannot be doubted, because it returns three different times to the road to Damascus, with Luke modifying his account each time. It is a matter of a document pieced together for apologetic reasons, so it would be difficult to produce three identical accounts.

Let's compare these versions. The first is situated in the narrative of Paul's life that Luke recalls.

> Now as he was going along and approaching Damascus, suddenly a light from heaven flashed around him. He fell to the ground and heard a voice saying to him, "Saul, Saul, why do you persecute me?" He asked, "Who are you, Lord?" The reply came, "I am Jesus, whom you are persecuting. But get up and enter the city, and you will be told what you are to do." The men who were traveling with him stood speechless because they heard the voice but saw no one. Saul got up from the ground, and though

his eyes were open, he could see nothing; so they led him by the hand and brought him to Damascus (Acts 9:3–8).

The second account is drawn from a speech Paul gave in 58 before a hostile crowd in Jerusalem:

"While I was on my way and approaching Damascus, about noon a great light from heaven suddenly shone about me. I fell to the ground and heard a voice saying to me, 'Saul, Saul, why are you persecuting me?' I replied, 'Who are you, Lord?' Then he said to me, 'I am Jesus of Nazareth whom you are persecuting.' Now those who were with me saw the light but did not hear the voice of the one who was speaking to me. I asked, 'What am I to do, Lord?' The Lord said to me, 'Get up and go to Damascus; there you will be told everything that has been assigned to you to do.' Since I could not see because of the brightness of that light, those who were with me took my hand and led me to Damascus" (Acts 22:6–11).

The third version recalls the words that Paul spoke at Caesarea Maritima in the palace of the Roman governor Festus to the Jewish king Agrippa. Paul was no longer addressing an agitated Jewish crowd but a dignitary:

"...At midday along the road, your Excellency, I saw a light from heaven, brighter than the sun, shining around me and my companions. When we had all fallen to the ground, I heard a voice saying to me in the Hebrew language, 'Saul, Saul, why are you persecuting me? It hurts you to kick against the goads.' I asked, 'Who are you, Lord?' The Lord answered, 'I am Jesus whom you are persecuting'" (Acts 26:13–15).

Think about it: in the first text, a light enveloped Saul and he heard a voice; his companions heard the voice but saw nothing. In the second, he heard the voice; the companions saw the light but did not hear the voice. In the third, he alone heard the voice and his companions only saw the light.

These variations could be disturbing. Looking at them closely, one notes that it is as a consummate writer of dialogue—which he is—that Luke makes Paul speak. Poor dramatists give the same speech—their own—to all their characters. The others diversify the style, the sense, and the tone according to each role. Therefore, Luke himself narrated the first version. In the other two he had his hero speak in the way he could best convince his different audiences: the crowd in Jerusalem and King Agrippa in Caesarea.

The main thing here is to rely on Paul himself; Jesus appeared to him. I think it would be helpful to cite once again the text of the man from Tarsus:

"Then he appeared to more than five hundred brothers and sisters at one time, most of whom are still alive, though some have died. Then he appeared to James, then to all the apostles. Last of all, as to one untimely born, he appeared also to me" (1 Cor 15:6–8).

One of the best informed commentators on Paul, Jurgen Becker,[4] goes so far as to suggest that from this one appearance of Jesus—even though it was silent—Paul was able to deduce "the sense of the message and the mission" confided to him—an entire theology! It would not be surprising that such an event would give rise to reservations or even doubts. From the moment that the encounter comes under the jurisdiction of the irrational, a positive explanation is no longer necessary. Rationalists refute such reasoning. For two thousand years, Christians have accepted it.

To discover "the sense of the message and the mission," it is necessary to scrutinize the texts. First, the essential one: "For I handed on to you as of first importance what I in turn had received: that Christ died for our sins in accordance with the scriptures, and that he was buried, and that he was raised on the third day in accordance with the scriptures, and that he appeared to Cephas, then to the twelve" (1 Cor 15:3–5).

Not surprisingly, these few lines—as long as we understand their content—are of the first, I would even say of immeasurable, importance. They are nothing less than *the most ancient witness to the Resurrection of Jesus.* The Letter to the Corinthians was redacted between 55 and 57. The Gospel of Mark—the first of the four—was written at the earliest between 65 and 70. The text will faithfully take up the outline Paul sketched. Around 80, Matthew and Luke will do the same. Is it necessary to underline the significance of these simple facts? They make of Paul the first written source of Christianity.

To the Galatians, he recalls, "The gospel that was proclaimed by me is not of human origin; for I did not receive it from a human source, nor was I taught it, but I received it through a revelation of Jesus Christ" (1:11–12). No ambiguity here: what he taught came from the encounter. Through Luke, he reports even the words he heard:

"I have appeared to you for this purpose, to appoint you to serve and testify to the things in which you have seen me and to those in which I will appear to you. I will rescue you from your people and from the Gentiles— to whom I am sending you to open their eyes so that they may turn from darkness to light and from the power of Satan to God, so that they may receive forgiveness of sins and a place among those who are sanctified by faith in me" (Acts 26:16–18).

Certainly Paul's writing of the Letter to the Galatians takes place much later than the vision of Damascus, but this allusion to his universal mission is fascinating.

DID THEY REALLY lead him "by the hand" to Damascus, as Luke claims? Suffering from sudden blindness, unable to follow landmarks, and in danger of tripping at every step on the stones along the road—even if he was being supported—Saul would almost certainly have been lifted onto one of the mounts that would have been part of the caravan.

Thus we see Saul of Tarsus entering Damascus, bounced around on an animal, plunged into an unconsciousness full of remembrances, consumed by an anguish so tenacious that, in his diminished state, he has no strength to fight.

Rising from the Syrian desert, between the last spurs of the Anti-Lebanon and the massif of the Jebel Druze, Damascus imposes itself—yesterday as today—as one of the most attractive cities of the East. The names with which it has been adorned reflect the dreams it has inspired: "seed of the beauty of the world," "calyx in the middle of the flowers," "halo of the moon on the earth." Even in the West, damask cloth, the blouses of Damascus, Damascus swords, and damascene armor have all become legendary. Travelers were enchanted to find there an "island of greenery." Even before entering the city, apricot trees and vines alternated as far as one could see. Having scarcely breached the walls, the freshness of the gardens irrigated by the river Barada reached to the terraces of the houses.

In the fourth millennium before our era, the site was already inhabited by human beings. Tablets—from Egypt and Mari—mention the existence of a civilization in the ninth century B.C. An inscription from the temple of Karnak cites Damascus among the cities conquered by Thutmose III. Having become the capital of the powerful Aramaean monarchy, the city was annexed by King David, hellenized by Alexander the Great, and conquered in 65 B.C. by Pompey, who made it the residence of the Syrian legate.

I passed through the eastern gate through which Saul entered—today the Bab Sharqi—a thick tower, without decorative motif, pierced by three openings. I set off on a long rectangular path that for more than twenty centuries has gone down into the city. Luke recalled its existence: "Now there was a disciple in Damascus named Ananias. The Lord said to him in a vision, 'Ananias.' He answered, 'Here I am, Lord.' The Lord said to him, 'Get up and go to the street called Straight, and at the house of Judas look for a man of Tarsus named Saul'" (Acts 9:10–11).

Around one and a quarter miles long and six and a half feet wide, this *Via recta* of the Romans led to a temple. Porticoes resting on Corinthian capitals extended along the way. Today it is unrecognizable: shops have usurped the line and greatly reduced the original width. Everything is sold there: rugs, fabrics, jewelry, copper trays, side arms. Noises and odors intermingle with the charm of ancient Arab streets.

It is useless to look for a few concrete souvenirs of Saul. Straight Street survives, but the house of the Jew Judas has disappeared. Meanwhile, three hundred yards from there, the "house of Ananias" is on display, or rather the sanctuary that the Byzantines built in the fifth or sixth century. After many reconstructions and restorations—the last one taking place in 1973—Saint Paul's presence has been reduced to nostalgia.

SAUL WOULD REMAIN three days at Judas' home. Eating nothing. Drinking nothing. Without the faintest light reaching his dead eyes.

In the history of the world, perhaps no other episode has provoked so much commentary and so many different or contradictory interpretations. Some have contented themselves with naming it *the Event*, pure and simple.[5] Would anyone dare to imagine the throes the man of Tarsus endured during these three days? A comparison—always risky—comes to mind: Jacob's wrestling with the angel.

Let us list, in the manner of a police report, the information we have on Saul on the day of the Event:

1) *Age: about 26;*
2) *Small in stature, of delicate complexion; yet having a certain physical strength nonetheless;*
3) *Born Jewish abroad, claiming his membership in the Hebrew people;*
4) *Pharisee of strict observance;*

5) *Having acquired from an eminent teacher an exceptional knowledge of the Bible and the Law;*

6) *Languages: Greek, Hebrew, Aramaic;*

7) *Marital status unknown;*

8) *For the past few months has demonstrated violent feelings and has manifested, with regard to Christians, a ruthless sectarianism;*

9) *At the time of the Event, was obsessed by this hatred.*

Is it logical to assume that one vision, however incomparable, or one voice, however supernatural, could lead to the radical change we will see in Saul? According to the modern exegete Alfred Loisy, "Paul's nervous system was eminently excitable and over-stimulated," as is demonstrated by the persecution he has just presided over in Jerusalem. This first vision—he will have others—"produced itself in an organism well prepared to take it or rather to produce it." Alfred Loisy explains:

> After having filled his imagination with this Messiah that he did not want, one fine day he had the impression of being before Jesus whom he was persecuting; he saw him, he thought he saw him as his faithful followers said he was in glory and as many among them had seen him; he was seized with the idea that Jesus was truly the Christ, and he found himself believing.

The objection that could be made to the author—and was made during his lifetime—is that Saul could not have been "filled" with the person of Jesus, since he hardly knew him.

Let us digress and move on to Daniel-Rops: "The fact is there, irrecusably as it will be for Saint Francis of Assisi or for Joan of Arc; it is not in the limbo of a conscience more or less troubled by dementia that the call, which would tear Saul from himself, resounded; it is in the very reality of the things of the earth, on an Asian road, in the hot sun of a July day."

Of the contacts Saul could have made with the Christians he persecuted in Jerusalem, Jurgen Becker draws this hypothesis:

> The discussions Paul had with them had permitted him to know their doctrine and its Christological note. Therefore, this Jesus appeared to him resurrected. For there, things became clear for him; it was not Paul who had to change Christians in the name of the Law or to persecute them, but it was for him to understand God in a new way, contrary to his attachment to the Law. He had himself to change, since this Jesus, on whom Christians based themselves to justify their transgressions of the Law, was alive.

Alive since he had appeared to Saul: "It was thus that he knew himself sent as an apostle to work among the nations without taking the Law into consideration."

Jurgen Becker's reasoning goes further: "If the God who raises the dead lifted him [Jesus] to his side, then the God of the fathers and the God of the Law had become *the Father of Jesus Christ.*"

Let us remember that, in the Old Testament, God almost always spoke to human beings. He ordered Noah to build an ark. At the time of Abraham, he descended to earth—accompanied, it is true, by two angels—to tell Sarah that she would bear a child; he made her laugh and then became angry when she did so. At the summit of Sinai, he gave Moses the tablets of the Law. The prophets received his word. Far from being surprised at this, the readers of the Bible—that is to say, all the Jews—considered these intrusions to be perfectly natural. The German writer Leo Baeck, himself a Jew, asked himself if this, Saul's first experience, was not the engine of his transformation. For a Jew like him,

> a vision had necessarily the significance of a call, the call to set off on a new path. From that time on he could no longer rightly pursue the old way. If a Greek had had such a vision, he would have reacted by reflecting or meditating on the thing, by speaking or writing on the subject. He would never have heard the Jewish commandment: Go, you must set out on the road. The Greeks did not recognize one God, who had every right over them and who was able to make of them his messengers. Only the Jews had always been aware that a revelation implied a mission, with the result that immediate readiness to follow the road prescribed was the first evidence of faith. Paul knew at once that the apostolic office had been assigned to him in the name of the Messiah.

This can explain many things, but not all of them.

THE EXCELLENT ANANIAS belonged to the large Jewish community of Damascus and no doubt had recently converted to Christianity. Before obeying the Lord, who commanded him to go restore Saul's sight, he balked: "Lord, I have heard from many about this man, how much evil he has done to your saints in Jerusalem."

The Lord replied, "Go, for he is an instrument whom I have chosen."

Ananias did not dream of discussing the matter further, and ran to the house of Judas. He found Saul in prayer. "Brother Saul, the Lord Jesus, who appeared to you on your way here, has sent me so that you may regain your sight and be filled with the Holy Spirit" (Acts 9:13–17).

Ananias laid his hands on him and immediately scales fell from the eyes of the blind man. In an instant Saul passed out of the night, where he opposed Jesus, to the light of faith in him. The episode is incorporated, always with identical details, in the very first Christian tradition. Let us return to the reading from Luke: "...And his sight was restored. Then he got up and was baptized" (Acts 9:18). Paul confirms that he was indeed baptized: "For in the one Spirit we were all baptized into one body—Jews or Greeks, slaves or free—and we were all made to drink of one Spirit" (1 Cor 12:13). And again: "Do you not know that all of us who have been baptized into Christ Jesus were baptized into his death?" (Rom 6:3)

Even before the baptismal water dried, Saul was hungry. So says Luke, "And after taking some food, he regained his strength" (Acts 9:19).

No one can adequately explain how the Event settled in Saul, how little by little the message became clear. He did not know Damascus, an imposing city, overpopulated and nothing like Jerusalem in its architecture, its customs, or its language. Anyone would have felt oneself at a loss there. What must it have been like for one who emerged enthralled by a tumult of ideas and impressions that assailed him without respite?

Some object that this is Saint Paul, and that he must have been spared such distress. Proclaimed a saint in 258, his canonization does not in any way mean that his encounter with Jesus removed Saul from the human condition.[6] The reasoning worthy of a Greek philosopher scattered throughout his letters, his enthusiasms, his bitterness, his anger, his hopes, his doubts—all bring him infinitely closer to us. That Paul felt himself to be guided by a higher power can be disputed with difficulty, but, in the history of religion, such is the case with many others. What simple logic demands here—and will demand—is that the historian search out how *the man* Paul reacted in this situation as in all things.

BARELY BAPTIZED, Paul sought the door of a synagogue; Luke shows him thus. That he would rush to a Temple of his Jewish faith is only to be expected. Faced with a great misfortune, a threatening danger, an intense interrogation, what believer—even a lukewarm one—has not felt driven to throw oneself down in a place of worship to pray?

Luke wants us to believe that "immediately he [Saul] began to proclaim Jesus in the synagogues, saying, 'He is the Son of God'"

(Acts 9:20). Really? Acts, it is true, depicts the astonishment of the hearers who recognize in this unexpected preacher the number one persecutor of Christians in Jerusalem. "Saul became increasingly more powerful and confounded the Jews who lived in Damascus by proving that Jesus was the Messiah" (9:22). So much the better for them. So much the better for him.

There are many meanings for the word "confound." We must stop at this one: "to disconcert, to trouble, to fill with astonishment or confusion." This is how we see the Jews of Damascus. Paul's discourse leaves them confounded.

How would you and I have acted had a similar fate befallen us? I wager that we would have hastened to Jerusalem to acknowledge our error and to proclaim the light in which we had just been bathed. We would have tried to inform the persecutors who, in our name, were determined to pursue these unfortunate Christians. We would have opened the prisons where they were languishing. In all humility, we would have sought to learn about this Jesus who had just favored us with an unheard-of gift. The men who had accompanied Jesus from the first days of his public life lived in Jerusalem. We would have begged them to tell us everything they knew about him.

Saul did not undertake any actions like this. Without any warning whatsoever, he disappeared from Damascus. Exit Saul. Such behavior seems like a desertion. Was he afraid? That would be understandable: in Jerusalem, he had just stirred up such suffering and hatred! Where could he go not to bear the gigantic burden that suddenly overwhelmed him? On the Mount of Olives, Jesus himself had prayed to his Father to spare him the agony that awaited him.

The first Christians did not understand Saul's flight any more than we. As proof of this, the Acts of the Apostles remains absolutely silent on Saul's sojourn in Arabia. By means of a sleight of hand, as staggering as it is deliberate, Luke wanted to ignore the exile in Arabia and, from the two sojourns in Damascus, he made one. After "a long enough time," he shows Paul going to Jerusalem to visit Cephas (Peter) and James, "the brother of the Lord."

Adopting another perspective, our astonishment could diminish, even disappear; in fact, would this Saul, ever permeated by a boundless presence, need to run to Jerusalem to seek knowledge of what he was already sure he knew now and forever? "That Paul did not go to

Jerusalem," declares Dieter Hildebrandt, "is and continues to be the sign that *he knew everything at once.*"

Can we, in the relation between God and human beings, learn everything in "the space of a somersault," to quote André Frossard? If we have faith, yes.

BEFORE HIS DEPARTURE, Saul did not seek advice from anyone. Not only does he not hide this fact, he insists upon it. Saul of Tarsus would never have become Saint Paul without this grandiose pride. We find a trace of it in the Letter to the Galatians: "I did not confer with any human being, nor did I go up to Jerusalem to those who were already apostles before me, but I went away at once into Arabia" (1:16–17). According to contemporary criticism, the letter was written in 56 or 57, thus twenty years after Paul's precipitous departure from Damascus. At the time, Paul was seeking to reinforce his own authority in order to be more clearly understood. How better to succeed in this than to show himself, from the time after the Event, free from all influence and all authority? They say that everyone recomposes his or her own biography at forty. In 56–57, Paul would pass his fortieth year.

HE WALKED.

The "way of the kings"—a thousand-year-old name—spread its stony trail under his steps. Going directly south, it allowed one to rejoin the port of Aqaba. Eyes burned by the sun, walking through a furnace that assailed his body and dried his mouth, could the man from Tarsus fail to recognize that he was reversing the road that the Hebrews took on the return of the Exodus? Without a doubt, as Lawrence and his Bedouins later would, Saul avoided walking at high noon, preferring dawn and dusk.

For days and days, he walked.

THE ARABIA OF SAUL'S contemporaries encompassed a precise region: the land of the Nabateans. Sprung from one of the many tribes that wandered the area, they seem to have settled, between the seventh and the sixth centuries B.C., in the kingdom of Edom known as the cradle of Herod the Great. In order to insure their predominance over the peoples of the surrounding area, these desert wanderers knew how to use a means no one would have expected of them: irrigation. In arid wastes, they made a harvest grow. With hardly more than a few tens of thousands of people, they established one of the most brilliant civilizations of their time.

With their caravans—camels being the only means of transportation—they plowed the East. Under King Aretas III, 1,500 tons of incense were taken to Rome each year. Pliny depicted these caravans that transported "the tortoise shell from Malacca and nard[7] from the Ganges, the bark of the cinnamon from the Himalayas ... and from India, diamonds and sapphires, ivory and cotton, indigo, lapis lazuli, and especially pepper, dates and wine, gold and slaves."

It was a peculiar kingdom incapable of setting limits. At its peak, it spread over modern Jordan, part of Syria, and the deserts of the East. Aretas III's capital was Petra.

Leaving the route of the kings, Saul would have branched off toward the west and gone down into a gorge that led precisely to Petra.

I remember it. In order to climb the hill from which height one could better see Petra at sunrise, my wife and children had left the hotel in the middle of the night. Since my cardiologist forbade me that kind of exploit, I simply calculated the hour I should catch up with them in the valley. Early in the morning, having avoided the mules offered in abundance, I set out on foot to rejoin the road that gave one access to these marvels. After having followed the bed of the wadi Musa and imitating Saul's example, I slid between two walls of high rocks, each 330 feet. Almost a mile later, there rose before me one of the most prodigious sites in the world: Petra, the red city.

The name comes from the Greek word for rock, *petra*. The miracle was born of water, wind, and the jolts of nature: together they have sculpted the sandstone as much as the limestone and juxtaposed the colors, yellow striped with blue to scarlet, mauve to dregs of wine. Humans have lived there for ten thousand years. From the third century B.C., fascinated by the décor, the Nabateans sowed monuments by the hundreds: temples and tombs often carved into the mountain itself.

When Saul reached Petra, the Nabateans were going through difficult times. The tetrarch of Galilee, Herod Antipas, had married the daughter of Aretas IV, their king. After this, he succumbed to a foolish passion for Herodias, the wife of his half-brother. Repudiated,

Aretas' daughter was sent back to him without any formal process, which, as we would expect, did not please the king of the Nabateans. Sorely tempted to make the son-in-law who had offended him disappear, he must have thought better of it for fear of incurring the wrath of the Romans, who were faithful allies of Herod. Aretas IV contented himself with causing a thousand worries to the Jews of the region. Evidently, Saul arrived at an inopportune moment. He would remain in Arabia no less than three years.

What did he do there?

Certain Fathers of the Church believed that he had only come to this region for the sole purpose of evangelizing the Nabateans. The argument they advanced is certainly still striking today: After the Event, how could Saul have kept quiet? However, must we deduce from this that the keeper of such a secret chose to confide it to the Nabateans? Should we picture the small man preaching, in a language he did not know, to a people he did not know? Was he ready then to evangelize people other than Jews, when he had not felt the strength—his departure from Damascus is the sign—to convince those of Syria?

Some have recalled the conversion of Saint Augustine, who felt the need of "stopping time" to put order in the "tumult"—he too experienced it—of his thoughts and feelings. Nietzsche said, "Whoever would be someday the bearer of an important message remains quiet for a long time; whoever wants to produce lightning must for a long time be a cloud."

Could Saul then have wanted to escape the awful question that perhaps obsessed his mind: *What if I dreamed it?* Pushing back a cry of terror. Feeling again, after having lost, the Lord's presence, only to lose it again—and to again find it.

These questions have no answers. The only serious clue we have comes from Saul. Having re-entered Damascus, he will have to clear up serious annoyances on the part of Aretas IV's envoy. The Nabatean king must have been in contact with Saul previously and a serious conflict must have arisen between them.

Let us again make the point. Regaining consciousness after the Event, Saul moved toward the Jews because he only knew the Jews. They pushed him away. It was impossible to return to Jerusalem; they would have avenged themselves against him for his tragic error in which he implicated his fellow citizens. Therefore, he had to go, no matter where,

without any other purpose than to leave behind him this too heavy burden. The Event? He would carry it in his heart. Outside Damascus there
was little more than the desert. He plunged into it. Of the money carried
from Jerusalem, he had enough to live for some time. After that? No
problem whatsoever. He was a tentmaker. When he began his apostolic
journeys, it was exactly what he would do: entering a city, he would set
himself to weaving.

We can conclude that King Aretas' anger might have been of a commercial nature. Was it due to a conflict Saul might have had with suppli-
ers or clients close to the king? When the danger defined itself—the
threat of prison?—Saul would have returned to Damascus. There is no
document to support this hypothesis. Still, it stands.

The day will come when Paul will compare what he received to a
treasure, all the while recognizing its fragility. "But we have this treasure
in clay jars, so that it may be made clear that this extraordinary power
belongs to God and does not come from us" (2 Cor 4:7).

Is not man himself a vessel of clay?

4

FIFTEEN DAYS TO KNOW JESUS

From the Atlantic to Mesopotamia, from Tingi (Tangier) to the depths of Egypt, the *Pax Romana* extended its hegemony, its omnipotence, its protection.

On his isle of Capri, in the luxury of one of the twelve villas he had built to house his debaucheries, Tiberius, the old emperor, saw his last days. He had raised much hope when Augustus had put him into power by force. Gradually, the unrestrained exercise of absolute power perpetuated suspicion and fear everywhere. Protected by a guard with a thousand eyes, he delegated to his minister Sajan, the doer of his dirty work in Rome, a spate of death sentences that appalled the senate. When would the merciless emperor pass from life to death?

Was it from Capri or from Rome that Vitellius, the legate of Syria, received instructions to put an end to the impieties of Aretas? The Nabateans had been too easily allowed to take Philadelphia, to occupy Gerasa, to annex Gamala. That they were now intensifying their pressure on Damascus came close to unbearable.

In March 37, ruled by the military logic of Pompey, the legions of Vitellius approached the city which trembled between the Nabatean threat and the Roman peril. To appease Aretas, the people of Damascus let it be known that Roman currency would no longer be used in the city. To protect themselves from Vitellius, they prepared Damascus for war, reinforced its defenses, and closed its gates. Saul no doubt slipped in at the last minute.

Tangled in his version of events, which would ignore the three years Saul spent in Arabia, Luke shows his hero returning to his preaching in Damascus as though he had just left yesterday. He depicts Saul's Jewish hearers becoming more and more exasperated by the repeated claim of "Jesus, Son of God." Let us understand these Jews: no one had ever let it be known that the Most High could have a son. Not a word from the prophets, not a verse in the sacred text. This was a scandal!

And the Christians of Damascus? Logic would suggest that for three years they had multiplied, and that the report of the persecution led by the man from Tarsus had been communicated and naturally amplified to the new converts. Far from a Saul who is sure of himself, we see him haunted by his disgraceful reputation and visibly uncertain about what to do.

"The Jews plotted to kill him, but their plot became known to Saul. They were watching the gates [of the city] day and night so that they might kill him" (Acts 9:23–24); that is what Luke believes he knows. Paul's version is altogether different: "In Damascus, the governor [*ethnarch*] under King Aretas guarded the city of Damascus in order to seize me" (2 Cor 11:32). In the Roman Empire the title "ethnarch" designated the governor of a province. Therefore, Aretas' envoy was an important person. According to Nabatean tradition, conquered or controlled regions became autonomous districts entrusted most of the time to members of the royal family. That the ethnarch of Aretas had to guard the city confirms the extent of the grievances the king nurtured on meeting Saul and, at the same time, shows that the Nabateans controlled Damascus.

Paul's short phrase casts the episode in a new light; the hostility of the Jews was not the essential cause of the danger he encountered. He wanted to escape from the ethnarch. The rest of the story permits no hesitation: "I was let down in a basket through a window in the wall, and escaped from his hands" (2 Cor 11:33).

The story of the basket was a success. It figures into all the tour books; it is echoed by guides of every language who point out, on the ramparts, what is left of a square tower whose foundations of enormous stones remain today. They repeat in their most authoritative voices, "It was from there that Saint Paul was lowered in a basket!"

"He rises from divine waters seized by such a fire," Saint John Chrysostom says of Paul, "that he did not even wait for the teaching of the Master." At this point in his story, the fire burns by its absence. Saul never ceases to disconcert. Impatient by nature, he now shows too much patience. After the Event, he was expected in Jerusalem but went instead to Arabia. In Damascus one would expect the messenger of Christ to confront, but he flees in a basket. At that moment, could Saul of Tarsus have been the loneliest man in the world?

I sense that the reader could be increasingly intrigued by all these texts: are we sure of their authenticity? How have they reached us?

In the New Testament, the canonical texts are arranged in an unchangeable order: the Gospel according to Matthew, the Gospel according to Mark, the Gospel according to Luke, and the Gospel according to John. Then come the Acts of the Apostles, the Letters of Saint Paul, the Letters of other apostles, and finally the Apocalypse. One could draw from this arrangement an idea ready-made; the publication of the Gospels must have preceded Acts and the apostolate of Paul. But this is a mistake. We know that at the time of the Event, no Gospel text had yet been disseminated. It would take a long time for that to happen.

We cannot rule out that several witnesses of the life of Jesus preserved some of his teaching in writing, on the condition that it was redacted as an afterthought. The idea of notetaking at the scene, so familiar in our time, had no counterpart in the ancient world. In the first century, writing was a skill exercised by professionals who prided themselves on their title of scribe. They acquired their knowledge after long years of study, and they practiced it for a fee. The scribe was the only one able to redact without making a rough copy. Although more rarely than we originally thought, he sometimes used wax tablets on which, with the help of a stylus, he etched what he was asked to write. When one wanted to approach a longer text, such as the Letters of Paul, it required the use of a material whose description has come down even to us: a board on which were fixed small cups to hold the ink; a stylus with a dry point to mark the lines; and a scraper to erase.

The scribe made his own inks: black beginning with black charred matter, red beginning with red earth. His pens—*calame*—came from rushes or from reeds. Apart from the wax tablet, he could choose between papyrus and parchment, both expensive. Papyrus was a kind of paper made of strips drawn from the stalk of a plant cultivated in Egypt and laid side by side to obtain "leaves" eight to sixteen inches long. Each side could be used. Parchment, costlier but more substantial, was nothing more than the skin of an animal—sheep, deer, or antelope—that had been tanned and bleached. Michel Quesnel, whose study of this subject serves as reference here, concludes that "on such material one could write about three syllables per minute, that is, seventy words an hour."

Imagine the apostles carrying such gear in their bags and using it, when there was a pause, to give written form to the words of Jesus. In almost all of the simplest settings, most people did not know how to read or write. They would have burst out laughing if anyone had claimed otherwise. But they would never have dreamed of disagreeing, if one had presented them as masters of oral transmission. This was the common lot: learning by heart the verses of the Law, Jewish children strengthened their memory to the point of over-development. The apostles are the best proof of this.

Many studies have focused on the dating of the Gospels and the Letters of Saint Paul. Today there is agreement on dates that are compelling but still just approximations. After the deaths of Peter and Paul, Mark redacted his Gospel, the first, between 65 and 70. The second Gospel, attributed to Matthew, one of the Twelve, was originally written in Hebrew and adapted in Greek by an unknown author. It came to light in the 80s, as did Luke's; he did not know Jesus but devoted himself to a profound inquiry of the witnesses to Jesus' life. The last, the Gospel of John, probably the youngest of the apostles, is a spiritual monument profoundly different than the others. Resulting from a long process of maturation, its redaction is situated in the 90s.

We come to a question that legitimately preoccupies us even more: How were these texts transmitted to us? Although the existence of the Letters of Paul is attested in 150, no manuscript from that era has reached us. The first manuscript of the Gospels, the *Vaticanus,* is dated from 331. Such a space of time is troubling. If the first documents about Louis XIV came to light just today, would we trust their authenticity? Three centuries between the redaction of the Gospels and the first manuscripts drawing them together is an enormous amount of time! Many believers remain obsessed by it.

They are wrong. Their concern should extend to the great classics of antiquity, whether Greek or Latin. Between the time when Euripides wrote and when the first copies of his works that we know of appeared, sixteen centuries had elapsed. For Sophocles, Aeschylus, Aristophanes, and Thucydides, fourteen centuries had passed; for Plato, thirteen; for

Demosthenes, twelve; for Terence, seven; for Virgil—the favorite—four. Would we argue that the works of Sophocles are not of Sophocles but of a monk forger of the Middle Ages?

For a long time it was the same for the Old Testament, which we knew only from later copies. This is no longer the case. After the Second World War, original manuscripts from the Dead Sea were discovered, bringing to light long passages from the Bible. With few exceptions, they are identical to the later copies. This should reassure the most skeptical.

I would add one collection of Greek papyri, copied around 200—the *Papyrus Chester Beatty*—which restores to us a Bible that is almost complete, including the Letters of Paul.[1]

The process for the survival of ancient texts is clear. One copy of the Letter to the Romans on papyrus would have covered a scroll twelve to thirteen feet long. The extreme fragility of the foundation of these texts led gradually to their disappearance. The last "survivors" must have perished at the hands of the monks when they recopied them onto parchment.

Paul died without ever being able to read a single Gospel. We can hardly believe our eyes when we come to these phrases in one of his letters:

> For I received from the Lord what I also handed on to you, that the Lord Jesus on the night when he was betrayed took a loaf of bread, and when he had given thanks, broke it and said, *"This is my body that is for you. Do this in remembrance of me."* In the same way he took the cup also, after supper, saying, *"This cup is the new covenant in my blood. Do this, as often as you drink it, in remembrance of me"* (1 Cor 11:23–25).

Incorporated into the Gospel, these lines of Paul are now pronounced each day at all the Eucharistic celebrations throughout the world.

WHEN WOULD SAUL admit that it was time for him to know the Son of Man in his earthly reality? Could he not see that his faith limped on one leg? He had missed hearing those who had seen Jesus, who had been there when the adulterous woman destined to be stoned was brought to him and who had heard him pronounce these words: "Let anyone among you who is without sin be the first to throw a stone at her" (Jn 8:7). Saul had missed the answer Jesus gave his mother when, at Cana, she asked him to put an end to the confusion of the hosts who did not have enough wine: "Woman...my hour has not yet come" (Jn 2:4). He had missed knowing that Jesus, an affectionate son, had still changed the water into wine. When would Saul decide to inform himself as he must?

A somewhat obscure text of Paul gives us pause; he would have had to wait three years before returning to Jerusalem. Three years in addition to his three years in Arabia? As troubled as we are by this confusing reference, specialists have arrived at a plausible explanation: the three years must be counted from the Event; they encompass the exile in Arabia and the two sojourns in Damascus.[2] We breathe a sigh of relief and, satisfied, fall into step with the journey just getting underway.

For Saul is finally walking toward Jerusalem.

THERE IT IS, the city at once feared and mourned, unchanging in its stone walls, the heart of the Jewish nation, where on the same days and the same feasts, all those who ran to its Temple to pay homage to the Eternal One found themselves. Hundreds of thousands of pilgrims sang and prayed always in the sacred place. Filled with the Most High, they returned scanning the hymn repeated a thousand times: "The LORD will keep your going out and your coming in.... My help comes from the LORD who made heaven and earth" (Ps 121:8, 2).

The Saul who re-entered the city of David a bit wearily could not help but feel the intensity of such living forces, the vigor of this religion and, in contrast, the fragility of those who believed in Jesus. He failed to see that that immense flux of pilgrims returning home harbored an invisible current. Many families returning to "Mesopotamia, Judea and Cappadocia, Pontus and Asia, Phrygia and Pamphylia, Egypt and the parts of Libya belonging to Cyrene"—Luke's wonderful list (Acts 2:9–10)—carried with them a secret confided to them by a relative, a friend, or a stranger: *the Messiah has come to earth.* This "spontaneous expansion" continued the dispersion that had begun after the execution of Stephen. Like Philip, Hellenist Christians sought refuge far from Jerusalem or returned in haste to their native land. In their turn, they spread the story of the crucified Messiah who, laid in the tomb, was raised on the third day.

Thus, little by little, the prophecy that Jesus addressed to the Twelve on the day of the Ascension was fulfilled: "You will be my witnesses in Jerusalem, in all Judea and Samaria, and to the ends of the earth" (Acts 1:8).

Luke shows Saul in Jerusalem trying to reunite with the faithful there, but "they were all afraid of him, for they did not believe that he was a disciple" (Acts 9:26). Here for the first time a person arrives on the scene whom we will meet again at many stages of Paul's life. Acts presents him this way: "There was a Levite,[3] a native of Cyprus, Joseph, to whom the apostles gave the name Barnabas"[4] (Acts 4:36). He will introduce Saul to the apostles. Of this meeting that we await, we only have this dry statement from Paul: "I did go up to Jerusalem to visit Cephas and stayed with him fifteen days; but I did not see any other apostle except James the Lord's brother" (Gal 1:18–19).

Just fifteen days to know Jesus! "Unbelievable but true," declared the little books that I read when I was a child. I wouldn't know how to say it better. Undoubtedly the care of the community absorbed the time of Peter and James, but all the same...!

What could Saul have learned in such a few days? The words of Jesus that Peter, by dint of repetition, knew by heart? The course of the Lord in Galilee and Judea sketched in broad outline? The first phases of a stammering theology, the progress of the fledgling community, the obstacles it met? The conversion that Peter underwent by baptizing the Roman centurion Cornelius, a pagan? Was the ex-fisherman from the Lake of Tiberias tempted to talk about his friends and himself, about how they had left their nets to follow this unknown Rabbi who then and there had recognized them? None of that seems to have interested Saul. Formerly adept at non-factual history, Saul was not concerned with relating details.

In the Letters of Saint Paul, Christ blazes on each page; Jesus passes unnoticed. There is not one allusion to the parables that simple people listened to so avidly. There is no Sermon on the Mount, no miraculous catches, no healings, nothing about the Temple from which the merchants were driven and where the son of Mary preached before being crucified. For Paul, "in Christ God was reconciling the world to himself, not counting their trespasses against them, and entrusting the message of reconciliation to us" (2 Cor 5:19). Jesus did not need a biography.

NOT ONLY DID PAUL acknowledge that he did not see anyone but Peter and James during these fifteen days, he also insisted on being believed: "In what I am writing to you, before God, I do not lie!" (Gal 1:20) If he reinforced his affirmation in this way, it was to make a point—essential in his eyes—that he did not *need* to see others.

Still, one must not neglect his encounter with James. Even if we do not want to take literally those who at that time—practically everyone—called James "brother of the Lord," his belonging to the family of Jesus was hardly in doubt. His influence would be revealed as considerable, not only over the first Church but also, paradoxically, over the unconverted Pharisees who would establish a rigorous piety within Judaism. When the primacy of Peter diminished, James would assume leadership of the disciples of Jesus. He would be known as the "first bishop of the Hebrews." The case of this Christian determined to remain fully Jewish would be weighed by Paul when he himself had to make his choice. The day would come when James would confront Paul on the road, determined to destroy the effects of his mission. Unfortunate religion that, newborn, would divide and fight itself.

We see Saul at the end of this brief sojourn, having gradually acquired self-confidence, walking in the street with Peter and James, which shocked the Christians who noticed. On several occasions, he would try to explain himself to people who were clearly hostile: "He spoke and argued with the Hellenists; but they were attempting to kill him" (Acts 9:29). They had not forgotten. What he had feared had happened: his reputation as persecutor had become for him Nessus' tunic. Luckily, not everyone wanted to harm him; having learned that some had reserved bad treatment for him, perhaps the worst, "they brought him down to Caesarea." The information should not be dismissed; from Caesarea, Paul will be "sent...off to Tarsus" (Acts 9:30). Defeat in Damascus, defeat in Jerusalem, defeat at Caesarea—it's a lot to take.

To be fair, we should look at the meaning of the Greek verb "to send back." *Exapostellein* can mean "to put far away" but, in the Septuagint and other contemporary texts, it also has the meaning "to send on mission." This is the sense Paul seems to evoke when he writes: "Then I went into the regions of Syria and Cilicia" (Gal 1:21). In this case, the facts are themselves deduced. Saul, having joined Peter and James, would have received from them a kind of apostolic mission to exercise in the neighboring provinces of his native city. Tarsus will serve as his base of departure.

No text informs us of his parents' reception: arms wide open, tears of joy, concern over his strange experience of God? Soon enough he would have gone back to cutting and sewing tents in his father's workshop; but one imagines him not well-suited to being dependent on his parents. We might suppose that his aging father would have confided growing responsibilities to him. We can picture Saul discussing delivery delays, the holding price, or simply—we are in the East—involved in haggling.

One of his biographers depicts him during these three years, "traveling around the province to sell his goods and to announce the Gospel, a bit like the Bible salesmen who, in South America, play the part of charlatans or sellers of elixirs."[5] Was this how the uniqueness of a destiny took shape, by making oneself at one and the same time an artisan and a preacher of the Gospel?

Once more uneasiness stirs within us. Even if Saul left Tarsus every now and then to make contact with some fledgling community, we have a hard time explaining these years of retreat with his family, in the most "bourgeois" situation possible. Does the Event no longer seethe in his mind, in his memory, or in his heart? At the family table, with the cares of his work, does he end up not thinking about it, without however striking it from his memory deliberately, as one does with a book one skims in the library knowing that, if the need should arise, one could refer back to it? The question altogether remains: why did Saul linger in Tarsus?

SINCE THE DEATH of Tiberius in 37—finally—a mad emperor reigned in Rome: Caligula. Great-grandson of Augustus, son of the popular Germanicus and Agrippina, and adopted son and successor of Tiberius, he was recognized without difficulty by the senate and the army. Caligula's nascent instability suggested to him the idea of having his subjects adore him as the "New Sun." Gradually this oddity transformed itself into a raging madness. Not only did he make his favorite horse a senator, but he was seized by a hatred of the Jews. In the East, imperial anti-Semitism would find a first-rate dwelling. A ruthless pogrom in 38 ravaged Alexandria, a Jewish city par excellence. In Antioch, the Jewish quarter was divided in squares; killing and pillaging took place there. The tensions between Roman authority and the Jewish community reached their climax in the year 40 when Caligula demanded that his statue be erected within the precincts of the Temple in Jerusalem. A year later, a tribune of the praetorian guard would slaughter the madman in his palace.

For fear of being massacred in his turn, his uncle Claudius—an epileptic and a stammerer deprived of all will power—cowered in a hiding place in the same palace. Discovered by the praetorians, he was proclaimed emperor on the spot. The disciples of YHWH could breathe again: an edict of Claudius assured the Jews of Alexandria freedom to practice their religion and informed those in Antioch of his wish for tolerance; their rights would be inscribed on bronze tablets. Providing its own leaders, the Jewish community of Antioch would from that time enjoy special legislation protecting family rights and the rules of worship, without, however, recognizing its members as full-fledged citizens.

At the same time, conversions to Christianity multiplied. They would pose problems not only for the increasingly irritated Jewish hierarchy, but in the very core of the new community of Jesus' disciples.

After the torment that followed the stoning of Stephen, a notable group of Hellenist Christians driven out of Jerusalem had sought refuge in Antioch. Everything leads one to believe that one of the Seven, Nicolaus, founded a Christian community there. Being prudent, its members began by "announcing the Word" to Jews only. They soon noticed that a number of pagans displayed an unusual interest in the religion of Moses. More astonishing still, these were not exceptional cases. They were numerous enough that they were given a name: the "God-fearers."

To understand what this name signified, it is necessary to imagine a "Greek" who, from childhood, had lived in the cult of the gods of Olympus and, when it came to offering them sacrifices, had always had an array of choices. He named the same gods, sometimes in Greek, sometimes in Latin: Zeus or Jupiter, Dionysius or Bacchus. He appealed to this multiple family with the agility of spirit that his ancestral culture allowed. They all passed there: Juno, Hermes, Venus, Eros, Apollo, Aphrodite, Mars, Minerva. Our man knew all about their existence or their roles in nature, their merits, their vices—for they had some—their affronts, their loves, their progeny. Nothing was more alluring, nothing more endearing, nothing more apt to arouse a dream; but our Greek friend was beginning to grow weary of the exploits of these too human gods. He wandered from there and would only have to take one small step but, out of loyalty, he had not wanted to think about it. Then one day someone whispered in his ear that some people in the city believed in only one God. Only one? This Greek was amazed and showed some curiosity. Who was he, what had this God done? They told him this God created the world and everything that lives. He watched over human beings, preserved them from the snares that threatened them, rewarded them if they did good, and chastised them if they did evil. The Greek could hardly believe it. He asked who were this God's faithful ones. They answered: the Jews. Like everyone in the world, the Greek knew of their existence, but where could one see them? In the synagogue. So it happened that the "God-fearers"—better named "God-seekers"—crossed the threshold of the private home where the Jews assembled. The idea of a place built for the sole purpose of praying together had not yet implanted itself in their minds.

Having discovered in this unsuspecting milieu fertile ground, the Christians would take the risk of recruiting there. They succeeded beyond all their hopes. To the "God-fearer" ready to become Jewish in order to discover the one God, they proposed Jesus, God and man, a Jew but infinitely closer to Biblical personages than they, until then, had tried to approach. The reasoning was simple: it was not necessary to pass through Judaism in order to meet Jesus. One could go to him directly.

THE PROBLEM OF the conversion of pagans went beyond simple questions of obedience to rituals. It required a fundamental option: from their early childhood, the faithful followers of Jesus who were of Jewish origin had kept the Law. But when pagans asked for Baptism by ignoring the whole Law, did the disciples have the right to admit "Gentiles" in the Church of Christ? This awesome question would be posed to the elders in Jerusalem controlled by the severe James. Was it permitted to live in contact with Greeks, Scythians, or others—all men who had not been circumcised? How to tolerate that the disciples of the Law, in sharing their meals, risked touching the meat of animals butchered outside the rules?

With distance exaggerating the scope of the debate, everything being reported in Jerusalem began to raise suspicions for James and his followers. They had no time to lose. To look into the matter closely, James had to send a trustworthy "inquirer" to Antioch. He found one in Barnabas, the same disciple who had introduced Saul to Peter and James. "A good man, full of the holy Spirit and of faith" (Acts 11:24), Barnabas was not only retained because of his Cypriot origin, which brought him close to Antioch by distance, but especially because he knew the Antiochene mentality.

As soon as he arrived, Barnabas set to work. He did not want to reconsider the conversions already obtained from among the pagans. But he insisted on meeting each new Christian, to bring to light the sincerity of each one's commitment. Among the pagans converted at Antioch, Barnabas discovered a profound faith that pleased him: "When he...saw the grace of God, he rejoiced, and he exhorted them all to remain faithful to the Lord with steadfast devotion" (Acts 11:23). He would quickly conclude that in this vast city the task was beyond his strength.

What to do?

It seems obvious that the memory of Saul—so complex, hated by so many people, but who, in Jerusalem, had moved him—would come to his mind. He inquired: What has become of him? "He has returned to Tarsus where he is making tents; he was confided a vague mission as apostolic delegate." "Who confided it to him?" "Peter and James." Barnabas could no longer doubt; he chose the man of destiny. Luke relates this in less than ten words; because for him the affair flowed from the source: "Then Barnabus went to Tarsus to look for Saul" (Acts 11:25).

Let's allow our imaginations to run a bit. Barnabas arrives in Tarsus. He inquires to find the house of Saul, at whose door he knocks. Saul's mother sends him to the workshop. For local color: pieces of tent that Saul assembles or the transactions he drafts. There is hesitation on both sides at the moment when they recognize each other; how one can change! The interesting turn Saul's baldness has taken…. "Naturally you will stay at the house." "But no." "But yes." The parents. Small dishes in larger ones. Barnabas' proposal. Silence. A few tears from Saul's mother at the prospect of losing her son once again. The old gentleman tells her to be quiet. Silence. Saul's question, weighty with meaning: "When do we leave?" "Tomorrow."

Who can prove that it didn't happen this way? Great undertakings often begin small. I love this comment of the historian Marie-Françoise Baslez: "The opportunity comes to him from Antioch and from Barnabas."

This is an excellent occasion to render to Barnabas the name under which he became a saint.

SAUL WAS THIRTY-FIVE years old. He walked.

Barnabas walked.

How could their conversation not have been concerned above all with the fundamental debate going on in Antioch? Logically everything would have carried the man from Tarsus, the student of the tolerant Gamaliel, toward the Hellenists. But since the affair of Stephen, they hated him. Saul's answer to the questions Barnabas put to him must not have kept Barnabas waiting. The encounter the man of Tarsus had with Jesus had made him a Christian without abrogating anything of his Jewishness. The essential thing he retained from it and the order that he received were to make known to *all human beings* that the Son of God was crucified to redeem the sins of *all*. Excluding the pagans for any reason whatsoever would be a great mistake. Barnabas could

count on one brother who, steeped in Greek culture, formed by crafts-
manship and business, would be everywhere at ease in announcing
Christ.

When walking, one not only exchanges general ideas. One informs
oneself or the other. They talked about Herod Agrippa I, who had recon-
stituted the kingdom of his grandfather Herod the Great. Agrippa could
do this because Caligula, his companion in debauchery, gave him northern
Palestine, Galilee, and Perea, to which Claudius had added Judea and
Samaria. In his zeal to make himself appreciated by his restive subjects,
Agrippa had begun to pursue the Christians. James, the son of Zebedee,
has been "killed with the sword" (Acts 12:2), the first of the apostles to
shed his blood. Recently Peter had been arrested but, as Barnabas was
ready to swear, an angel had opened the doors of his prison. Freed, he had
warned James, the brother of the Lord, as well as the elders. They were
now in a safe place.

What of Agrippa? When in April of 44 he was addressing a speech
from the royal tribune, "the angel of the Lord struck him down" (Acts
12:23). Flavius Josephus did not get wind of the same kind of death:
"He entered the theater at dawn, dressed in a robe entirely of silver and
admirable fabric.... Then he was stricken with an intestinal malady and
died three days later." Luke adds, "he was eaten by worms and died"
(Acts 12:23). Luke's angel of the Lord does not strike with a light hand.

And then, they arrived at Antioch.

WAS SAUL PREOCCUPIED with the past of the city he now entered?
Would it interest him that Seleucus I, named The Conqueror, had founded Antioch three centuries earlier; that it had become the capitol of the
Seleucid Empire; that thirteen sovereigns had reigned there until 64 B.C.,
when Pompey had despoiled Antiochus XIII of his throne? The Seleucid
genius had profited magnificently from a unique position on the
Mediterranean. Very quickly the city attracted traders, merchants, outfitters of ships, bankers. It also emerged as the most cosmopolitan of cities,
streaming with riches and extreme passions. In the second century B.C.
the Seleucid Empire already shone from Greece to the Hindu Kush. The
rival of Alexandria, Antioch counted five hundred thousand inhabitants.
In the first century, when Saul reached it, it was little changed.

It was very difficult for the man from Tarsus to grasp the contradictions of such a city. Evoking Seleucia, the port of Antioch, Juvenal had

grown indignant to see embarking there each year "depraved beings" born of a "secular corruption" ready to descend upon Rome to infect it. This entry on a subject without ambiguity would inspire Renan. From sources, none of which escaped him, he drew a striking description of Antioch. We see it, this "city of races, of games, of dances, of processions, of feasts, of orgies" where reigned "an unbridled luxury, all the folly of the Orient, the most unwholesome superstitions, the fanaticisms of the orgy." On the great avenue, which crossed the city from one side to another, rolled "the waves of a population futile, frivolous, fickle, riotous, sometimes spiritual, occupied with songs, parodies, pleasantries, impertinence of all kinds." Renan imagined there, "like an intoxication, a dream of Sardanapalus," where there unrolled "pell-mell all the delights, all the debauchery, without excluding a certain delicacy."

Let us beware of Manichaeism; in this city of all follies, people also read and admired Aristotle, and dramatized Aristophanes and Euripides. The schools were the most quoted in the Near East, and the libraries were glutted with works. From afar, people came to admire the temples where the people prayed.

That one of the most decisive debates of Christian history was held in such a setting and such a climate leaves us, twenty centuries later, incredulous. Yet, it was so.

Surely the first thing that astonished Saul in Antioch was to discover the name that the brothers of Jesus now bore: "It was in Antioch that the disciples were first called 'Christians'" (Acts 11:26). Whatever belief we claim, we can't but sense the emotion in seeing such a word emerge: a word called to such a prodigious future; a word that will embrace such faith, holiness, and spirit of conquest in the best and sometimes worst sense of the term. The source of the word is the Greek *christianos*, formed from *Christos*, the Christ. Strangely, it was forged in non-Christian surroundings. Those concerned, who until then had called themselves *brothers, saints, believers, disciples, the Way,* seem to have welcomed it without reticence, since they hastened to adopt it. The biographer feels relieved to be able finally to write "Christian," without circumlocution, notice, quotation marks, or explanatory note.

Perhaps from now on we should see Saul through the mosaics and paintings that, plausibly born of portraits more ancient still, give us the invariable image of a man with a haughty look, thin, bald, with a large forehead and a beard cut to a point.

Did he feel that the Church of Christ was in the process of coming into its own? From all parts it was organizing itself. In Antioch it was to a group of five exemplary men that he returned—beside the "Assembly" —to lead the community. In the midst of such authorities, Saul figured solely as a zealous disciple. Although Barnabas recommended him, he would have to prove himself. The disciples of Stephen were far from having forgotten their persecutor from Jerusalem. Did the others only know what happened to him on the road to Damascus? After a long enough time Saul must have given up boasting of it; exposing the Event to doubts—logical and plausible—would have been unbearable for him. His letters demonstrate that he senses himself always in immediate dependence on Christ. He will never deviate from this certitude.

For an entire year, Saul lived with Barnabas in a charismatic community, fasting and praying in the company of the "regulars" of the local Church. He preached in the synagogues but also elsewhere in the city, and that was something new. One tradition, long evoked at Antioch, shows him speaking near the Pantheon and notably to hearers who have been romanized. He taught more willingly than he baptized. From day to day, from month to month, Barnabas became convinced of the excellence of his choice. There is no doubt that Saul was deeply influenced by him, or by the friendship that united them for so long. Both remained celibate, while others among the leaders of the Church—such as Peter and James—were married. Barnabas, though the offspring of a rich family from Cyprus, would persist, like Saul, in working with his hands in order not to burden the community. On the list of the five principal members of the Christian community of Antioch, Barnabas has a right to the first place, Saul to the last (Acts 13:1).

Was it because he was searching so desperately for light that Saul would be struck by what some would identify as an obvious encouragement, others as a more unusual call to order? "This falls upon you," say those who have been its object. The vision that Saul received would mark him forever. Refusing out of humility to express himself in the first person singular, he would later allude to it in these terms:

> I know a person in Christ who fourteen years ago was caught up to the third heaven[6]—whether in the body or out of the body I do not know; God knows. And I know that such a person...was caught up into Paradise and heard things that are not to be told, that no mortal is permitted to repeat. On behalf of such a one I will boast, but on my own behalf I will

not boast, except of my weaknesses. But if I wish to boast, I will not be a fool, for I will be speaking the truth. But I refrain from it, so that no one may think better of me than what is seen in me or heard from me, even considering the exceptional character of the revelations. Therefore, to keep me from being too elated, a thorn was given me in the flesh, a messenger of Satan to torment me, to keep me from being too elated. Three times I appealed the Lord about this, that it would leave me, but he said to me, "My grace is sufficient for you, for power is made perfect in weakness." So I will boast all the more gladly of my weaknesses, so that the power of Christ may dwell with me.

Therefore, I am content with weaknesses, insults, hardships, persecutions, and calamities for the sake of Christ; for whenever I am weak, then I am strong (2 Cor 12:2–10).

To those who go on repeating only the blessings of visions without reference to poverty, what a response!

A THORN IN THE FLESH. The phrase has caused rivers of ink to flow. All the illnesses that can befall the human body have been proposed: osteoarthritis, tendonitis, chronic sciatica, gout; tachycardia, angina, acute itching, scabies, anthrax, boils, hemorrhoids, fistula, eczema, leprosy, shingles, plague, rabies, fever of Malta, skin infection; stomach pains, diarrhea, stones; chronic ear infection, sinus, bronchitis; retention of urine, infection of the urethra, malaria, parasites, ringworm; headache, gangrene, running sores, abscesses, chronic hiccups, convulsions; epilepsy. Which to choose? As Paul passed victoriously through numberless trials and did not die at a respectable age but under the executioner's sword, one must exclude illnesses that kill with one sure blow: plague, leprosy, rabies, gangrene. Also excluded are those that would have weakened him too much to pursue his mission for very long: angina, malaria, running sores, even hiccups comparable to those suffered by Pius XII. More simply, one must return to the meaning of the word and what it suggests. A thorn is matter of some kind, particularly of wood, which, having entered into the skin by accident, is able to give rise, with certain movements, to an acute pain. In the present circumstances, one must imagine a thorn remaining in place during almost one's entire life. Most of the illnesses suggested do not fall into this category. Arthritis pain remains at the top of the list. While in Chaplin's first films rheumatics made people laugh, those who suffer from it never find it amusing. Certain arthritics reveal themselves to be veritable martyrs; in Paul's time there was nothing to bring them relief. We can also add here recurring kidney stones. One of Paul's letters alludes to an illness that immobilized him for several months. This is not the thorn. Illnesses are occasional; the thorn is permanent.

The thorn must not cloud the issue: the man who came through the vision he evokes in the Second Letter to the Corinthians emerges touched to the depths of his soul. The great mystics found rare words to relate the grace of which they were the object.

We can be sure of one thing: the vision arrived in the nick of time. A new Saul was born. Although most first-generation Christians considered that the most important thing for a Jewish convert was to persuade other Jews to rally to the Messiah, Saul confirmed his other ambition: to make known the message of Christ to those who were not Jews.

AMONG CHRISTIAN JEWS the discussion continued. Those who refused to come to terms with the Law emphasized their disagreement with those who wanted at all cost to open themselves to the world. From one part and another, people tensed and persisted. Saul affirmed himself as one of the most ardent among the "liberals." Confrontation would find its favorite ground: circumcision.

The camp of Barnabas and Paul did not deny that the question had to be posed. They simply wondered; the pagans who asked for Baptism had not been circumcised as the Law required. Was it necessary, before receiving them among the faithful followers of Jesus, to deliver them to the rabbi's blade whatever their age: twenty, thirty, forty? These pagans were loathe to agree. Would they deprive Christ of the faith to which they witnessed?

Each one entrenched himself in these positions.

One day when Barnabas, Symeon, Lucius of Cyrene, Manaen, and Saul gathered to celebrate the worship of the Lord, they perceived together an order that they felt came from elsewhere. It was clear: *Set apart for me Barnabas and Saul for the work to which I have called them.*

"Then after fasting and praying they [Symeon, Lucius, and Manaen] laid their hands on them and sent them off. So, being sent out by the Holy Spirit, they went down to Seleucia; and from there they sailed to Cyprus" (Acts 13:1–4).

For the second time Barnabas would play an essential role in Saul's life. After having drawn him out of his retreat in Tarsus, Barnabas would lead him into the country that he knew best because he was born there: Cyprus.

5

SAUL BECOMES PAUL

In the spring of A.D. 45, three Christians made their way to Seleucia, the port of Antioch: Barnabas, Saul, and a man by the name of Mark. He was the cousin of the former and one who would make a name for himself. One of the Gospels would be attributed to Mark, something we should not overlook.

Nineteen hundred years later, in the company of Cornélie Scheffer, to whom he would dedicate his book *Saint Paul*, Ernest Renan will also leave Antioch for Seleucia. It is, he writes, "a short day's walk." We motorists are brought back to reality by this horseman, Renan, a former seminarian in his eighties, whose doubts haunted him and whose weight hampered him.

Let us follow the three Christians, whose tunics grew heavier with dust, and this Ernest Renan, whom I imagine gaily dressed in the manner of one of Jules Verne's travelers.[1] The author of *L'Avernir de la science* observed the same countryside as did Saul. From the year 45 to the year 1861, certainly it changed little. Renan crossed and described hamlets— things and people—scarcely removed from the villages of the Bible. They became, then, a source for approaching the itinerary of Saul, who was then Paul. The proof: "The route follows at a distance the right bank of the Orontes River, overlapping the last waves of the mountains of Pieria and crossing, by fording them, the many streams of water that descend it. There are woods on all sides pruned of myrtles, of arbutus, of laurels, of green oaks; wealthy villages are suspended on the ridges cut from the mountain." Twenty miles separated Antioch from Seleucia. Midway, the route crossed a gorge from which one noticed the sea. "The wooded summits of the mountains of Daphne form the horizon of the southern coast."

One would have hoped that the emigrants noted by Juvenal would not have overly crowded the dock, and that the wind, falling from the mountains, would not have raised from the gulf a "strong swell" noted by Renan, so that "the quays, the piers formed by enormous blocks" might still exist. In the twenty-first century, only vestiges remain—such as breakwater and walls—near the Turkish village of Magaracik.

As their ship reached open sea, our three Christians could consider before them "the beautiful arc of the circle formed by the coast at the mouth of the Orontes"; to their right, "the symmetrical cone of the Casius"; to their left, the torn slopes of Mount Coryphae"; behind them, "the snows of Taurus and the coast of Cilicia that closed the gulf of Issus."[2] Renan did not embark. Standing on the black sand of the shore, he was content to salute the sea where three conquerors of Christ had set forth.

ESTABLISHING IN THE first century a catalogue of physical trials that could afflict man, Seneca situated shipwrecks on a par with fires and landslides. Throughout antiquity, travelers preferred sea travel because it was infinitely more rapid and less exhausting than land travel, but they always recognized the risks. The dangers were so real and frequent that the ancients found it necessary to dictate rules to alleviate them in part. The most exacting of these were that ships could only sail in the good season, from May to September, so that sailors and passengers would not become "playthings of the wind." Texts of the time curse the greed of ships'outfitters; most shipwrecks occurred because of the overloading of the ship with merchandise and passengers. In 64, if Flavius Josephus was shipwrecked in the Adriatic, it was because his ship took on six hundred passengers.

No ship was intended to receive passengers only. They were welcomed but in addition to the "cargo," a generic term to designate goods and animals, especially oxen, cows, and sheep. To the large carriers, *naves onerariae,* were compared the coasting vessels, *naves orariae.* When Barnabas, Saul, and Mark embarked, they knew in advance that they would not receive any special treatment. They had to bring at least a blanket and a mat for sleeping on the deck. Very rarely it happened that the back of the boat, raised up in a poop deck, comprised cabins—*dietae*—

always reserved for the more distinguished passengers. In the best of cases, a tent was put up for the common folk, meant to protect them from the heat of the sun. Certain people found themselves relegated "to the bottom of the deck," an unenviable lot since the hold received all the waters of the ship, including the most malodorous; the word "stinking" says it all. The passengers had to provide themselves with food for the whole voyage; the captain furnished only drinkable water.

Barnabas, the chief of the expedition, must have paid the ship's owner the price of the crossing. The traveler who had not reserved his place in time could, at the last moment, bargain with the captain. This haggling never seemed to end. For a relatively short distance—130 miles—the *oneraria* chosen by our three Christians was probably a ship more long than round, with a single mast to which was attached a rectangular sail less high than wide. Without a rudder, it had in the back two long oars fixed from two parts of the stern in "steerage holes" and rejoined by "spindles" attached to a bar, the *clavus*, by which the helmsman guided the ship.

Those who embarked with them would have seen the three men as travelers like others. We know that they were undertaking an "expedition from Alexandria in reverse." From the East, it would lead Paul to the far West and to death beneath the sword of the executioner. Until this point the message of Christ had made itself heard only within the borders of the eastern Mediterranean. It would resound on two continents.

We don't doubt for an instant that Saul felt deeply the will to evangelize the pagans. Would he, like the apostles, "tell the story" of Jesus to those who did not know him? He was incapable of it. Faced with this fundamental difficulty, was he worried? He who came from years of occupying himself with weaving, with making tents and the profit to be drawn from it—did he not all at once experience the feeling of being presumptuous? I doubt it. Even if for a while he could have relegated the Event, he now gave it its full priority. It was up to him to communicate to everyone the essential news: *Christ is risen.* If Jesus had conquered death, it was to save humankind. Everyone: "The Gentiles have become fellow heirs, members of the same body, and sharers in the promise in Christ Jesus through the Gospel" (Eph 3:6). If death waited for each one at the end of the road, at the moment the fear of vacillating flowed from this unknown event that threatened. Paul claimed: *Christ brings you salvation.* He insisted that one could retrace every road, even the most evil. Every fault could be forgiven. "Death, where is your victory?" Paul had become the messenger of "the good news of Christ," more simply the Good News: "Although I am the very least of all the saints, this grace was given to me to bring to the Gentiles the news of the boundless riches of Christ, and to make everyone see what is the plan of the mystery hidden for ages in God who created all things" (Eph 3:8–9) He wanted to transmit this theme to those to whom he went. He would do it in his own words, and this would be so exacting, and at times so obscure, that one wonders how so many people were able to understand and accept it. That is another mystery.

ON BOARD, Barnabas, Saul, and Mark spent some thirty hours squatting or stretched out among the sacks and bales on a bridge made noisy by bellowing and bleating animals.

The day dawned. In the flash of their whiteness, the cliffs of Cyprus loomed in the distance. The white houses in the port of Salamis stood out against the deep blue of the sky.[3] Though Roman since before 58 B.C., the island remained almost totally Greek in its language, its writing, and its way of life. This did not displease the quasi-Greek Saul. As for Barnabas, he rediscovered "his" island, and that was all there was to say.

Today, north of Famagusta, there are vestiges recalling the ancient grandeur of the city: thermal baths, a gymnasium, a Roman theater. Saul saw them all. The Jewish community of Cyprus was particularly prosperous. Flavius Josephus affirms this by specifying that it sent wine from Cyprus to the Temple in Jerusalem. The principal resource of the island lay in its copper mines. Their yield was such that Rome confided the government of the island to a proconsul. Herod the Great, always anxious to grow in power and round off his fortune, obtained from Augustus "half the revenue of the copper mines of Cyprus and direction of the other half." But Barnabas, Saul, and Mark had not come to seek copper in Cyprus.

"When they arrived at Salamis, they proclaimed the Word of God in the synagogues of the Jews" (Acts 13:5). As we can see, they did not waste a minute. They addressed themselves first of all to the Jews of the city, numerous since the time of the Ptolemies. This inaugurated a method—singularly effective—that Paul would later make his principal striking force. To evangelize the pagans, one would always begin by preaching to the Jews. From this fact, the Diaspora would reveal itself as the principal agent of the expansion of Christianity.

The eagerness of the Jews to welcome their coreligionists has become proverbial. Does a Jewish traveler arrive somewhere? He looks for the Jewish quarter, runs to it, and they open their arms to him. In the Middle Ages, the Jew Benjamin of Tudele traveled through all of Europe "without having seen anything but Jews." Why would things have been any different in antiquity?

It was Saturday, the Sabbath day, when our missionaries arrived in the synagogue. They were surrounded, questioned about their families and the country from which they came. People were eager for news; the travelers brought some. Jesus himself had proceeded this way: "He went to the synagogue on the sabbath day, as was his custom. He stood up to read" (Lk 4:16). Barnabas and Saul were careful not to speak too soon of a Messiah named Jesus. Better to allow a week to pass.

I cannot believe the general wonderment that would have accompanied their speaking and of which Luke makes himself the echo. Let's imagine we have come to announce to believers, brought up in an ancient religion and one that has never grown old, that they must change a whole side of their faith. Some would refuse to listen, while others would protest. Barnabas and Saul would not allow themselves to be affected by this behavior that would become their daily bread. They would consider it a success if anyone wanted to know more. One single convert signified a victory. Sometimes the whole business went wrong. A hearer became angry, cried imposture, sacrilege. This translated into violence, sometimes to the point of punishments reserved for heretics, whippings regulated by the rabbis, or specifically Roman scourgings administered by lictors. "Five times I have received from the Jews," says Paul, "the forty lashes minus one. Three times I was beaten with rods" (2 Cor 11:24–25).

TWO ROUTES PRESENTED themselves to the travelers. Would they choose that of the high mountainous plateau, the most direct, which followed the course of Pedias? From a bird's-eye view this represented ninety-three miles through a mountain whose scale did not suggest a pleasure party. If approached in the summer, one was certain to endure insupportable heat. In the first century, the poet Martial was already complaining of it.

Everything suggests that the trio chose the other route, that of the coast. Certainly it meant an extra thirty miles. But apart from being incomparably easy, unlike the other way, it offered an advantage that our missionaries could not have passed up. It traversed through cities with synagogues: Citium, Larnaca—planted in the middle of countryside that inspired Homer—and Amathus.

They went around the mountainous massifs of Troodos. Our missionaries covered about twenty-two miles a day, a distance slightly less than the one presented, in my childhood schools, as the average daily distance of a man on foot: twenty-five miles a day.

Don't feel sorry for them. In the spring, the air was light, the countryside enchanting. To their left, on the slopes of mountains whose summits were still white, trees bloomed—cherry or apple. The artistically pruned vineyards announced the arrival of grapes from which savory wine would be made. Orange trees offered fruit that would give juice when squeezed. Olive trees proclaimed the promise of excellent oil that would be exported afar.

To the right of the walkers, the sea, made choppy by innumerable capes and promontories, displayed the whole palette of blues, adding the sound of the surf to the fascination of the spectacle.

The more the trio walked, the more distressed they grew: other than the cult of Apollo, celebrated in the north of Curium, the island lived entirely under the sign of Aphrodite. Born according to legend from the froth of the sea, the Greek goddess of love found herself conveniently assimilated to Venus of Rome; the Roman conquest of 58 B.C. did not disturb her cult, her temples, her priests, or her faithful. Salamis, Amathus, Idalium, and Paphos, the principal cities of the island, remained devoted to her. They celebrated her countless loves, her sensuality without limit—even her infidelities—and the children that her lovers gave her: Harmony, Eros, Anteros, Priapus, Hermaphrodite. That she openly favored illicit loves suited the people well—accommodating Aphrodite!

On the heights of Amathus rose the sanctuary most frequented by inhabitants of the island as well as by strangers eager to participate in the feasts celebrated there. Young priestesses demonstrated such religious enthusiasm that on certain days great crowds flocked there to the point of a veritable Stakhanovism.

How to overcome such a faith that flattered so well the desires, the instincts, and the weaknesses of human nature? How oppose to it the rigors and prohibitions of a Law which, as that of the one only God, risked striking one with fear? No doubt such a question obsessed Paul until the day when he understood; there were many who, unconsciously weary of an ancient laxity, were searching for new rules.

IN EACH PORT, the pious men repeated their routine. At the synagogue, Barnabas probably spoke first, because of his double primacy as chief of the mission and a Cypriot. He favored the concrete image of Jesus. He showed him preaching love and forgiveness on the roads of Galilee as on those of Judea, curing the sick, choosing to die on the cross to save all humanity.

After Barnabas it was Paul's turn. He felt little confidence in his oratorical skills; he himself recognized that "his speech [was] contemptible" (2 Cor 10:10). What did it matter? Barnabas spoke of the man Jesus. Paul cut to the essential, demonstrating that this Jesus was the Son of God and at the same time God himself. From anecdote Paul passed to abstraction. No one could doubt its demonstrative force, but this was hard for certain of his listeners. Fortunately they had points of reference: Saul leaned especially on the Bible, which always elicited a lively interest among Jewish hearers. He underscored the passages that announced the coming of a Messiah and affirmed that they applied very exactly to the person of Jesus Christ. As he would do in his letters, he certainly developed the theme of the Resurrection, the epicenter of his reasoning. The words may have jostled each other in his mouth, but those who heard him were struck by this little man who stammered because his faith was so strong. And Mark? We must conclude that, for the moment, he confined himself to listening to Saul. Later he would learn many other things by listening to Peter.

Did the trio win conversions? Acts assumes so, nothing more. We might dream of a big catch, new Christians drawn as a crowd to follow the three men. Let us content ourselves with the dream. The walkers finally reached the new Paphos, for an earthquake had destroyed the ancient one and the emperor Augustus himself ordered the reconstruction. The Roman proconsul Sergius Paulus resided there.

It was believed for a long time that this high Roman functionary was known only from Acts, which mentions "the proconsul, Sergius Paulus, an intelligent man" (Acts 13:7). This was too little. Patient researchers allow us today to attribute much better defined traits to this Roman.[4] Belonging to the third generation of colonists who had settled on the

Anatolian plateaus, Paulus was a native of central Galatia. The owner of a vast estate in Venissius, he preferred to confide its operation to freedmen and to undertake a career in the imperial administration; he would one day be a senator. If there is no document to confirm his nomination as proconsul of Cyprus—a mediocre post in the eyes of Rome—we know that his predecessor remained in place from July of 43 to July of 44: the mandate lasted one year. The encounter of Sergius and Saul therefore took place logically between July of 44 and July of A.D. 45.

At Paphos magic ruled the city. It was all but accorded the rank of a religion. Its zealots referred to doctrine with roots in Egypt and Mesopotamia. The proconsul readily welcomed in his palace a magician more in demand than the others, a certain Elymas also called Bar-Jesus, indicating Jewish origins. After being amused by his tricks, Sergius opened one of those debates that so delighted intellectuals in antiquity. At that time, "philosophers transformed themselves into sophists and sophists into magicians."[5] This was so true that having learned of the presence in Paphos of three preachers on an unknown god, Sergius Paulus—"a prudent man," according to Luther—determined to meet them. He "summoned Barnabas and Saul and wanted to hear the word of God" (Acts 13:7). We would rather believe that, being lonely on his island, the proconsul wanted to distract himself by calling these unusual visitors. Totally destitute, the trio found themselves the next day thrown into a luxury of which they had little idea. Welcome, greetings, questions. Barnabas explained. And Paulus was astonished: Who is this Messiah? In the background, the magician Elymas was disturbed. He too had come to inform himself; what if it was a matter of disloyal rivals? Suddenly he exploded: Let these men bring proof of their words! And let the proconsul beware!

The violence that Saul carried within him and that he tried to tame to his betterment awakened at once. His face darkened with anger. He thundered: "You son of the devil, you enemy of all righteousness, full of all deceit and villainy, will you not stop making crooked the straight paths of the Lord?"

Petrified, the audience listened to him. Saul launched an ultimate thrust at his adversary: "And now listen—the hand of the Lord is against you, and you will be blind for a while, unable to see the sun."

"Immediately," says Luke, "mist and darkness came over him, and he went about groping for someone to lead him by the hand." Was this a miracle that Paul had performed? All hypnotists of some experience could obtain similar results. To this thrust, Luke adds, "When the proconsul saw what had happened, he believed" (Acts 13:8–12). This is admirable to read but less convincing. History does not record at that time any conversion of a personage of such rank. If this had been the case, the one concerned would today be honored on the altars. Here Luke translates his desires into realities.

AN EVENT CHARGED with consequences will flow from these memorable interactions: *Saul will change his name.* He asks that we call him Paul and will call himself so for the rest of his life. From Paulus to Paul, we cannot deny the connection. Could the proconsul's influence have been so great? Some, like Saint Jerome, advanced the hypothesis that the Roman adopted Saul. A gratuitous supposition; if a certain intimacy seems to have been born between the two men, it remained more philosophical than religious. Would immersion in a territory so deeply Greek perhaps have led Saul to abandon his Jewish name? *Paulos* in Greek means small; apart from the physical reality of his size, did he want to confirm in his own eyes his condition as servant reduced to nothing by the fact of the infinite power of God?

Under Roman standards, so many nations, peoples, and languages coexisted that the substitution of one name for another was commonplace. Another striking example was that of Simon, chief of the apostles, having become first Cephas and later Petrus.[6] For a time the man from Tarsus will be Saul *known as* Paul. Soon enough, Saul will disappear and only Paul will remain. Farewell to the memory of the first Jewish king.

Another decisive change: in Cyprus, we see Paul pass insensibly from the second role to that of chief of the mission. The transition is indicated with a discretion that Acts intends. In his Letter to the Galatians, Paul will confirm it. With a modesty we can only admire, Barnabas erased himself without discussion. Did he understand that Paul's entire character designated him to be the master? Until this point the text always speaks of "Barnabas and Saul." It will now be "Paul and Barnabas."

At Paphos the boats relaunched, setting out in all directions. They only had to choose which one to take. The fall of 45 was approaching, the fateful time when travel by sea was forbidden. Among other destinations, Ephesus was proposed. They would be sure to find many Jews there, as everywhere in Asia Minor. Paul did not seem to consider it. He preferred Attalia. It is useless to speculate who initiated the decision; the name

Sergius Paulus comes immediately to mind, the man from central Anatolia, who possessed great goods and contacts that would not fail to be very useful.

Only thirty-six hours of navigation were required before reaching the gulf at the end of which the majestic Attalia sprawled. All the sailors in the Mediterranean knew how to find it in a time of storm, for it was an incomparable haven.

I searched for Attalia in Antalya, the Turkish site most advertised by tourist agents throughout the world. Of the Roman presence, I found only Hadrian's gate, an impressive entrance of white marble. Relative to the history of Paul, its only fault is to have been built sixty-six years after his death. In the museum, the Phrygian and Greek rooms prevail over the effigies of a few emperors. As for the *Dancer,* an exciting bacchant seven feet high in white and black marble, it is worth the detour, even if we strongly doubt that Paul would have taken the trouble to see it.

It is difficult to imagine the missionaries of Christ strolling the streets of this seaside resort of 700,000 inhabitants, more European than Turkish. The only place we are sure to have admired in common is the high cliff at the end of the gulf, which all travelers see before their eyes as their boat approaches. At the time of Paul, it formed the socle [the lower part of a Roman wall] on which the city had been built. It is the same today.

THE REGION IN which Paul, Barnabas, and Mark disembarked was called Anatolia.[7] The Romans ruled there as masters. Not only did the people consent to such mastery, they rejoiced in it. Most had submitted without resistance at the time of conquest. Ancient political alliances had disappeared, like those of Phrygia, Caria, and Lydia, as well as the king-doms of Pergamum, Bithynia, and Pontus. All this part of the Empire begged the favor of being designated as "friend of Caesar." The cities prayed that they might be accorded the title of "metropolis" or of "most illustrious," as Tacitus and Dio Cassius attest. The cult of Augustus had become the dominant religion. Temples to the emperor-gods were raised up everywhere. Was it a sincere cult? We would rather lean toward the notion of a platitude producing advantages.

From Attalia, the trio reached the city of Perga in less than a half-day's walk. In the *Verrinse* Cicero denounced the pillages of the quaestor Caius Verres; did he not go so far as to tear away the gold vestments from the statue of the goddess Artemis, protector of the city? Of the appearance of Perga, almost everything was ignored until 1946, the year when Turkish archaeologists began to excavate the marvelous site that slept beneath the earth. When I visited it, they were still working there.

Nothing can give a better idea of a Roman city in Asia Minor. Paul saw it imprisoned by its walls. He entered it between two Hellenistic towers of thirty-nine feet high and, unless he decidedly chose to remain insensible to the external world, he could not have failed to be impressed by their majesty. In widening the city, the Romans later tried to conserve the vestiges of the ancient wall; thank you, Romans!

Having crossed the monumental door, an avenue paved in marble offered itself to the man from Tarsus and his companions. Three hundred yards long and twenty-two yards wide, it stretched from one end to the other of a canal where the water flowed in abundance. Porticoes allowed people at the same time to walk in the shade and to make purchases in the shops. If Paul had felt ill in Perga, he could have consulted the doctor whose office opened to the east, in the thirty-ninth stall beginning from the monumental gate—a mosaic still confirms it today.

None could ignore the major edifice of Perga: the imposing sanctuary that rose at the end of the avenue. At the foot of the acropolis, on two stages, waters from neighboring sources collected to be offered to the canal. How could Paul not have tread to the right of the grand avenue, the mosaic pavement of the agora—a square of eighty-two yards on each side—where in the freshest hours the whole city could be found? He must have passed through one of the marble doors that gave access to the adjoining roads. The pagan temples would undoubtedly not have detained him. Certainly he would have favored the synagogue.

It would have been from the synagogue that Paul, Barnabas, and Mark would have made inquiries. "They would announce the word in Perga," says Luke. Where would they have done so, if not before their brother Jews?

Surprise: when they left the city, there would only be two of them. Mark abandoned them. He seems to have been repelled by the horrifying depiction they must have offered him of the voyage to come; at least this is what is generally thought. I would propose a different explanation. Not everyone was like Barnabas. It is quite possible that Paul's increasingly egocentric personality proved in the end to be intolerable to the young man. At the announcement of Mark's desertion, as the fall of 45 came to an end, we can imagine well enough what the goodbyes must have been like: Mark's tears, the conciliatory words of Barnabas, the cries of Paul.

6

ON THE ATTACK FROM ANATOLIA

We rolled along the excellent route that, from the exit for Antalya, rises immediately northward. It was literally dug into the mountain. In the back of the car, Anne Helen, my oldest daughter, and her friend Aurora did not take their eyes off the dense woods that stretched from one part to the other along the road. Taken as they were with the meaning of our trip, were they looking there for the shadows of Paul and Barnabas? My wife Micheline Pelletier was driving, photographic equipment always at hand. I had all the leisure to scrutinize the wild expanse of the Taurus mountains in which our two missionaries, twenty centuries ago, had immersed themselves. I imagined them, on the road barely outlined, walking and panting into the heart of the forest, their faces scratched by branches, wearily climbing the sharp cliffs, sliding on rocky trails down to the very bottom of ravines.

To confront the dangers and demands of such an expedition, they had to have equipped themselves: sturdy shoes, a mantle with a hood (the *birrus*) and a hat with a wide brim (the *petase*). The canvas tent was indispensable; we can guess that someone we know chose it with great care. They would have to cook, so they had to carry basic accessories. It would be impossible to stuff all of that in bags. The ass or the mule came in handy here, for these ideal beasts were surefooted in the mountains. To rent or even buy one of these was not ruinous; the travelers would then only have to worry about themselves. The indispensable walking staff would help them there and, on occasion, would allow them also to keep at bay the wolves, bears, and other wild animals that moved in the areas along the water. Not to forget the brigands who, hidden in their dens, managed to hold off the Roman police, so effective in the rest of the Empire.

Without relief the crushing backdrop that also marked our own journey bore down upon them, the same summits snow-covered until the heart of summer. It is well understood that they had no map, no compass. It was useless to rely on the few guideposts along the way. The stars remained, but one had to wait for nightfall and pray that clouds did not veil the heavens. Even today villages are rare. Paul and Barnabas could have walked many days without meeting a human being. The prospect of a tavern developed for the most part into a false hope. From time to time, a farm or a woodcutter's house appeared. Hospitality was rarely denied strangers; the barn was always there with its welcoming hay. Each time the travelers stopped they replenished their supplies, as best they could, with a few things, for they had little money. They filled their gourds with goats' milk, which would break the monotony of water from springs and streams.

When the hills were less rough and the descents less dangerous, they exchanged the conversation of walkers: commonplaces, observations on their progress, the difficulties of the road, natural needs. All at once, a confidence slipped out almost in spite of oneself. Long periods of silence were surely filled with prayer. How could it be otherwise on the part of two men so passionately motivated? To address the Lord directly, to confide to him their whole selves, to offer him themselves, to implore his aid, at times to call on him for help—all of this situated itself in the logic of such a project. For want of an echo, dialogue with God could be short-lived. Therefore, prayers learned long ago returned to their lips. These could only be Jewish prayers, for Christian prayers did not yet exist. The first among them, the Our Father, dictated by Jesus, would not appear until much later, with the publication of the Gospels. Neither Paul nor Barnabas would have seen this as inconvenient: Jesus himself recited Jewish prayers. Their assurance of being Christians without ceasing to be Jews was further strengthened.

I imagine Paul always small but muscled by the distances covered, jaw tight, determined, almost aggressive.

The certainty that they were acting according to an order that came from God carried them, motivated them, and sustained them—him and Barnabas. They could not postpone even for a day the announcement that the Messiah—the *Son of God,* Paul hammered it out—had visited humanity and that, therefore, a hope out of all proportion had opened to all. The stories of mystics, great and small, demonstrate that such faith increases strength a hundredfold. It even permits the annulment of the laws of nature; human beings have lived for years, even in the twentieth century, without food.

The vegetation changed. We told ourselves that it resembled the Swiss Alps. All at once, at a detour in the road, a lake emerged between the trees. At that instant what came to our minds was probably the same relief the two men felt when they saw it, after what trials! By the actual route that cuts to the shortest, this represented eighty-one miles. One must at least triple the distance for men on foot who ascended by climbing. Paul and Barnabas knew by hearsay this lake they found on their route; they knew its name. Today, Lake Egridir is the fourth largest lake in Turkey; with a breath-taking beauty, thirty miles long and two to ten miles wide, no one can forget its turquoise blue color. Often frozen in winter, it resembles a Siberian lake. In summer, fed by two hundred sources, its waters are lukewarm. When we stopped by its shores, the wind was blowing violently and the short waves pressed against the shore. In the distance, the rocky mass of Sultan Dag crushed everything. It rises here more that one and a half miles high.

To follow their route, Paul and Barnabas walked around the lake. They may have been tempted by a fisherman's proposal to take them to its northernmost point. They refused, as it was too expensive. Furthermore, going north would have taken them away from the road to Antioch of Pisidia: forty miles by today's route.

THE DANGERS PAUL later mentioned are not literary artifices: "on frequent journeys, in danger from rivers, danger from bandits, ...danger in the wilderness, ...in toil and hardship, through many a sleepless night, ...cold and naked" (2 Cor 11:26–27). From this list we can imagine the travelers' happiness on approaching this other Antioch, but also their astonishment on entering it.

Paul certainly knew large cities: Jerusalem, Damascus, Antioch of Syria, and even Tarsus merited no disdain. Did he imagine a Roman metropolis in the midst of a region Luke considered barbaric and wild?

What to say of these buildings that dated back only seventy-five years? The walls that the two men discovered were Roman. After having passed through the gates, Roman certainly, they were in the presence of two perpendicular avenues bounded by porticoes: one ran from south to north and bore the name of the emperor Augustus; the other ran from east to west and was erected under the sign of Tiberius. The latter would lead them up to the monumental gate with three arches, adorned with magnificent emblems of the victory at Actium. These gave access to the center of a vast esplanade surrounded by a portico of two stages carved into the rock—the place of Augustus. In the middle of it stood the principal temple of the city, naturally dedicated to the emperor god Augustus.

Founded by the Seleucid king in the third century B.C., it was a very sparse area when the Roman armies occupied it in 25. The decision Augustus made to establish a Roman colony there caused it to develop. The veterans who were demobilized after Actium obtained land there that they cultivated, on one condition: that they establish order among the population, which they were perfectly prepared to do. The *colonia Caesarea,* an intersection of roads, became the engine of the romanization of Pisidia.[1] Antioch wanted to be a replica of the capitol of the Empire: administration, religious traditions, division into quarters, a corps of citizens. People took up the habit of calling it "little Rome." In his will, the emperor Augustus mentioned the Pisidian colonies as one of the better accomplishments marking his reign.

Paul and Barnabas' first concern was to find lodging, and, as soon as possible, to wash, an urgent concern of all Jews. After that they could relax their hardened muscles and anoint their aching feet with oil. If Sergius Paulus had given the two travelers letters of recommendation, doors must have opened to them and they must have found asylum. Then, burning with impatience, they kept the Sabbath.

By all indications many Jews lived in Asia Minor at that time, "as many as in Egypt," which does not mean that it was so in Galatia. Flavius Josephus gives an account of the favorable treatment the Romans granted them: the trade that they practiced drew the Jews closer to them; they more often spoke Greek or Latin than the indigenous peoples did. The texts, among others those of Cicero and Philo of Alexandria, confirm the existence of strong Jewish communities able to claim their rights and unafraid to appeal local decisions by the Roman authority. They even obtained exoneration from common charges. If a dispute set them in opposition to the native population, most of the time the Romans found in favor of the Jews. But such disputes seem to have happened infrequently, for we see pagans and Jews living on good terms. After having intrigued the population, the customs of the Jews ended by seducing them. Many "God-fearers" frequented the synagogues. Some readers may be astonished: "God-fearers" in Antioch of Pisidia? They were everywhere, providing a remarkable opportunity for Christians.

For Paul and Barnabas the hour had come: "And on the Sabbath they went into the synagogue and sat down." They were observed, drawing only simple curiosity with regard to strangers. Interest would come later. "After the reading of the law and the prophets, the officials of the synagogue sent them a message, saying, 'Brothers, if you have any word of exhortation for the people, give it'" (Acts 13:14–15).

They had been waiting for just such an invitation. Paul rose and offered a long discourse on the theme of the continuity of Israel's history. It would take all of Luke's talent to transcribe it.

"You Israelites, and others who fear God, listen."

We cannot help but think of Peter speaking in the Temple, of Stephen expressing himself to the Sanhedrin, even more because their speeches too come from Luke's pen. All the chapters of the Bible unfold:

"The God of this people Israel chose our ancestors and made the people great during their stay in the land of Egypt, and with uplifted arm he led them out of it...."

The desert, the return to Israel, the division and distribution of the land, the judges, the prophets, the kings—nothing was missing.

"[God] made David their king. In his testimony about him he said, *'I have found David, son of Jesse, to be a man after my heart.'*"

There was nothing to prevent nodding heads, eyelids struggling not to close. These words had been heard time and again. In what concerns us, the understanding of such a discourse is essential. It permits us to discover the sense and the arguments used from this epoch by the man from Damascus. Paul's voice swelled. The synagogue awakened.

"Of this man's posterity God has brought to Israel a Savior, Jesus, as he promised."

Attention mounted.

"My brothers, you descendants of Abraham's family, and others who fear God, to us the message of this salvation has been sent."

"Others who fear God": in a public gathering, they were the useful minority. Paul did not miss this opportunity. He pursued it:

"Because the residents of Jerusalem and their leaders did not recognize him or understand the words of the prophets that are read every Sabbath, they fulfilled those words by condemning him. Even though they found no cause for a sentence of death, they asked Pilate to have him killed. When they had carried out everything that was written about him, they took him down from the tree and laid him in a tomb. But God raised him from the dead; and for many days he appeared to those who came up with him from Galilee to Jerusalem, and they are now his witnesses to the people. And we bring you the good news that what God promised to our ancestors he has fulfilled for us, their children, by raising Jesus; as also it is written in the second psalm, *'You are my son; today I have begotten you.'*"

Paul affirmed that the resurrection of Jesus is something unique:

"Let it be known to you therefore, my brothers, that through this man forgiveness of sins is proclaimed to you; by this Jesus everyone who believes is set free from all those sins from which you could not be freed by the law of Moses" (Acts 13:16–39).

He would reprise this demonstration tirelessly from now on, enriching his reasoning by developing certain arguments and clarifying what may have seemed obscure. What Jew other than Paul would have dared to claim that the Law of Moses had limits and could be transcended? Until then, only one: Stephen. And he had died because of it. Paul not only fell in step with him, he went even further than Stephen had. What revenge, O Stephen!

Stage by stage, month by month, year by year, obstacle by obstacle, a theology was being built.

For Schalom Ben-Chorin, an already-cited Jewish specialist in the history of religions, who was a disciple and friend of Martin Buber, Paul's behavior in the synagogues registers very exactly within the framework of the traditional office: reading from the *parsha* (the chapter from the Torah chosen for the week), then from the *haftarah* (a corresponding passage from the Prophets). Then comes the *drash* (the homily). For this interpretation, "one often calls on a rabbi passing through or on another learned guest. It goes the same in our day." Ben-Chorin considers it consistent with the tradition that

> in the synagogues of the Diaspora, one would readily have invited Paul, who could present himself as a disciple of Gamaliel, to preach a certain kind of sermon. He would begin therefore by presenting a traditional interpretation of the Scriptures (essentially in the sense of Hellenistic Judaism); then he would announce the message of Jesus, which was routinely experienced by his Jewish hearers as scandal.

But not always. Scandal was not produced in Antioch of Pisidia. On the contrary, Paul was immediately asked to treat the same subject the following Sabbath: "When the meeting of the synagogue broke up, many Jews and devout converts to Judaism followed Paul and Barnabas, who spoke to them and urged them to continue in the grace of God" (Acts 13:43).

"Devout converts to Judaism"? Simply put, "God-fearers." The title evolved in the course of ages. They spoke from that time of "worshipers," a term to which was frequently added "uncircumcised"; it is impossible to be more precise.

There is every indication that the hearers—Jews and pagans—were deeply moved by Paul's discourse. The story of the two men having arrived from who knows where and the strangeness of their announcement spread throughout the village to the point of becoming the main topic of conversation. At the service the following Saturday, the synagogue welcomed a record crowd. In the midst of pagans eager to hear the strangers, the Jews found themselves in the minority! "But when the Jews saw the crowds, they were filled with jealousy; and blaspheming, they contradicted what was spoken by Paul" (Acts 13:45).

Who cannot imagine this house in which people were crushed, where they perspired, and from which the crowd undoubtedly overflowed outside? As on the previous week, Paul spoke. At the first word about Jesus, cries of anger burst forth.

In order to understand such a reaction, we must return to Ben-Chorin. He knows that of which he speaks:

> The Jews—even if it is a matter of Hellenistic and liberal Jews of the Diaspora—hold with certainty the sense that there is here a departure from their tradition, an illicit interpretation. Contrary to what many Christian theologians may have thought, this sense does not flow from Paul's affirmation of the messiahship of Jesus. That is not where the scandal lay.... Had Paul contented himself with announcing the Messiah in the person of Jesus,

he would not have provoked this insoluble conflict with the synagogue that marks his whole life. The affront lies in the fact that in part, in the eyes of the Jews, he depreciates the Law in the broadest sense of the term, and that, on the other part, he advocates absolute equality between pagans and Jews, which ends by suppressing the election of Israel.

To deprive the Jews of being the *chosen people* was in effect to demand a great deal. The best proof of this was found that very night. When the Jews let out a stream of insults, the rest of the audience protested: "Let him speak!" The pagans wanted to know more about this Jesus who had begun to make them dream. Paganism was constantly enriched by new gods: why not this one?

This violent confrontation was happily contained to just words. Would Paul and Barnabas have to tone down their speech? Such was not in their nature. The presence in the synagogue of a majority of pagans was a chance not to be missed. They recalled the Jews to order, saying, "It was necessary that the word of God should be spoken first to you."

A volley of protests provoked the foreseeable reply: "Since you reject it and judge yourselves to be unworthy of eternal life, we are now turning to the Gentiles."

The Jews were silenced at once; they were dumbfounded. From that time on Paul and Barnabas, changing course, would address themselves to the pagans. "For so the Lord has commanded us, saying, *I have set you to be a light for the Gentiles, so that you may bring salvation to the ends of the earth.*'"

"When the Gentiles heard this," says Luke, "they were glad and praised the word of the Lord; and as many as had been destined for eternal life became believers" (Acts 13:46–48).

Once again Luke's enthusiasm carries him away. We can believe that some conversions occurred on that day, and others on the days that followed. But to claim that "the whole region" was won, as we read in Acts 13:49, Luke would have had to state precisely the lapse of time presupposed by such a conquest. We guess today that it could have taken a year. Certainly we can admit that they had great success, since Paul confirms it in his Letter to the Galatians, where he boasts of having convinced pagans who "did not know God" and who were "enslaved to beings that by nature are not gods" (4:8). This refers to the Anatolians faithful to their ancient cults—that is to say, honoring Men who healed the living, men and beasts; Sabazios, the risen one, and a phantom horseman who promised immortality.

What region could have been more ready for the preaching of Paul and Barnabas than this one whose original mythology referred to gods who saved and, perhaps, to just one god?

To reach the heavily protected perimeter of the ruins of Antioch of Pisidia, we crossed the small city of Yalvac. Before all else, we saw the aqueduct. Its many arches gather in the distance, a long curve toward the mountain. Throughout the countryside, small mounts too regular provide shelter for the ruins not yet uncovered.

At the entrance to the site, we climbed a steep slope toward a monumental gate. Only a few pillars remained of it. The gate gave access to an esplanade as well as to the avenue dedicated to Tiberius. On the left a long paved road ran up to the semicircle of a theater constructed in the second century B.C. that Paul may have seen. Surprise: the avenue passed through a tunnel under the benches of the theater. I reached one of the highest of these. Under the grassy expanse that stretched in the open country at my feet, I looked for the quarters of the city that were still to be excavated. Does the synagogue, where so much began, lie here under the brownish earth where only Roman baths have so far been uncovered? It was a beautiful, warm morning. A single worker, protected by a red helmet, worked among the stones.

PAUL AND BARNABAS never ceased to score points, and the anger of the Jews reached a high mark. The women were the most vociferous and assailed the notables of the city with their complaints. In other cases, the Romans, anxious about the harmony between the social classes of a population trying to integrate themselves in the Empire, would have refused to intervene in such a debate. But the Jewish ladies who protested so loudly were of excellent social condition—and rich. The result did not delay in coming: the occupiers blamed the disturbers.

They were thrown out of the city. "So they shook the dust off their feet in protest against them, and went to Iconium. And the disciples were filled with joy and with the Holy Spirit" (Acts 13:51–52).

WHO WOULD KNOW the Galatians were it not for the great letter that Paul addressed to them? They were a Celtic people who came from the

Balkans in the third century before our era. On meeting conquerors hurtling down from the East toward the fertile land of the West, they showed their spirit of contradiction by choosing to settle on the rough Anatolian plateaus. After the battle of Philippi, the Galatian king Amyntas received from Antony the government of Pisidia, then that of Galatia, one part of Lycaonia and of Pamphylia, and saw himself confirmed by Augustus as ruler of this considerable region. At the end of Augustus' reign (A.D. 25), the Romans secured the whole area, pure and simple, to form a Roman province. Why burden oneself with allies when one can reign as master?

It is easy to reach Iconium—modern Konya—by car: 112 miles, of which eighteen are through mountains. But on foot? Paul and Barnabas now approached the gorges whose black and mangled rocks were themselves enough to arouse fear. At every turn in the road they could expect to see robbers. The villages that received them have long since disappeared.

We can imagine their relief on reaching the paved road again. Barely settled in Asia, Rome extended to that point the prodigious network of roads that already furrowed Europe and would always symbolize the Empire's omnipotence. Originally, the intention was purely military; it was a means of facilitating the rapid deployment of the legions. In 6 B.C., the emperor Augustus gave the order to open another system of roads on the territory that is today Turkey. The engineers set to work and traced the roads from Antioch of Pisidia; one, crossing East toward valleys and mountains, cut over the Sultan Dag and, by means of a narrow gorge, rejoined Iconium; another stretched from Antioch of Pisidia toward the northeast to reach Cappadocia.[2] In honor of Augustus, the two routes were given the name *Via Sebaste;* the Greek "Sebastos" is equivalent to the Latin "Augustus."

Threading through the plains and mountains, usually in a straight line, and sowing them with works of art, builders multiplied the marvels. They forgot none of the required rules followed in Europe and Africa: thirteen to twenty-six feet wide, the standard foundation composed of a base of masonry covered by a layer of concrete, in all up to six feet thick. The paving stones were so skillfully cut that no cement was needed to join them together. All this was the work of the legionnaires reinforced by local "volunteers," naturally recruited by force. Did the expression "Roman handiwork" come from there? Of note is the fact that this system of roads—in the third century of our era—would end by reaching the

Persian Gulf! We have to ask ourselves about the insufficiency of the ver-
dicts pronounced by the people of antiquity; it is necessary, urgent even,
to declare Roman roads the eighth wonder of the world.

Here our travelers would extend their steps on solid pavement.
Unless, parallel to the road, they preferred to walk on ground better suited to strolling. Walkers who read this will understand.

The abundance of buildings, new or under construction, surprises one
who crosses the suburbs of Turkish Konya. They are agreeable to look at
with their vivid colors; one must respond to the reality of a constantly
growing population.

It is impossible to discover the least remembrance of Saint Paul in this
modern metropolis of 600,000 inhabitants. Konya, whose whirling
dervishes were celebrated in the thirteenth century by the Tekke of
Mevlana, is above all consecrated to the prophet Mohammed. The
mosque that the sultan Selim offered to his father Suleyman the
Magnificent is impressive. Also interesting is Alaettin Camii, the most
ancient (1220), where there stand forty-two antique columns topped by
capitals torn from Roman monuments; they are all that remain of what
Paul may have seen.[3] The city took its name from the emperor Claudius:
Claudiconium became Iconium. At the time of Paul the cult of Heracles
and the Phrygian deities—Zeus, Magistos, and Cybele—were chiefly celebrated there.[4]

Paul and Barnabas again used the strategy that had finally brought
them such good results at Antioch of Pisidia: visit the synagogue on the
Sabbath day, and accept with eagerness the invitation to speak. As a
result, "a great number of both Jews and Greeks became believers," to the
great displeasure, it must be said, of the Jews who remained stubborn;
they "stirred up the Gentiles and poisoned their minds against the brothers" (Acts 14:1–2).

The Jews were not the only ones to become indignant; the conversion
of certain pagans also scandalized some of their own. Anger gathered
together the two camps, who formed a league against the intruders. They
decided to seize them and, to put it simply, stone them. Forewarned, Paul
and Barnabas stole away in time and rejoined the Roman road that, at the
time, ended in Lystra. It was a day's walk in the heart of one of the most

beautiful sites that can be seen in central Anatolia. An immense circle of notched mountains, whose colors go from ochre to gentle green and then pass to a somber green, dominated the high plateau.

We wanted to see Lystra, which today has been replaced by the village of Hatunsaray. There is no trace of the Roman road. As we approached, the hairpin turns of the actual route tightened. A sign that said "Lystra" led us astray. We found ourselves on a road that we hoped would lead us to evocative remains. Our error soon became obvious: all that remains of Lystra are rare vestiges buried underground. What emerges from this city, founded by Augustus in 6 B.C., are scattered stones, a fragment of wall, and in the yards of a few houses sarcophagi that have become troughs. It is a large and very poor village with houses enveloped in clay, whose walls of dried earth are covered with branches. A small mosque stands there now. The natives were astonished to see us. Nothing here recalls that in Lystra Paul almost lost his life.

THROUGHOUT THE REGION, the contemptuous judgments of antiquity were never lacking. Strabo barely spares it: "A high plateau, cold and bare, without shade, water very rare and wells extremely deep." Vast herds of onagers [Asian wild asses] were pastured there, but the region had so little water that it was necessary to buy it at stages. Cicero, who lived there as proconsul, showed nothing but disdain for this population, ignorant and not very civilized. In spite of the efforts of Roman veterans, Lystra still presented itself, when Paul and Barnabas arrived there, as a large village grown artificially and barely humanized by the cultures to which the new grants attached themselves.

How does one preach the Good News to a population that speaks neither Greek nor Latin nor Hebrew? Paul and Barnabas persisted in their efforts. The first astonishment having passed, the people became accustomed to seeing them. Some asked about the origins of these strangers. When Paul spoke, they came to listen, not understanding a word he said but admiring the balanced linkage of his phrases and the impassioned tone that sustained them.

That day in the midst of the small crowd that had gathered, an invalid did not miss a sound of the mysterious language: "In Lystra there was a man sitting who could not use his feet and had never walked, for he had been crippled from birth." The poor man stared intently at Paul, who met his gaze. The man from Tarsus, "seeing that he had the faith to be healed," ordered, in a loud voice: "Stand upright on your feet."

The man understood the invitation by the tone of voice and the gesture that accompanied it. He obeyed. He jumped up. He walked!

Imagine the wonder of the people of Lystra. They ran up, they gathered, they were moved. They wanted to see and to touch the crippled man who had been healed. Struck more than all the others, an influential Lystrian drew the conclusion, evident to his eyes, of this miracle. He exclaimed in Lycaonian dialect, "The gods have come down to us in human form!"

The language not only convinced them, but it corresponded so closely to what these people had just experienced that they took up the cry. Not a moment was lost before they identified these gods: Barnabas, taller and stronger, was surely Zeus. As for Paul the speechmaker, he was without doubt Hermes, messenger god of the Olympians, Mercury to the Latins. The hypothesis became reality. They prostrated themselves and prayed to these gods that they now recognized. The priest of Zeus-outside-the-walls, a temple built in front of the city gate, was also convinced. He ran up, brandishing crowns and pulling bulls behind him. It was necessary immediately to offer sacrifice to these two gods who honored the city by their visit! Stupefied, Paul and Barnabas searched in vain to understand the meaning of this activity. The truth dawned. They wavered between astonishment and anger. To be taken for gods—they who had given themselves to the duty of transmitting the word of the true God! Seeing that protestations did not suffice, and without any way to foresee what was to come, our two Christians tore their cloaks, a striking gesture in antiquity: "Friends, why are you doing this? We are mortals just like you."

Someone who spoke Greek was present in the crowd. He did his best to translate Paul's urgent explanations. They listened with attention:

> "We bring you good news, that you should turn from these worthless things to the living God, *'who made the heaven and the earth and the sea and all that is in them.'* In past generations he allowed all nations to follow their own ways; yet he has not left himself without a witness in doing good—giving you rains from heaven and fruitful seasons, and filling you with food and your hearts with joy" (Acts 14:8–17).

Intractable, Paul made room here for strategy. It would have been useless to make a frontal attack on these pagans whose reactions they could not have foreseen. That would have risked putting into question the very essence of the mission. Therefore, he said no more. A heavy silence followed. The faces were marked with sorrow, which at least was not discontent. How they were deceived, these Lycaonians! "Even with these words, they scarcely restrained the crowds from offering sacrifice to them" (Acts 14:18).

Between the missionaries and the Lycaonian people the door remained open. Some men demanded that this living God be explained to them. The interpreters translated. Little by little, Paul and Barnabas learned basic Lycaonian vocabulary. Conversions multiplied. Two women were the first to ask for Baptism: Eunice and Lois, her mother. A young man named Timothy followed them, the son of Eunice. Almost a child still, his Greek father had raised him in the language of Pericles. Deeply moved by Paul's discourses, he begged to go with him. *Be patient!* said Paul.

Rumors of these successes reached Iconium and struck with full force the Jewish community, who believed they had rid themselves of such dangerous characters. The Jews of Iconium descended upon Lystra to enlighten the natives and put an end to the boasting imposters. Their anger was contagious. In an instant, the inhabitants of Lystra completely turned around. They bore a grudge against Paul especially; by healing the crippled man, this magician had set them on an evil path! They seized him and pushed away Barnabas, who had flown to his rescue. Still furious, those from Iconium asked the Lystrians what they would do to this false Hermes. Their answer was unambiguous: "Stone him!"

At that moment how could Paul not have thought of the Calvary of the unfortunate Stephen? Like him, Paul was dragged outside the city and thrown to the ground. The furious mob gathered stones and the avalanche crashed down upon him. When the people of Lystra and the Jews saw Paul inanimate, they thought he was dead. Leaving the body, face against the ground, they left.

Firm in their new faith, the first Christian converts ran behind Barnabas. They bent toward Paul. His heart was still beating; his head intact. Apparently his injuries were not fatal. To survive a stoning was practically unheard of. If they had known, would the executioners have held back their hands? Apart from exceptional luck, this confirmed the intensity of life that burned in the small man. To affirm, as Luke does, that on the following day Paul took to the road in the company of Barnabas, raises a misunderstanding of the gravity of the injuries that such an ordeal must necessarily have entailed. To go from Lystra to Derbe—the last anticipated stage of the mission—they had to walk eighty-seven miles. It would have been impossible for one who had been stoned to take that on in the state he was in. We must rather believe that a family, converted in Lystra, gave Paul shelter, hid him, and cared for him. A few days later, Barnabas borrowed a wagon, stretched Paul out in it, and in several stages led him to Derbe, where a Roman colony had been established. There, Paul would be able to get back on his feet and resume his mission.

Nothing of Derbe remains today—absolutely nothing. We recognize that the tell of Kerti Huyuk, in the southeast of Konya, marks the site. At the time of Paul it was an important city. We read in Acts that the two missionaries gathered there "disciples numerous enough," but there is nothing mentioned about the length of their stay.

Luke's silence does not facilitate the dating of facts. The Letters of Paul are no more helpful; they contain no reference to the situation of the external world. Luke reports voluntarily on historical events, but his "chronological reports" are often incorrect. He uses easily the expression "there is little," which brings the historian help that is very relative. One must resign oneself to approximation in remembering that ancient authors—whether Greek or Latin—did not overly preoccupy themselves with chronology. The notion in itself will not see the light for a very long time.

How much time was required for the wounds of one who had been stoned to heal? How much time to convert a people? It is easier to answer the first question than the second. Let us wager on several months.

WHY DID PAUL, restored, not choose to go to Tarsus directly? Was it because winter had come? To cross the Taurus in that season was not a tempting prospect. Writers often spoke of the "uncrossable" Taurus. Knowing Paul's obstinacy, we must look elsewhere for the answer. Perhaps he considered it necessary to consolidate the "churches" and, along the lines of the councils that we find at the head of Jewish communities, to install on site responsible people: "And after they had appointed elders for them in each church, with prayer and fasting they entrusted them to the Lord in whom they had come to believe" (Acts 14:23).

Neither Paul nor Barnabas seems to have hesitated. After their goodbyes to the new community of Derbe, they returned to the road. They would pass again by way of Lystra, Iconium, and Antioch of Pisidia. We can imagine the risks they took each time they revisited these cities. What remained of the converts whom they had baptized? Joy; they persisted in living as Christians. The two missionaries remained as long as they could in the company of their new brothers and sisters. A visit of a few days would not suffice to confirm the future of these communities that history will show became churches in the fullest sense: "There they strengthened the souls of the disciples and encouraged them to continue in the faith" (Acts 14:22).

Paul received a precious lesson. These churches that he had birthed were almost exclusively composed of pagans. Faced with the systematic obstruction of the Jews, he had found in Asia Minor men and women disposed to receive the great message, peoples immersed in parallel mythologies. The other lesson to be drawn from this Asiatic odyssey was that nowhere had there been a question of circumcision. Everything can be summed up in the words Paul would later address to new communities: "It is through many persecutions that we must enter the kingdom of God" (Acts 14:22).

7

UNDER THE SIGN OF CIRCUMCISION

etracing one's steps is most difficult because we already know the depth of the gorges that we will run down and the height of the slopes we will climb. We will hear anew the thousand noises announcing the dangers that we escaped from earlier and that risk turns into reality now. In the hurry to arrive or the fear of not arriving, how do we know what got the better of Paul and Barnabas on the road to Attalia? They had no way of measuring time except by the notches in their walking sticks. Between the branches, one watched for the moment when, in the violence of the light that each knew from experience, the sea and the sky would suddenly appear. Each false hope came as a defeat.

Happiness! Behold *Mare nostrum*. Hearts beat, spirits lifted. In Perga as at Attalia, they would rediscover established churches, very much alive. When they tore themselves away from them and finally set sail, we can estimate, from the logical rhythm of their adventures, that their mission must have lasted two years.

THEY HAD AN UNEVENTFUL crossing. At the end of the journey, the ship lowered its sail before the port of Antioch—the other one, the one in Syria. When they disembarked, it is difficult to believe that the contrast did not seize these men who had come from crossing wild mountains and living alongside peoples whose simplicity was almost primitive.

Of the enormous city nothing had changed—not the swarming crowds, nor the pride of proclaiming themselves a free city, nor the movement of business, nor the grand airs that those whom the city had enriched gave themselves, nor the misery of those who had only their arms to offer.

For two years our missionaries had not sent any news; how could they have done so? Among the Christians of Antioch, worry had grown in proportion to the time that had passed. Finally Paul and Barnabas returned and recounted the story, alternating failures and conversions. Filled with wonder, the Christians listened to them. But not all; certain members did not hide their hesitation in learning that the two men had baptized pagans especially. So antagonism remained between Jewish Christians and pagan Christians, and that necessarily upset Paul.

According to Pierre-Antoine Bernheim, who wrote a biography of the apostle James, in the first century the Jews adopted a "relatively tolerant" attitude toward pagans and idolaters. The hostility, even hatred, that one still met was directed especially at pagans "who worshiped other gods in the land of Israel and against those who, outside Israel, opposed the intention of YHWH [Yahweh]." The prophecy of Isaiah affirmed that "the mountain of the LORD's house shall be established as the highest of the mountains, and shall be raised above the hills; all the nations shall stream to it" (Isa 2:2). Twice Isaiah put these words in YHWH's mouth: "I am coming to gather all nations and tongues; and they shall come and shall see my glory" (Isa 66:18). The desire for expansion seemed evident. Meanwhile, other books of the Bible—in particular, Leviticus, Ezekiel, Ezra, and Nehemiah—condemned all contact with Gentiles. Nothing is simple in this field.

The behavior of the Jewish contemporaries of Paul reflected the same diversity as the Bible. The phenomenon of "God-fearers," nevertheless, marked an opening. If pagans frequented the synagogues, drawn by a monotheism that represented for them an immense novelty, it was because the doors were not closed to them. Flavius Josephus, evoking what he had seen among the Jews of Antioch, was astonished at "the number of Greeks that they attract to their religious ceremonies," making "of them in a way a part of their community."

That the Jews, having become Christians, opened their ranks to pagans offered then nothing extraordinary, and Paul could not but see it. Two camps dug in: the first required that a pagan, in order to obtain Christian Baptism, become Jewish; the second, which had all the sympathy of the man from Tarsus, identified with the "freedom that comes from

Jesus."[1] For Paul, Baptism created Christians even if they did not eat *kosher*, even if they did not have circumcision, "For the kingdom of God is not food and drink but righteousness and peace and joy in the Holy Spirit" (Rom 14:17).

Could these positions still meet? At so little distance from the death of Jesus, were we moving toward a schism that would put an end to an incredible hope?

Good will would react in time. On both sides the decision was made to refer to a supreme authority: the church of Jerusalem. A mission including representatives of the two camps set out for Jerusalem. The presence of Paul and Barnabas at the head of the delegation was a presentiment of the positions it would defend.

"I went up again to Jerusalem," Paul would write, "taking Titus along with me" (Gal 2:1). Of this Titus, Paul tells us that he was born of a pagan family and was not circumcised. Luke furnishes an important detail: "So they were sent on their way by the church [of Antioch]" (Acts 15:3).

THEY HEADED FOR the holy city by a land route. "And as they passed through both Phoenicia and Samaria, they reported the conversion of the Gentiles, and brought great joy to all the believers" (Acts 15:3). In Jerusalem, the elite of the Church awaited them.

We know about the meeting from both the Letter to the Galatians and the Acts of the Apostles. The consequences that flowed from it in the history of Christianity were such that certain people later boldly designated it the "Council of Jerusalem," which leaves one to suppose an official and formal assembly. Instead it was a meeting of a private nature bringing the few representatives of the church of Antioch that we know—Paul and Barnabas—face to face with James, Peter, and John. To Paul's despair, former Pharisees spitefully defended the Jewish Christian point of view. They repeated without respite that it was necessary to circumcise the pagans and to require that they observe the Law—all the Law—of Moses. Always brutal in the heat of controversy, Paul will speak of "false believers secretly brought in" (Gal 2:4).

We must pause a moment and look at the person of James, who will play a major role concerning Paul's fate. The Gospels show James, like most of the members of Jesus' family, reserved and rather hostile toward him during his ministry. Everything changed when the Christ rose. That Paul in First Corinthians grants James a place apart is striking; he presents James as having been favored with an appearance of Jesus for him alone. From then on, we see James persuaded that the return of Jesus was imminent and that the Kingdom of God was also. Yahweh's promise to Israel was going to come true.

A representative and spokesman whom the Christians respected, he would be able, by way of Jewish piety, to serve as an example for the most zealous members of the community. As soon as he escaped from the prison of Agrippa I, Peter ordered: "Tell this to James" (Acts 12:17). We estimate that it was at the same time, when Peter fled from Jerusalem— in 43 or 44—that James replaced him, not only as head of the church of the city but as head of the Christian movement. By attaching such importance to winning the support of the church in Jerusalem for his opinions, Paul proved the reality of James' preeminence. For Paul, the three "acknowledged pillars" of the Church were James, Peter, and John (Gal 2:9). The order of the names indicates a hierarchy, without any doubt.

The discussion bogged down. Hallowed with the sacred authority that all recognized in him, Peter intervened: "Now therefore why are you putting God to the test by placing on the neck of the disciples a yoke that neither our ancestors nor we have been able to bear?...We believe that we will be saved through the grace of the Lord Jesus, just as they will" (Acts 15:10–11).

None could minimize the importance of this remark. Peter admitted that the rules imposed upon the Jews by the Law were so hard that the majority of the sons of Abraham could not submit to them. Paul and Barnabas described with spirit "all the signs and wonders that God had done through them among the Gentiles" (Acts 15:12). They were heard with marked attention. James spoke. Beginning with Paul, each one awaited his opinion.

"Therefore I have reached the decision that we should not trouble those Gentiles who are turning to God...."(Acts 15:19)

Thus James swept away hesitation. The apostles and the elders decided to send to Antioch two delegates, Judas and Silas, "leaders among the brothers" (15:22), who would travel with Paul and Barnabas. A letter was confided to them that put forth very exactly James' proposal: "For it has seemed good to the Holy Spirit and to us to impose on you no further burden than these essentials: that you abstain from what has been sacrificed to idols and from blood and from what is strangled and from fornication. If you keep yourselves from these, you will do well. Farewell" (15:28–29).[2]

Although writing many years after the meeting, it is clear that it deeply marked the man from Tarsus, for he was still excited when he dictated the story. He remembered having agreed to go to Jerusalem "in response to a revelation" (Gal 2:2) and recorded the words that he had pronounced before the assembled Church: "Then I laid before them...the gospel[3] that I proclaim among the Gentiles" (2:2). He mentioned the strong opposition that was raised among the Jewish Christians: "We did not submit to them even for a moment.... Those leaders contributed nothing to me" (2:5–6). Most striking is that Paul remembered having been heard: "...When they saw that I had been entrusted with the gospel for the uncircumcised, just as Peter had been entrusted with the gospel for the circumcised..." (2:7). He would not doubt that: this historic division of preaching was inspired by the Lord. The final scene is impressive: "When James and Cephas and John, who were acknowledged pillars, recognized the grace that had been given to me, they gave to Barnabas and me the right hand of fellowship, agreeing that we should go to the Gentiles and they to the circumcised" (2:9). One simple condition was placed before them: they were asked never to forget the poor. The man from Tarsus would know how to remember.

Was Paul's timid triumphalism meant to convince us? In vain do we reread his letter and the Acts of Luke. Sadly, we see on the part of the mother church a sort of tolerance granted with condescension to a minority.

SCARCELY ARRIVED IN Antioch, Judas and Silas, though official delegates of the church, did not hesitate to make common cause with the pagan Christians. Highly affirming, they "said much to encourage and strengthen the believers" (Acts 15:32). If Judas returned a little later, Silas insisted on remaining in place. We learn suddenly that Peter himself had decided to make the journey. To what end? The news must have made the community anxious. Very few of them, perhaps none at all, had met the chief of the apostles, but he had immense prestige. As far as symbol was concerned, these people were not wrong.

The arrival of the fisherman from the lake of Tiberias could not but produce the usual effect: enthusiasm and veneration. Immediately the Christians watched the apostle's behavior. Those who rallied around Paul's position did not hide their joy when they saw Peter voluntarily sharing meals with pagans. It was very evident that he did not behave thus by chance.[4] We are present at the first episode of what will be known as "the affair of the tables." It must be understood that it was a matter of those tables at which, in memory of the last meal of Jesus, the faithful sat not only to eat but to pray. Let's remember that the food taken in common represented one of the first options of the Christian community emerging in Jerusalem; it was a matter of a Eucharist to which the gathering for the meal constituted the link.

So among the Christians of Antioch, was everything for the best in the best possible world? That would be an illusion. In Jerusalem, anxiety had changed into distrust. The mother church, inspired by James, judged that Peter was going too far. They dispatched to him new messengers whose mission could be summed up this way: "It is not because certain pagans have recognized YHWH and his Messiah that they became full members of the people of God. [...] The Jews who have recognized Jesus, those who form the true Israel, must maintain their identity and respect a certain level of ritual separatism vis-à-vis these pagan Christians."[5]

The new delegates from Jerusalem had scarcely arrived in Antioch, and Peter wavered. Let us reread Paul: "I opposed him to his face, because he stood self-condemned; for until certain people came from James, he used to eat with the Gentiles. But after they came, he drew back and kept himself separate for fear of the circumcision faction" (Gal 2:11–12).

Are we surprised that this reversal stung Paul to the quick? We can hardly accuse Peter of cowardice. For the sake of Christ, Peter had known prison and scourging, and he would die a martyr for his faith. But Paul, beside himself, would have been able to make an allusion to the cock that sang out three times to punctuate three denials. However, to reassure the reader, this is nothing but pure hypothesis.

The tragedy was that certain Christians, impressed, would follow Peter's example. The height of insult was that dear Barnabas—companion and brother—was among them. In Paul's eyes this could not be worse. We sense he was on the verge of despair: "So that *even Barnabas* was led astray by their hypocrisy," he wrote (Gal 2:13). A storm in Antioch. By sheer bad luck, Peter and Paul found themselves unexpectedly face to face. We can picture them, the one very embarrassed, the other boiling with fury: "I said to Cephas before them all, 'If you, though a Jew, live like a Gentile and not like a Jew, how can you compel the Gentiles to live like Jews?' We ourselves are Jews by birth and not Gentile sinners" (2:14–15).[6]

Paul against Peter? Who could have believed that this would ever happen? Raised to his short height, sure of himself as he always was, the maker of tents taught a lesson to the one whom all recognized as the rock of the Church:

> Yet we know that a person is justified not by the works of the law but through faith in Jesus Christ. And we have come to believe in Christ Jesus, so that we might be justified by faith in Christ, and not by doing the works of the law, because no one will be justified by the works of the law. But if, in our effort to be justified in Christ, we ourselves have been found to be sinners, is Christ then a servant of sin? Certainly not! But if I build up again the very things that I once tore down, then I demonstrate that I am a transgressor. For through the law I died to the law, so that I might live to God. I have been crucified with Christ; and it is no longer I who live, but it is Christ who lives in me. And the life I now live in the flesh I live by faith in the Son of God, who loved me and gave himself for me. I do not nullify the grace of God; for if justification comes through the law, then Christ died for nothing (Gal 2:16–21).

What dialectic! We can discern in it the premises of the Letter to the Romans, the legacy of Pauline thought. Paul's position at Antioch would be weakened by the confrontation. The affair became even more worrisome because not only were there two camps that clashed at Antioch, but the entire Church appeared literally split. In the common gatherings from then on there met fundamentalist Hebrews, pagan converts, the uncircumcised, and others who had been circumcised. We see the Hellenists, the old partisans of Stephen—although always proclaiming themselves Jews—detaching themselves more and more from the practices of the Torah. They also grew more pessimistic about a conversion of all the Jews.

Paul himself persisted. In the Letter to the Romans, he would repeat with force that Jews and pagans had the same Lord, and that God had never rejected Israel. Even more, the new Christians must never forget that they would be nothing if God had not, through Abraham, chosen the Jewish people. He used the famous comparison of the root and the branches of the olive tree: "And if the root is holy, then the branches also are holy. But if some of the branches were broken off, and you, a wild olive shoot, were grafted in their place to share the rich root of the olive tree, do not boast over the branches. If you do boast, remember that it is not you that support the root, but the root that supports you" (Rom 11:16–18). Conclusion *ne varietur:* Christianity is a branch of Judaism. This is an obvious fact.

HOW COULD PAUL have felt at ease in the midst of conflicts which, according to the concept forged on the road to Damascus, could only appear to him derisive? Unhappy, no doubt bitter, everything pushed him to rediscover these great expanses where the struggle, with full clarity, came down to winning new souls for Christ. Suddenly we learn that he set off again toward the churches that he had founded. He burned to know what had become of them.

Would Paul and Barnabas team up again? Despite the "desertion" of his friend, Paul approached him, but Barnabas demurred. Was it, as has been maintained, because Barnabas wanted to bring Mark along and Paul, never one to forget, rejected the young man who had earlier gone "missing"? I rather believe that Paul bore a grudge against Barnabas for his having rallied to Peter. He told Barnabas so, and—we know him—no doubt he went too far. Barnabas did not bear it well. Their friendship died. Barnabas would return to Cyprus in the company of Mark.

It was impossible for Paul to leave alone. He would take Silas, a Jew from Palestine, the very one who had reported the decisions of the Jerusalem meeting to the Christians in Antioch. To say that a long collaboration would be formed between the two is not sufficient. Silas would devote himself body and soul to Paul, illustrating the strength of feelings and the passionate loyalties that the man from Tarsus would arouse in people throughout his life. A Roman citizen like Paul, Silas would go so far as to adopt the name Silvanus, which etymologically means "god of the forests."

This time they didn't take a ship. Although Paul had refused the land route in returning after the first journey, since the Taurus mountains were inaccessible in the winter, he now chose it because it was spring. "[Paul] went through Syria and Cilicia, strengthening the churches" (Acts 15:41). Already many churches were flourishing in Syria. Climbing northward, the two men crossed the wooded mountains of the Amanus—in our day Kizyl Dag. They came down toward the gulf of Issos, which bathed the plain where Alexander the Great, in 333 B.C., crushed Darius III, king of the Persians. That day, the East had been opened to Hellenistic thought.[7]

Having crossed Adana, a familiar place of his youth, Paul returned to his beloved Tarsus. How can we not suppose that he would stop there? It was twenty-seven years since the young Saul, knapsack on his shoulder, had left home for Jerusalem; thirteen years since Barnabas had come to look for him to lead him to Antioch. If his parents were still living, they would have been beyond their sixties, old age at this time. It was impossible for the two men to stop for very long, for the mission spurred them on. In following the flow of the Cydnos, they planned to cross the barrier of the Taurus mountains.

I too have followed this road. Like other travelers, I felt disappointed because this range, presented as formidable—and it is in other places—hardly seems so today. A driver's reaction? The route we took did not pass by the famous Gates of Cilicia, which would be illusory. To find them, one must leave the car and, on foot, sink into a narrow pass dug vertically between two walls: one hundred and thirty yards high and scarcely twenty-two yards wide. We can understand then how the reputation of the Gates was forged. We dream of conquerors of all kinds—the Persians, the Greeks of Alexander, the Romans of Caesar—who, in traveling over the pass, imprisoned between these walls of stone, must have felt rise within them the unpredictable anguish they transmitted to future generations.

THE ROADS BECAME more and more straight. Breathing in the midst of tangled trees, did the two men lend their attention to the frame that surrounded them? The countryside changed unceasingly. At first rocky, later dry, it changed completely twenty-five miles out from Tarsus, where conifers abounded. At 4,160 feet our walkers crossed the last pass and came out on a high plateau where I reassured myself for them: for several days they would not have been able to rise or to descend. Did they walk beneath a pounding rain like the one that struck our windshield in April? If they arrived there later in the season—which, given the length of the road, is probable—they would have traveled under an implacable sun. This was no better. In every season they would have had to struggle against the wind, which the Turks curtail today with thousands of young poplars.

They came to a countryside that Paul thought he recognized; no doubt it was Derbe. How could he not have recounted for Silas the pitiful state in which he had arrived in the village and the convalescence from which so many conversions had followed? The two men appeared and people recognized Paul; they rushed up and surrounded them. Ten houses offered to receive him and his companion. It was a joy to discover a community that had endured but little spiritual damage. Then followed a closer inspection, preaching, and a common fast. They did not leave

Derbe until they sensed that these Christians were solidly attached to the right teaching they had received from Paul.

SOMEWHERE IN GALATIAN territory, an illness would root Paul to the spot. We sense him as though stricken. Later remembering this sad episode, he will show himself in retrospect frightened by the state in which the faithful saw him: "Though my condition put you to the test, you did not scorn or despise me, but welcomed me as an angel of God, as Christ Jesus. For I testify that, had it been possible, you would have torn out your eyes and given them to me" (Gal 4:14–15).

When Paul speaks of the disgust that he would have aroused, let us remember that to meet a sick man suffering gravely and visibly was then considered to be a bad omen. People would have hastened to avoid him.

How long did he need to recover? He does not tell us. But it is certain that he soon took to the road again.

In Lystra each one tended to forget the stoning. Paul met once more the young Timothy, unrecognizable at eighteen, a fervent Christian who reminded him of the promise he had made three years earlier. Paul made inquiries: "He was well spoken of by the believers in Lystra and Iconium" (Acts 16:2). There was no further reason to postpone such a step. Overjoyed, the adolescent would be quickly disillusioned: before leaving, Paul assumed the duty of having him circumcised.

Circumcise Timothy! But why? Let us open Acts: "Paul wanted Timothy to accompany him; and he took him and had him circumcised because of the Jews who were in those places, for they all knew that his father was a Greek" (16:3). Really? Is that the whole reason? I ask the reader's permission to speak—this one time, I promise—directly to Paul.

Dear and great Paul, what happened to you in Galatian territory? For ages you had been fighting so that pagans could become Christians without having circumcision imposed upon them. Your position was accepted in Jerusalem in the eyes of your most reluctant brother Jews. Of a Greek father and a Jewish mother, Timothy was already Christian at the time of your first journey. The Jews of the region must have known this and, according to what we know, were hardly alarmed by his conversion. To please them, did you have to compromise yourself? Don't try to deny it. Dear and great Paul, the more we follow you, the more we admire you. How can you disappoint us like this? One owes one's friends frankness, all the more for those whom one admires.

As they went from town to town, they delivered to them for observance the decisions that had been reached by the apostles and elders who were in Jerusalem. So the churches were strengthened in the faith and increased in numbers daily (Acts 16:4–5).

By dipping into the various Letters of Paul, we can get a clear idea of the communities to whom he gave birth. He would write to Titus: "I left you behind in Crete for this reason, so that you should put in order what remained to be done, and should appoint elders in every town, as I directed you" (1:5). For these presbyters—an unchanging reference to the rules of Judaism—he would gradually set obligations. They should be "...blameless, married only once, whose children are believers, not accused of debauchery and not rebellious" (Titus 1:6). The *episkopos*—who would later become the bishop—had as his principal mission to show vigilance; no community was totally safe. To Timothy:

> Now a bishop must be [...] temperate, sensible, respectable, hospitable, an apt teacher, not a drunkard, not violent but gentle, not quarrelsome, and not a lover of money. He must manage his own household well, keeping his children submissive and respectful in every way—for if someone does not know how to manage his own household well, how can he take care of God's church? (1 Tim 3:2–5)

In the Letter to the Philippians, Paul presents the deacons—instituted by the Twelve in Jerusalem—as assistants to the *episkopoi* (cf. 1:1). Again to Timothy: "Deacons likewise must be serious, not double-tongued, not indulging in much wine, not greedy for money; they must hold fast to the mystery of the faith with a clear conscience." To Timothy once more: "[The deacons' wives] likewise must be serious, not slanderers, but temperate, faithful in all things. Let deacons be married only once, and let them manage their children and their households well; for those who serve well as deacons gain good standing for themselves and great boldness in the faith that is in Christ Jesus" (1 Tim 3:8–13). This hierarchy was not put in place right away, but the rules prefiguring it were decreed very early. What was essential was to convert and, in the second place, to certify the firmness of the new Christians' convictions. The rest would follow.

How did these communities address God?

I desire, then, that in every place the men should pray, lifting up holy hands without anger or argument; also that the women should dress themselves modestly and decently in suitable clothing, not with their hair braided, or with gold, pearls, or expensive clothes, but with good works, as is proper for women who profess reverence for God. Let a woman learn in silence with full submission. I permit no woman to teach or to have authority over a man; she is to keep silent. For Adam was formed first, then Eve; and Adam was not deceived, but the woman was deceived and became a transgressor. Yet she will be saved through childbearing, provided they continue in faith and love and holiness, with modesty (1 Tim 2:8–15).

Here then we directly confront the anti-feminism for which Paul will be eternally reproached. We have not exhausted the subject, but an example emerges from the preceding text. The origin of this attitude in regard to women followed exclusively from the Book of Genesis, which was written seven centuries before Paul was born.

When Acts informs us that Paul and his people covered "the region of Phrygia and Galatia" (16:6), it must be understood that the mission only revisited the region explored at the time of the first journey. Derbe, Lystra, and Pisidian Antioch were situated in southern Galatia, and Iconium was at the edge of Phrygia and Lycaonia. Now that the mission was accomplished, where to go?

Leaving Pisidian Antioch, Paul hesitated, facing a choice that must be understood spiritually as well as geographically. He had to choose between the southwest by the *Via Sebaste,* which would lead him directly to Ephesus—an attractive prospect a priori—and the northern route, which would permit him to reach the Roman province of Bithynia. A sudden repulsion—he was sure that it came to him from the Holy Spirit—turned him away from Ephesus, where, it is true, other missionaries had preceded him from the first days of evangelization. Nowhere did Paul like to be second.

These "forces of the Spirit" that regularly intervened in Paul's life must not be treated lightly, for Paul existed only through them. Since Damascus, he had remained listening. He felt every impression so much that it reinforced him in the certitude that God had chosen him. He did not doubt it; he would never miss the messages of the Father or the Son. He had believed this since the time he wrote: "God...had set me apart before I was born" (Gal 1:15). To admit such pride, to dare go so far, one must believe from the depths of one's soul. If pride had dominated him, we could very well fear being the victims of the greatest deception in history—which is not so.

LOGIC INCLINES US to think that Paul and his people crossed modern Ankara; Midas Sehri, the capital of King Midas; Gordion, where Alexander the Great cut the famous knot; and that then they stopped in Pergamum, where a Jewish community resided. Paul harangued the Jews without result. Today, at the summit of a peak, an acropolis remains that shelters superb temples. They must have left Paul indifferent; one should never think of him as a tourist.

The stubborn Renan followed these same roads, as narrow as in Paul's time—about six and a half feet wide—where he often found ancient paving stones. The writer honestly confessed that this ride on horseback for days and days tired him. He consoled himself with stops that he judged to be "delicious"; one must water the horses. "An hour's rest, a piece of bread eaten by the side of limpid streams, running on beds of pebbles, sustains you for a long time." Everything Renan saw during his journey enchanted him: abundant water, infinitely varied mountains "that we would take for dreams if an artist dared to imitate them: summits serrated like a saw, sides ripped up and torn to shreds, strange cones and vertical walls, where all the beauty of the stone is spread vividly." And the trees! "Long lines of poplars, of small plane trees in large beds of diverse torrents, superb clumps of trees whose feet plunge into the fountains and which soar in somber tufts from the base of each mountain." Mounted on his horse, he thought of Paul, of Silas, and of Timothy who walked these roads.

FROM NOW ON the three travelers have a goal: Troas. It is their destination for a simple reason: one night, a Macedonian appeared to Paul in a dream and begged him, "Come over to Macedonia and help us." Following this vision, "we immediately tried to cross over to Macedonia, being convinced that God had called us to proclaim the good news to them" (Acts 16:9–10).

We? What is this about? Here it is not Paul who is expressing himself. This unexpected witness is perfectly well known to the reader: it is Luke, who until now has shown himself as a chronicler, an informer of the first order. When he writes, "...passing by Mysia, they went down to Troas," he narrates, yet is not himself involved. But now we read in Acts:

"When he had seen the vision, *we* immediately tried to cross over to Macedonia" (16:8 and 10). It is clear that Luke has ceased to be only a chronicler. He has entered the action. For now, and on three other occasions, he will be a witness reporting what he sees.

When and how did Paul and Luke come to know each other? We do not know. We must limit ourselves to saluting the moment when Luke first met his favorite subject. If the thirteenth apostle has gradually taken the place he occupies in Acts, it is because of this meeting. It happens to all of us; we come across someone—a man, a woman—whom we feel the imperious need to see again. This was exactly the case with Luke. We can be sure that it was not there, on the road to Troas, that he and Paul met each other for the first time. If they had, Luke would not have been able, as he did, to cast the "young man" who would guard the garments of Stephen's executioners. Logic inclines one to believe that Luke had been observing Paul for a long time. When he joined him to see him act directly, Luke crossed a stage.

What do we know of the author of the Acts of the Apostles? In the first place, a very ancient tradition ascribes to him the role of a physician. We shouldn't imagine him exclusively occupied with scrutinizing the behavior of the twelve apostles and particularly of the thirteenth. Today we meet physicians, excellent in their profession and who, at the same time, are passionate about art or literature. The physician Luke was a born writer. He reminds me of those journalists who, before writing the biography of a contemporary person and meeting their subject's friends and enemies, interview the person themselves, insisting on "discovering their subject" in the field of his or her activity. When I mention Luke, I often want to refer to him as "our special envoy."

A myriad of specialists have scrutinized each page, each paragraph, and each line Luke wrote. Without a doubt, Greek was his native language. According to Edouard Delebecque, "his deep knowledge of the best Greek language, even his atticism, shows from one end of his work to the other, and more particularly there where, free of his sources, from the milieu that surrounds him, he can become altogether himself, that is to say, a lettered man formed in Greek literature."

In his work we find many reminiscences of the writers of Greece. Of all the authors represented in the New Testament, he is "the only one to obey at every turn all the usages and particularities of the classical language." Obviously Luke is a storyteller, even when he narrates episodes he has not witnessed. The picturesque does not interest him by any means, and yet with just a few words he sets a scene. Of Tabitha, whom the other Christians believe to be dead, he writes: "Then she opened her eyes, and seeing Peter, she sat up" (Acts 9:40). Speaking of the taste of the Athenians, he emphasizes their attraction for "the latest novelties." Hardly well sketched out, his dialogue is no less forceful. He has the Ethiopian queen's eunuch, who is reading in his chariot, questioned: "Do you understand what you are reading?" (Acts 8:30). Always keeping himself at the level of his subject, he never conceals his own voice, whether tinged with elation or irony, which translates itself in the lively and spontaneous movement of his story. Luke would have been an excellent novelist.

His name appears in the Letters of Paul, designating him as one of the apostle's collaborators, of little importance. Such effacement will allow Jean-Robert Armogathe to make the argument that the Luke of the Letters and that of Acts are one: "If it were a matter of supporting the book of Acts by the authority of its author, we would rather have had recourse to other companions of Paul, more prestigious and better identified." A good point. From the second and third centuries, Irenaeus, Tertullian, and Origen named Luke the author of the Acts of the Apostles. The preface of the third Gospel, which Luke wrote at the same time, clearly shows his intention. Addressed to "Theophilus," to whom he dedicates his work, Luke insists on being clear: "Since many have undertaken to set down an orderly account of the events that have been fulfilled among us, just as they were handed on to us by those who from the beginning were eyewitnesses and servants of the word, I too decided, *after investigating everything carefully from the very first,* to write an orderly account for you" (Lk 1:1–3)—a need that certainly applies to Acts as well.

When he met Paul, Luke was already a Christian. He had personally survived the problems, obstacles, conflicts, and dangers that accompanied his own conversion. Like all believers, he asked questions; Paul answered them. He went through doubts; Paul dispelled them. Luke understood that a signal opportunity had presented itself to him, the kind one meets just once in a lifetime. Thus little by little a portrait of Paul would emerge to which Luke, through an exhaustive investigation, would put the finishing touches. A Jew molded by Hellenism, Luke would establish himself for all generations to come as the exemplary disciple: trusting, submissive, devoted, and gifted with that rare quality that is admiration.

8

BEYOND THE AEGEAN

W as Paul the greatest traveler of his time? I thought so for a long while, but studying other authors revealed my error to me. Paul was a determined traveler, motivated for a cause, but like many others. Pliny the Younger made fun of this excitement to travel, which drove people out of their homes to the point that "they ended up ignoring what was at their doors." History has preserved the memory of a merchant who rounded Cape Malea seventy-two times. According to Hervé Duchêne, a great expert of ancient travel, this feat had "the prestige that Cape Horn has enjoyed since the time of the great sailing ships."

What about Paul's record? A contemporary of Paul and fellow citizen of Tarsus, Apollonius of Tyana, apparently surpassed it. Philostratus, his biographer, shows him covering Asia Minor, India, Mesopotamia, Cyprus, Greece, Crete, Italy, Spain, Sicily, Chios, Rhodes, Egypt, and Ethiopia!

Paul took the same routes that merchants and numerous traders also used. In addition, politicians, soldiers, and physicians traveled these roads, along with those whom we would call tourists and crowds of pilgrims determined to sanctify themselves in the temples that abounded in Europe and Asia. A thirst for exploration often accompanied their piety, as still happens today.

Concerning Paul's travels, the Acts of the Apostles is content with very brief notations like the one that punctuates the rest of this story: "We set sail from Troas and took a straight course to Samothrace" (16:11). Beyond this, the ancient authors are there to inform us. Thus we know that Paul, Silas, Timothy, and Luke, embarking from Troas in the spring of 49, took one of the "round ships." They were called this because they referred to the large boats rather than the streamlined sailboats intended for long journeys and for transporting great quantities of merchandise. Equipped with a mast to which was attached a large square sail reinforced by a jib-like sail that helped to tack the ship, these round ships were indifferently named *olcas, gaulos, ploion.* A simple oar planted in the rear served as a rudder.

Sailing toward Samothrace, how could the man from Tarsus not have been obsessed by the mission and the risks that awaited him? Was the ship transporting a Paul sure of himself? The hesitations that dwelt within him on the roads of Asia and of Bithynia did not reveal a determined man. No Christian had ever gone where he was going to announce the word of Christ. Would this virgin territory let itself be worked by him? Until then having recourse to the synagogues had been his principal advantage. The region toward which he was heading—Macedonia—had fewer Jewish communities than Asia. We know of only one in Thessalonica and in Philippi. Besides, the proud man from Tarsus did not want to walk in anyone's footsteps. Later he would open up to the Romans: "I have fully proclaimed the good news of Christ. Thus I make it my ambition to proclaim the good news, not where Christ has already been named, so that I do not build on someone else's foundation" (15:19–20). He would avoid the areas that, according to the first letter attributed to Peter, had already been evangelized.[1]

Paul and his friends passed a short night on the island of Samothrace, a large green mountain coming up out of the sea. Its sanctuary at the summit of Mount Fengari had made it famous: there a colossal marble goddess spread her wings. Later broken and buried by an earthquake, it would be recovered by a French consul in 1863. Today *Victory of Samothrace* is the pride of the Louvre.

Early the next morning, they returned to the sea. Depending on the season, it took four or five days to cross the Aegean. In June we can bet it took four. Bypassing the island of Thasos, they landed in Neapolis (modern Kavala), on those shores, among so many others, that later so strongly moved Lord Byron: "O Greece! Very cold is the heart of the man who can see you and not feel what a lover feels over the ashes of the one he loved!" It is impossible to believe Paul felt such emotion. Rather, I see him taking in with a glance—and not a very benign one at that—the temple of Athena

Parthenos planted on the ridge of a promontory. In such a state of mind, to disembark in Greece would have been equivalent to self-flagellation.

Straight and proud, the *Via Egnatia* presented itself to Paul. Without leaving its path nor ceasing to walk its slabs of stone, he could go by way of Philippi, Thessalonica, and Edessa and reach the port of Apollonia on the coast of modern-day Albania. A ship would easily have taken him to Brindisi, where he would have found the *Via Appia*, which led to Rome.

All the people of his time felt an attraction to Rome. Paul was no exception. Fascination with the all-powerful—even when it surrounds itself with hatred—is a specifically human phenomenon. Paul acknowledged it. But he did not race ahead. He set off on the *Via Egnatia*.

HOW MANY PEOPLE have commented on "the total change of worlds" that would have awaited Paul the moment he passed from Asia into Europe? Yet the notion of Europe did not exist in his time. To affirm that the man from Tarsus left the wilds to join civilization is more nonsense. He passed from one Roman province to another, that was all. On the two shores of the Aegean Sea, people spoke the same language, Greek. Without losing touch, a single family spread itself over one shore to the other. Throughout the Aegean, commercial trade never ceased. The cloth business, for example, ignored frontiers, even coastal ones. Philippi, a Greek city, was populated by business people who had come from Asia Minor; inscriptions mention them as benefactors of the city. After three centuries the amazement that Alexander the Great always aroused united peoples from West and East. Besides certain business correspondents of his father's whom he could identify, Paul had relatives on the other side of the Aegean: Jason in Thessalonica; Sopater in Berea; Lucius in Cenchrae, a port of Corinth.[2] In the conquest of souls, Paul advanced well-armed.

Eight miles covered on the *Via Egnatia*, and behold, the fortified city that Philip II, the father of Alexander, built in 356 B.C., granting it his name. He immediately endowed Philippi with a theater; thus did warriors behave. Well preserved, it can still be seen on a hillside. A few columns and the frame of a door are about all that remain of the city where Demosthenes resided. Two miles from there, in 42 B.C., a famous battle took place that pit Antony and Octavian against Brutus and Cassius. Conquered, Caesar's murderers killed themselves. Today one is moved by the few slabs of the *Via Egnatia* in which the chariot wheels have inscribed their double furrows and on which Paul certainly walked.

Luke entered Philippi at the same time as Paul. We find him full of life:

> On the Sabbath day we went outside the gate by the river, where we sup-
> posed there was a place of prayer; and we sat down and spoke to the
> women who had gathered there. A certain woman named Lydia, a wor-
> shiper of God, was listening to us; she was from the city of Thyatira and
> a dealer in purple cloth. The Lord opened her heart to listen eagerly to
> what was said by Paul. When she and her household were baptized, she
> urged us, saying, "If you have judged me to be faithful to the Lord, come
> and stay at my home." And she prevailed upon us[3] (Acts 16:13–15).

This Lydia came from Asia Minor. The trade that she practiced confirmed certain ties in the textile business from which Paul would be able
to benefit. Installed at Lydia's, he would connect with two other women:
Syntyche, a name that means "encounter," and Euodia, which is translated "easy path"—not without irony at times. Thus three women figured in
at the start of Paul's apostolate in Europe. It was only the beginning; as
soon as the first appeared, others would come to him, serve him, take him
in, and often convert. Even more, in a number of churches Paul founded,
he would confide weighty responsibilities to women.

THE SUCCESSES PAUL won among the Philippians form the principal
theme of the letter he addressed to them. As a whole it gives an account
of the close bonds forged in the weeks or months that followed his
sojourn in Philippi: "I thank my God every time I remember you, constantly praying with joy in every one of my prayers for all of you,
because of your sharing in the gospel from the first day until now"
(1:3–5). Paul would never cease to offer as an example to other communities the fidelity of the converts from Philippi. But a grave incident
would suddenly compromise the success that was going so well. Paul
and his coworkers loved to return to the riverside where they had met
Lydia. One day they came across a young slave girl, endowed with
the gift of clairvoyance, and exploited shamelessly by her owners.
Seeing them for the first time, this clairvoyant cried out, "These men
are slaves of the Most High God, who proclaim to you a way of salvation" (Acts 16:17).

Those involved hardly seemed to have paid any attention to these
predictions. So, at each visit the apostles made, the woman repeated her
game. Exasperated, Paul finally suspected that the "gifts" in question
came to her from an evil spirit. Approaching her, he ordered the spirit and

commanded it to leave them in peace: "I order you in the name of Jesus Christ to come out of her."

"And it came out," says Luke, "that very hour" (Acts 16:18). So much for the slave's clairvoyance! As a result, her masters saw themselves deprived of a substantial source of revenue. Angered, they lodged a complaint. Paul and Silas were summoned before the magistrates who were charged with dispensing justice. Not only did the "plaintiffs" give voice to their accusation, they enlarged the grounds dangerously: "These men are disturbing our city; they are Jews and are advocating customs that are not lawful for us as Romans to adopt or observe" (Acts 16:20–21).

The magistrates considered the accusation to be so serious that, without a trial, they expelled the accused from Philippi. Before being expelled, however, they would be scourged.

"Scourged" is a word that certain commentators note without dwelling on it, as though it were a mere formality or a matter of procedure. Speaking frankly, scourging—*verberatio*—was a dreadful torture, sometimes deadly. The poet Horace explains that the victim was "torn by whips to the disgust of the torturer." The instrument of torture? The *flagellum,* a whip with a short handle to which were attached long, thick strips. So that the blows would better tear the skin and the flesh, balls of lead or bone fragments of sheep were fixed at the end of each strip. The blows rained down on the victim's back, hips, and the nape of the neck. Each time the whip crashed down, a searing pain assaulted the victim. We read with dread the testimony of a man who, in another time, had to endure the same agony: "The pain goes from the neck to the tip of the toes, radiates as far as the fingernails, [and] pierces the heart as though a knife had been planted in the body.... The interval between blows is of an agonizing length.... The blood rises to one's mouth, gushing from the lungs or from some internal organ torn by the contractions provoked by the horrific pain."

As Roman citizens, Paul and Silas should never have been treated this way. Were they scourged because they were not able to plead their right? They couldn't brandish their Roman citizenship as we would a passport today. Citizenship could only be proved by the testimony of a known person: relative, friend, or correspondent. It doesn't seem that Paul had access to such guarantors at Philippi.

Tottering from the pain, the men were thrown into prison after the scourging. Hobbles of wood attached to the wall, called *stocks,* were fixed to their ankles. Night came. They suffered; sleep eluded them. Around midnight, perhaps to relieve their pain, they began to sing praises to God. Wakened with a start, the other prisoners understandably reacted with a tumult of protest. When a muffled roar shook the prison, their anger changed to fright. Was it an earthquake like the ones the populations of these regions had been subjected to so often? All the ancient literature attests it. In the *Bacchantes* of Euripides, we read: "The bonds detach themselves from their feet, and the bolts of doors open themselves without any human intervention."

Suddenly, in Paul and Silas' cell the wall collapsed, the hobbles fell apart, and the door broke open. The jailer suddenly appeared, feeling his way in the darkness. He saw no one. Believing that his prisoners had escaped, he thought himself dishonored and lifted his sword to kill himself. No doubt he must have joined words to this gesture, for Paul stopped him in time: "Do not harm yourself, for we are all here."

The man ran to find a light, and on returning, discovered Paul and Silas. Throwing himself at their feet, stammering that he owed them a life, he freed them immediately while Paul declared: "Believe in the Lord Jesus, and you will be saved, you and your household."

The jailer brought them to his home, washed their wounds, and, according to Luke, asked immediately to be baptized. He even offered a meal to his unforeseen guests before returning them to prison. A new irruption of this best of jailers awakened them the next day. The man was filled with happiness as he informed them, "The magistrates sent word to let you go; therefore come out now and go in peace."

But Paul refused categorically. "They have beaten us in public, uncondemned, men who are Roman citizens, and have thrown us into prison; and now are they going to discharge us in secret? Certainly not! Let them come and take us out themselves" (Acts 16:28–37).

These words were reported to the magistrates who, alarmed to learn that they had ignored the law, ran to present their excuses, freed the two men, and asked them to leave the city without delay.

Still suffering from the aftereffects of the scourging, how could they obey? Luke attests that they remained some time in this city. As for Paul, he would never forget that the Christians of Philippi spontaneously offered him financial help, which he accepted: "You Philippians indeed know that in the early days of the gospel, when I left Macedonia, no church shared with me in the matter of giving and receiving, except you alone. For even when I was in Thessalonica, you sent me help for my needs more than once" (Phil 4:15–16).

Luke does not appear to have accompanied Paul when he finally left the city. With Silas and Timothy, Paul headed south. His goal: Thessalonica.

PAUL AND SILAS dragged themselves along as they walked. Timothy did his best to help them. They had to cover ninety-three miles. Given the excellence of the roads, they should have averaged fifteen miles a day, thus making it a journey of six or seven days. Paul and Silas' condition would have made it necessary to double that number.

They crossed Amphipolis; they entered between sea and mountain; they passed—probably without noticing—the tomb of Euripides. Dense trees, vigorous vegetation, and rapid waters came together to produce an agreeable temperature. Without the least transition everything suddenly changed: the heat became torrid, the air burned one's lungs, and clothes stuck to one's skin. They walked alongside lakes whose water was warmer still than the atmosphere. At noon, flocks huddled, motionless and overwhelmed, in the shade of the trees. Much later Renan remembered: "If it were not for the buzzing of insects and the song of birds, who alone in creation resist this prostration, we would think ourselves in the kingdom of death."

After Apollonia, they penetrated a marshy country infested with malaria. Luckily, they emerged from it unscathed. They worked hard to climb the hills that overlooked the gulf of Thessalonica. Far ahead of the travelers, a mountain rose: Olympus. We can imagine Paul taking in the kingdom of Zeus with an indifferent, even scornful, look. Dismissing these gods whose existence he denied, he fastened upon, above the harbor, the spectacle of the large city that he discovered at his feet.

Cassander, King of Macedonia, founded the city in 315 B.C. Searching for a name, he gave it that of his spouse Thessaloniki, the sister of Alexander the Great. The Romans seized the city in 68 B.C. Having become the capital of an expanded Macedonia, it obtained the status of a free city in 42 B.C. From that time on the Roman proconsul resided in Thessalonica.

Of all the places where Paul would stay, this was the first that I visited. In the summer of 1955, leaving Yugoslavia—whose roads had greatly compromised the shocks of our pre-war automobile—we found with relief those of Greece and, at Thessalonica, a large modern city. A French-speaking gas pump attendant advised us against calling it "*Salonique*," the name familiar to the French soldiers of the First World War; they owed the name to the Turks and it was little appreciated. Besides, since the Second World War, Thessaloniki has been its official name. Curiously, the strongest memory I have of the city is the military cemetery. A group of old Parisian soldiers had commissioned us with laying a spray of flowers there. The rows of French graves dating from 1915–1918 struck our hearts.

Paul's contemporaries gladly made fun of this city thrown between an acropolis and a muddy coast. In the course of centuries, the mud gave way to a second port of Greece, and the city became the second in the country.

In 1955, I was little interested in Saint Paul, but very much interested in antique souvenirs. We found them in the center, near the road *Egnatia;* a memory persists here that touches me today more than it did then. The arch of Galerius marked for us the survival of part of the palace, used as an official residence until the sixth century of our era, and which must have known Paul. Not far from there rose the Rotunda, the imperial mausoleum later transformed into a church and then a mosque.

It took us some time to learn that the city where the Jew Paul preached had become, after 1492, the most important Jewish metropolis of the Mediterranean. After their expulsion from Spain, twenty thousand Sephardic Jews sought refuge there. No trace of them remains; the forty-five thousand Jews who lived there in 1943 were deported to Auschwitz.

WHEN PAUL, SILAS, and Timothy entered the city through the East Gate, they saw a continual flow of strangers drawn by its commerce and wealth.[4] The city's status dispensed it from the principal Roman taxes, and a place where one pays fewer taxes always acts like a magnet. Paul would note especially that a number of Jews had taken up residence there for more than a century.

We know that Paul, having just arrived in the city, went to the home of his relative Jason, who opened his house to him as Jewish hospitality required. Learning that the traveler had no resources, and moved by his wounds, Jason procured for him the means to ply his trade as a tentmaker. "Though we had already suffered and been shamefully mistreated at

Philippi, as you know, we had courage in our God to declare to you the gospel of God in spite of great opposition" (1 Thess 2:2).

The number of Jews in the city gave hope of a fruitful harvest of conversions. Paul went to the synagogue the following Sabbath and revealed to these people a Jesus whom they did not know. Luke shows them listening attentively not just that day but in the course of the three following Sabbaths: "[He] argued with them from the scriptures, explaining and proving that it was necessary for the Messiah to suffer and to rise from the dead, and saying, 'This is the Messiah, Jesus whom I am proclaiming to you'" (Acts 17:2–3). Not only did they listen without balking, the news of Paul's preaching spread in the city. Certainly not all the Jews—and even less the non-Jews—of this metropolis suddenly welcomed the Good News. We estimate that less than one percent of the population could have known of the surprising preaching of the man from Tarsus. It is not by chance that Luke insists: "Some of them were persuaded and joined Paul and Silas, as did a great many of the devout Greeks and not a few of the leading women" (Acts 17:4). If the phrase "great many" rightly raises doubts, we know the names of a few of these "God-fearers," notably a Greek named Aristarchus and the Roman Secundus. Each time that a "God-fearer" asked for Baptism, Paul legitimately saw justification of the option he had defended in Jerusalem.

That the Jews of Thessalonica ended by showing a hostility almost identical to that of the Jews from Pisidian Antioch cannot surprise us. The heterogeneity of the Jewish community explains the alternation of rejection and adherence. We count in Thessalonica (along with Samaritans, kept firmly apart) Roman Jews working in the administration and Jewish dealers from Italy who belonged to the same corporations as idolators from the Orient. Paul spoke the language of each. He showed himself without too many illusions as to the merciless competition that reigned in business circles and wanted to be clear as to dissolute mores of the population. In the first letter that he would address to them, he would exhort the converts to make still more progress. "You must aspire," he says, "to live quietly, to mind your own affairs, and to work with your hands, as we directed you, so that you may behave properly toward outsiders and be dependent on no one." They must abstain from "immorality." Let each one of you "know how to control your own body in holiness and honor, not with lustful passion, like the Gentiles who do not know God; that no one wrong or exploit a brother or sister in this matter" (1 Thess 4:1–12).

In the First Letter to the Thessalonians a theme arises that permits us to explain the flight from conversion in the first days of Christianity. Jesus had announced that he would return to earth, and no Christian doubted it. Paul went further: confirming the certainty manifested by the Christians of Jerusalem, he preached that this return was imminent—an announcement that filled people with wonder.

FOUR SABBATHS WITHOUT characteristic opposition was too much for those among the Jews whom Paul had irritated from his first speech. They decided to take action. Recruiting "some ruffians in the marketplaces they formed a mob," sowed disorder in the city, and attacked the house of Jason, crying that they wanted to hand Paul and Silas over to a gathering of the people. By chance, both men were absent. Jason was taken from his home and dragged along with a few other Christians before the magistrates of the city, who were called *politarchas*. For the benefit of these serious dignitaries, the accusations were read: "These people who have been turning the world upside down have come here also, and Jason has entertained them as guests. They are all acting contrary to the decrees of the emperor, saying that there is another king named Jesus."

What prompted the aforementioned *politarchas* to require bail to free Jason and his friends? At least Jason was far from being needy; he paid what was required. In haste, he found Paul and Silas and implored them to leave the city right away. Night having come, he made them leave with Timothy for Beroea, where they arrived after a walk of four days (Acts 17:5–10).

Cicero referred to Beroea, forty-six miles southwest of Thessalonica, as an *oppidum devium* (outside the route), which is metaphorical but exact. The site spreads over the east side of Mount Vermio and dominates a plain that crosses the rivers Aliakmonos and Axios. Not far from there rose the gigantic palace of the king of Macedonia. In 1977 the tomb of Philip II, the father of Alexander the Great, was found there.* It con-

---

* Editor's note: More recent archeological studies have determined that these remains were not those of Philip II. For details see http://www.archaeology.org/online/features/macedon/ Source: *Archaeology*, April 20, 2000, "Not Philip II of Macedon," by Angela M. H. Schuster.

tained the bones of the man who was stabbed by his bodyguard Pausanias in the summer of 336. A gold casket housed the most extraordinary of treasures: Philip's wreath, made of gold oak leaves and acorns; his purple cloak; his shield; and his swords and breastplate. Once one has contemplated these objects, it is impossible to forget the incredible effect of the grandeur and power that once emanated from them.[5] What suggested to Paul this site where all, from Philip II to Alexander the Great, evoked the radiance of Greece? Literally immersed in this history learned and loved from childhood, was he able to remain indifferent to it?

At the synagogue of Beroea, Paul found the Jews "more receptive than those of Thessalonica." The proof: "They welcomed the message very eagerly and examined the scriptures every day to see whether these things were so." The success that flowed from Beroea cannot be doubted. "Many of them therefore believed, including not a few Greek women and men of high standing" (Acts 17:11–12).

These results provoked a reaction that we know well: some good souls ran to Thessalonica to announce the conversions in Beroea. This took time. Informed and angry, the Jews of the city pounced on Paul's trail. This also took time. Convinced that their hosts were not cut out to resist the approaching pack, the people of Beroea persuaded Paul to take shelter. Leaving Silas and Timothy, who would be all right there—since the hatred was focused on Paul—they removed the apostle right under the nose of his pursuers and escorted him all the way to the coast. Paul probably embarked at the small port of Dion or at Pydna, today near Katerini. Several converts from Beroea boarded the ship with him.

The end of autumn 49 was approaching. It would have taken three seasons to establish, in Thessalonica and in Beroea, vibrant communities that would continue. When the ship left shore, Paul was in a position to take stock of his work in Macedonia. The first thing that could be said with certainty was that he had received no help from the church of Antioch in Syria. The funds he had collected had come to him from the emerging church of Philippi and from his own work. More importantly, the converts were becoming themselves "converters." He had seen newly baptized Christians rush through the province to announce the Good News to their relatives and friends. The presence of women in the community, at Philippi as well as at Thessalonica, represented an obvious advantage for the future. No less promising were the conversions of "God-fearers"; the announcement that the Son of the God of the Jews had come to earth swept away their hesitations. It is necessary to give credit to those who believe that this mission to Macedonia may have been perhaps "the most fruitful of those that Paul had undertaken until then."

On the boat, Paul must have thought mostly of the future. Half of his culture was Greek. The poets he had read, the philosophers he had studied, even his dreams—all carried him toward Athens. In Tarsus, he had been taught the grandeur and the genius of this unique city. No one at that time could boast of a philosophical spirit without appealing to this city, the mother of philosophy, art, science, and politics.

The heavy sailboat slid alongside the shores of Thessalonica and, under his eyes, passed these coasts that had filled generations with wonder. Perhaps Paul eventually accepted the real challenge that these gods of Athens, who were also those of Rome, represented. To claim that the one true God had become the son of a Jewish carpenter—was that not a challenge impossible to sustain among people who, for the most part, did not even know where Jerusalem was located, and for whom all they knew of Judaism was where the grocer or the money changer ran his stall in their quarter? Paul was too intelligent not to feel such a challenge, but too stubborn to give up the impossible and announce Jesus to the Athenians. Perhaps his mood darkened and his faithful followers may have had to withstand more outbursts of temper than usual.

The ship took the strait of Euripus, which separated the island of Euboea from the continent. To the south, one would hope that the Cape of Sounion and the marble columns of the temple of Poseidon had moved Paul. They sailed along the coast of Apollon. On the port side, they passed the island of Egina and that of Salamina. There Solon, the precursor of democracy, had incited the Athenians—by his poetry, they say—to conquer. There, too, Themistocles, with Aristides, won memorable victory over the Persian fleet.

Tradition has it that the ship that carried Paul did not put the voyagers down at Pireas but at the port of Glifada. The brothers at Beroea did not want to let Paul travel alone the nine miles that separated him from Athens. Satisfied to see him safe, they later brought the order from Paul for Silas and Timothy to join him as soon as possible.

At the edge of the second half of the first century, the glory of Athens was intact, but we must face facts: Greece was no more. The taking of Corinth by the Romans in 146, and their domination that was confirmed everywhere, sounded its death knell. On March 1, 86 B.C., after having imposed his yoke in Rome, Sulla seized Athens, delivering it to merciless massacres and shameless looting.

One must read the bitter pages that famous travelers such as Polybius, Cicero, Strabo, and Pausanias have left behind; the appearance of freedom officially granted by Rome was but a mask. These ancient writers show us countrysides that became deserts. They describe ruined cities, abandoned temples, the pedestals of stolen statues, the Peloponnesus stricken to death, and the cities of Thebes and Argos reduced to the rank of simple villages. What a decline! Corinth alone seems to have been spared.

Throughout the world of that time Athens continued to fascinate men of thought. Cicero came there to be initiated into the mysteries of Eleusis. Horace, Virgil, Propertius, Ovid, and so many others insisted on spending long sojourns there. With the sole intention of studying at the Academy, the Lyceum, the Garden, and the Portico, students rushed there from all over Italy. When Paul surveyed the city, motley crowds jostled each other. On the agora, the political and artistic center of the city where history was written, and where the first plays and first choreographies were presented, only gossips could be found. Here Luke holds up a mirror: "Now all the Athenians and the foreigners living there would spend their time in nothing but telling or hearing something new" (Acts 17:21). We imagine Paul as much disconcerted as he is alone—which he detested—and overwhelmed by the superabundance of temples, altars, and a hundred images of a religion whose faithful were evidently far from endangered. "He was deeply distressed to see that the city was full of idols" (Acts 17:16). He found a little peace only in the synagogue where, true to himself, he lectured not just the Jews, but the "God-fearers" as always. The Sabbath having ended, and feeling hard-pressed to find an audience, he could only resort to announcing Jesus in random encounters. The agora was full of philosophers who each taught under a portico. Why not mingle with them? Luke, who must have won the confidence of Paul himself, unless it was of Denys the Areopagite, the first convert of Athens, has drawn from this encounter one of the most living pieces of his work. It all sounds right: "Some Epicurean and Stoic philosophers debated with him. Some said, 'What does this babbler want to say?'[6] Others said, 'He seems to be a proclaimer of foreign divinities'" (Acts 17:18).

We can understand the Athenians' astonishment in seeing this small bearded man persist in announcing the resurrection of an unknown Jew. Who cared? Of what importance was such an announcement? Yet, some Athenians eventually demanded that he come with them, in order to expose his strange theory more completely.

On a hill to the west of the Acropolis, where the High Council of Athens once held its meetings, a kind of assembly of wise men, charged essentially with questions of education, still sat. "They took him and brought him to the Areopagus" (Acts 17:19). If Paul let himself be pushed around, it was because such a request, even if expressed a bit rudely, was the answer to all he hoped for.

Luke is in his element. Recording the speech of Paul, his idol, must have brought him real pleasure. Whether he wrote it from an outline supplied by Paul or according to the testimony of people who had heard it, the text only confirms the apostle's tactical gifts. He would not address the Athenians in the same manner as the brave souls of Lystra or Derbe. He was fully conscious that he was dealing with men who were not only enlightened, but uniquely subtle. They were philosophers? Then Paul would speak the language of philosophy:

"Athenians, I see how extremely religious you are in every way. For as I went through the city and looked carefully at the objects of your worship, I found among them an altar with the inscription, 'To an unknown God.'[7] What therefore you worship as unknown, this I proclaim to you. The God who made the world and everything in it, he who is Lord of heaven and earth, does not live in shrines made by human hands, nor is he served by human hands, as though he needed anything, since he himself gives to all mortals life and breath and all things."

Paul's opening held the attention of his audience. Now he had to maintain the advantage. "From one ancestor he made all nations to inhabit the whole earth, and he allotted the times of their existence and the boundaries of the places where they would live, so that they would search for God and perhaps grope for him and find him—though indeed he is not far from each one of us."

They continued to listen, so he expounded even more.

"For 'In him we live and move and have our being,' as even some of your poets have said, 'For we too are his offspring.'"

The last part of the sentence was none other than a citation from the *Phenomena* of Aratus,[8] who wrote in the third century B.C. Perhaps here Paul registered a favorable murmur. Then he struck:

"Since we are God's offspring, we ought not to think that the deity is like gold, or silver, or stone, an image formed by the art and imagination of mortals. While God has overlooked the times of human ignorance, now he commands all people everywhere to repent, because he has fixed a day on which he will have the world judged in righteousness by a man whom he has appointed, and of this he has given assurance to all by raising him from the dead."

Even if the name of Jesus had not been pronounced, the announcement that God had charged a human being to make known to his fellow men the day when the world would be judged—why judged?—and especially the proclamation of the resurrection of this unknown man caused them to laugh. Epicureanism and Stoicism, two philosophies with which the Greeks at that time identified, agreed in refusing a personal god distinct from the universe. Hellenism did not conceive of survival except in the mind of those who kept alive the memory of the deceased. The climate recreated by Luke's talented writing appears so obvious, it's impossible to doubt its reality. "When they heard of the resurrection of the dead, some scoffed; but others said, 'We will hear you again about this'" (Acts 17:22–32).

Paul had known failure before. He would know it again. But we can be sure that this one instance was the most stinging. They had not insulted him, they had not led him to prison, they had not scourged him, but they had laughed at his words. I imagine him falling silent under their mockery. His shoulders fell; it seemed as if his whole body deflated. The Areopagus would no longer take interest in this negligible quantity. The wise men dispersed.

Paul remained alone. They had not only jeered at the sacred certainty he held from Jesus, they had also wounded his self-esteem. It was more than he could bear.

He would never want to see Athens again.

9

CORINTH

Leaving Athens in the twenty-first century by way of the Corinthian highway that borders the sea is a formidable enterprise. One has to merge with an endless line of trucks, vehicles of all sizes and speeds, and snails on wheels, all of which—bumper to bumper—drag themselves alongside smelly refineries; tanks that are emptied only to be refilled immediately; mechanics' shops; and the car cemetery, where the "carcasses," randomly piled, suggest an image of badly assimilated contemporary art. All of this spreads itself out on our right for many miles.

To the left of the two-lane highway, at the heart of a sea too obviously polluted, immobile freighters—desperately in need of paint—wait for cargo.

As we move away from the capital, the image of desolation blurs and nature takes the upper hand. The smell of pines replaces that of fuels. Above the sea, blue once again, a crimson splendor displays itself, which Paul, lost in the bitterness of his humiliation, must not have been aware of. We beheld this "halo" created in the distance over a chaplet of islands, seemingly so dreamlike because one could discern nothing of what lay on their surfaces.

Unless Paul preferred to reach Corinth by sea—but he usually avoided the least expense—he would have spent three days on this road, designated as the sacred Eleusinian Way. At the end of the journey, the spectacle of a great bay awaited him. Joseph Holzner, the great traveler, saw this place as "a lake surrounded by steep rocks and strewn with small islands." Above the bay, Corinth rose at the bottom of a natural circle. In the background, the mountains of Egina sheltered the highest-placed sanctuary in Achaia. Further on were "the steep rock faces of Megara," and again, "the mountains of Argolide covered with pine forests." From this city and from what went on there was born, throughout Greece, a long murmur of unwholesome and prurient curiosity. This feeling was diametrically opposed to the will that animated Paul: to preach to this mass of humanity, far removed from all ideals, the resurrection of Christ.

One stage awaited him in Cenchreae, one of two ports of the great city, surrounded by green hills. Cenchreae was separated from Lechaion, the second port, by an isthmus almost four miles wide. To travel by sea from one to the other, a person had to go around the whole Peloponnesian peninsula, which was an expensive waste of time. Ingenious aediles had the idea of building on the isthmus a tile road—*dialkos*—in order to haul commercial vessels between the two gulfs, the lighter ones transported on a carriage, the others set on cylinders. It took two days, sometimes three, for hundreds of slaves, shoulders torn by cords—and at times by whips—to push and pull them to the other side.[1]

This was Cenchreae, where "the masts of the ships are as tight as the trunks of a pine forest."[2] One cubic house, as there were so many, stuck to all those that surrounded the port. A young couple lived and worked there, two weavers who had arrived the year before. He was named Aquila, she Priscilla. If they are introduced to us in Acts, their existence is confirmed by the Letters of Paul, which present them under the names of Aquila and Prisca (Priscilla being a diminutive in his eyes). Addressing himself later to the church he founded in Corinth, Paul would write: "Aquila and Prisca, together with the church in their house, greet you warmly in the Lord" (1 Cor 16:19). They were Jews, but Christian Jews. When in the year 49 the Emperor Claudius had promulgated an edict that drove all Jews from Rome, they had had to flee. According to Seutonius, the Jews of Rome never ceased "to keep unrest alive under the instigation of a certain Chrestos." No one can deny the relationship, in sound at least, between Chrestos and Christ. The truth is that this imaginary Chrestos was born of a confusion of Jewish converts to Christ—there were some then in Rome in 49—who were considered responsible for this unrest.

For Aquila and Priscilla, Cenchreae must have been but a simple port of call on their way to Asia. To their surprise, they discovered there the Corinthians' urgent need for display tents on the eve of the Isthmian games of the year 51. Unable to resist such a piece of good fortune, the couple remained and opened a shop. Suddenly one day a person who was not much to look at appeared there. Informing them that he came from Athens, he introduced himself as Paul of Tarsus and called himself Christian. How did he locate them? No text specifies. A believer would voluntarily admit the inspiration of the Holy Spirit. Others might argue that Paul would have asked at random where he could find work and would have been sent to the right address. When the stranger announced that he was a tentmaker, he was hired on the spot. Very quickly the young people discovered that he was suffering from wounds poorly healed that remained from a scourging. How could one not see them seized with pity and love?

Aquila and Priscilla were totally unaware that they had just recruited "a tornado." The man was never reluctant to work, but, in those rare idle moments, he began to pray. Immediately he was transfigured. That he would have proclaimed verses from the Bible would be exactly like him. That Priscilla and Aquila remained stunned by him would not astonish us any more.

Paul worked with his hands, he prayed and meditated, but the day came when he took his leave. The goal of his journey was not Cenchreae but Corinth. Logic suggests he waited for his wounds to heal before setting out.

Destroyed in 146 at the time of the Roman invasion, the ex-capital of the Achaean League remained deserted during the next hundred years. In the year 44 B.C., just one century before the arrival of the apostle, Julius Caesar had the city rebuilt and populated by freedmen and women. Hence its population was particularly heterogeneous. Renan saw in it "a collection of people of all kinds and all origins." The Greeks no longer recognized themselves in the new city. They were disgusted by the bloody circus games the Romans popularized; the Corinthians delighted in them. Hence "a city very populated, rich, brilliant, and frequented by numerous strangers; an active center of commerce; one of these mixed cities; finally, a different world."

Leaving Cenchreae for Corinth, Paul traversed a steep valley five miles long. All around him there lay vineyards that even today yield the succulent grapes of Corinth. For a man who had crossed the Taurus three times, these few miles would have been child's play. Bypassing the great amphitheater against which the tomb of Diogenes was placed, he reached the outskirts of the city. Before entering one of the doors in the wall, it would have been impossible that his gaze not be drawn by the extraordinary rocky peak that, almost 2,000 feet high, dominated Corinth. It was a spectacle so rare that it always struck those who have contemplated it; I too have witnessed the peak. At the time of Paul, the site was called Acrocorinth, and it has kept this name today. We can believe that Paul was displeased to learn that its summit sheltered a temple to Aphrodite. Did he start to get the feeling that he was being pursued by this insolent goddess?

Coming from an Athens of little expanse, comparable enough to a medieval university city, he entered the largest city he had known since Antioch of Syria. Through the Propylaea, the monumental doors with three arches, he immediately came to the agora, a large place bordered on the north by shops, and on the south by a grand portico. To affirm that Paul must have remained before the scene openmouthed is not something the biographer needs to say; these buildings covered with marble left everyone speechless. Beyond the shops on the north and surpassing them by its mass, Paul could not have ignored the overwhelming presence of the temple of Apollo, originally built in the sixth century B.C. Having person-ally experienced the emotion, in the middle of a field of ruins, of finding on the spot seven of its columns that miraculously escaped the earthquake of 77, I can assess well enough what those who saw it intact must have felt: fifteen enormous columns on the long sides, six on the short sides.

Wandering among the scattered stones that rise in the short grass, I imagined Paul slipping into the streets where "a colorful crowd, buzzing, always hurrying, rushing up from all the corners of Europe and Asia," jos-tled one another.

The veterans, the freedmen, and the slaves of Caesar found themselves encouraged by the unearthing of riches buried in the tombs they pillaged with delight. Certain fortunes were born of this. The poet Crinagoras cried out his great sorrow at this Corinth that he would have preferred to see

> More deserted than the sands of Lybia rather than
> To see you given up entirely to these good-for-nothings.

Paul would not find there any of the aristocracy of olden times but the *nouveaux riches* or the heirs of pioneers made rich. Among the number of converts from the highest social group, he would count Erastus, endowed with a municipal office; Caius, proprietor of a large villa; and Stephanas, whose name evokes let us say a suspicion of vulgarity. "Consider your own call, brothers and sisters: not many of you were wise by human standards, not many were powerful, not many were of noble birth"—a humiliating situation that he corrected on the spot by revealing the advantages to be drawn from it: "God chose what is foolish in the world to shame the wise" (1 Cor 1:26–27). If anyone had enrolled in the right line of Jesus, it was certainly Paul here.

In this Roman colony, Latin remained the official language. But Greek, arising from its origins, did not cease to gain ground. Corinth deserved anew the name of "opulent" with which Homer had already gratified it. The transit of merchandise through its ports was the source of its economic power. From its shops came a great number of ships. Cenchreae and Lechaion prided themselves on having invented the galley with three rows of oars. Carpets, cloth, and materials of all kinds came out of its workshops. Its bronze armor had no equivalent in the West. On the fertile soil of the region, thousands of slaves grew wheat, vegetables, and fruit in abundance, and cultivated the vineyards from which a highly prized wine was made.

The Isthmian games, revived by Caesar and celebrated in honor of Neptune, attracted to Corinth every four years a crowd happily prodigious with its coins. That Paul attended the games of April–May 51, and that he was struck by the spectacle of masses of humanity sitting elbow to elbow; that he was seduced by poets who confronted each other in hurling their verses like gifts to the delighted audience; that he was impressed by the athletes jousting to break records—we find traces of all this in the First Letter to the Corinthians: "Do you not know that in a race the runners all compete, but only one receives the prize?" The parallel obsessed him: "Athletes exercise self-control in all things; they do it to receive a perishable wreath, but we an imperishable one. So I do not run aimlessly, nor do I box as though beating the air" (1 Cor 9:24–26). For Timothy, who had attended with him, Paul, approaching the end, would again evoke the games of Corinth: "And in the case of the athlete, no one is crowned without competing according to the rules" (2 Tim 2:5).

In the past the city had placed itself under the sign of Poseidon, recalling its maritime vocation by waving a trident [a spear with three prongs]. Aphrodite Pandeme supplanted Poseidon. For a long time at the top of the Acrocorinth, a thousand priestesses in the service of the goddess—the *hierodules*—prostituted themselves in cells bizarrely arranged behind rose bushes. Even if their numbers were declining in Paul's time, enough of them remained to afflict a man who preached asceticism and continence. Paul discovered at Corinth what we today call sexual tourism.

The ascent of the Acrocorinth tempted all those who had the available time and money: the eager, who came only for this; travelers passing through; dealers who bought or sold; sailors of ships resting in ports. The "Corinthian disease" would arise from there and would end by spreading to all the regions of the Empire. Corinth's reputation became such that a young girl who threw away her virginity was said to have *corinthized* herself. Even more, the word *corinthias* designated the pimps. "Everyone cannot go to Corinth," related a certain proverb, meaning that the priestesses were too expensive and all the more were the numerous bars of the ports where strong drink flowed like water. The moral corruption of Corinth, extreme among the Greek cities, inspired dramatists—Aristophanes of the first rank—but also poets and writers: Horace, Juvenal, and Cicero.

Paul must have confronted this climate to which other people adapted so profoundly. Others might have backed away from the task to be accomplished. Not him. He would remain eighteen months in Corinth, when he had reserved just twelve for his last sojourn in Antioch. We see him changing residence here at least four times.

Meeting a woman—again—would reveal itself as a weighty consequence for his mission. Here it was a matter of a certain Phoebe, a businesswoman full of worldly wisdom and, as such, a great traveler. Converted to Christ and being a woman of substance, she would support the activity of the man from Tarsus, represent him if necessary in court, and especially bear witness to his Roman citizenship. Around Phoebe the nucleus of a Christian community would establish itself at Cenchreae. Much later, Paul would commend her to the Romans as "our sister Phoebe, a deacon of the church at Cenchreae." His wish was that she be welcomed "as is fitting for the saints" and that, if she should be in need, they would help her, "for she has been a benefactor of many and of myself as well" (Rom 16:1–2).

HAD SILAS AND TIMOTHY forgotten Paul? Without warning they now reappeared! We can imagine an effusive introduction of the old faithful to the new. Luke affirms that from the minute his two companions arrived,

"Paul was occupied with proclaiming the word" (Acts 18:5). The man from Tarsus confirms that "the brothers having come from Macedonia" brought him subsidy.

After their arrival, Paul would be able to write the Letter to the Thessalonians, which he had been contemplating. His thought was so dense and so rapid that it was impossible for him, not being a professional writer, to transcribe it alone. All the letters, beginning with this one, would be dictated, and the scribes would designate themselves by name. Here it became: "Paul, Silvanus, and Timothy to the church of the Thessalonians..." (1 Thess 1:1).

At this unique moment, the little man to whom we were ready to give alms was in the process of giving shape to Christianity. The humble worker was transformed into a fiery prophet, trying his hand at improvising a text in which he sought to put his whole thought; progressing laboriously; stumbling over words, phrases, ideas; correcting himself; raging against himself and—it goes without saying—against those who, pen in hand, alternately attempted to fill the papyrus. At times Paul would fall into a profound silence. Nothing could be heard but flies buzzing. Suddenly, a dazzling reprise would develop in a single outburst, so quickly that the others could not keep up with him. Hence they would protest while he furiously replied. In short, moments that we deeply regret not to have witnessed.

The first phrase of the letter to the Thessalonians proclaimed with unbelievable power that Paul was perfectly aware of what he was undertaking. It addressed itself to "the church of the Thessalonians in God the Father and the Lord Jesus Christ" (1:1). No one has underlined the force of such words better than Dieter Hildebrandt: "There does not exist evidence before this wherein the term *Jesus Christ* is employed; no document more ancient attests to this name for the Messiah. And nothing previously allows this new faith to show through more. It is in all simplicity that Christianity greets posterity."

As much as the future epistles would appear marked especially by doctrinal questions, this one expressed without restraint the force of the feelings Paul experienced at Thessalonica:

> We were gentle among you, like a nurse tenderly caring for her own children. So deeply do we care for you that we are determined to share with you not only the gospel of God but also our own selves, because you have become very dear to us.... As you know, we dealt with each one of you like a father with his children, urging and encouraging you and pleading that you lead a life worthy of God, who calls you into his own kingdom and glory (2:7–12).

What gave importance to Paul's success in Thessalonica was the way in which he referred to them:

> For the word of the Lord has sounded forth from you not only in Macedonia and Achaia, but in every place your faith in God has become known, so that we have no need to speak about it. For the people of those regions report about us what kind of welcome we had among you, and how you turned to God from idols, to serve a living and true God, and to wait for his Son from heaven, whom he raised from the dead—Jesus who rescues us from the wrath that is coming (1 Thess 1:8–10).

If some of Paul's Letters will be marked by seriousness and admonitions, this one is full of the satisfaction that he owed to a community faithful to his teaching and no longer sacrificing to pagan gods. The message dwelt on a point to which we sense Paul wanted to give particular importance. He had learned that some Christians of Thessalonica had just died—a natural death—plunging this very new community into mourning, but especially raising serious questions.

To understand, it is necessary to return to Jerusalem at the beginning of Christianity. The first faithful, contemporaries of the death and resurrection of Jesus, wanted to hold back from the announcement of his return to earth the idea that it was imminent. Some even refused the teaching that was proposed to them as useless in their eyes, since all would be revealed by Jesus himself when he returned. It is necessary to meditate without ceasing on this primordial reality: the first generation of Christians lived in the certitude—indeed the expectation—of the end of the world followed by Jesus' return. Paul himself believed it and would not cease believing it. In the Letter to the Romans, his last writing, he would insist again: "You know what time it is, how it is now the moment for you to wake from sleep. For salvation is nearer to us now than when we became believers; the night is far gone, the day is near. Let us then lay aside the works of darkness and put on the armor of light" (13:11–12). Perhaps we must seek in this argument one of the principal reasons for Paul's success. We must wait for his own death for Christians to renounce envisaging a precise epoch for the return of Jesus.

The first generation of converts were persuaded that they would soon be the objects of Jesus' favor and thought that their lives were assured until his return. The first Christians of Thessalonica who died brought to bear on this unnuanced conviction a terrible contradiction. Paul's difficulty came in that he himself could not but be stupefied by these deaths. Meanwhile, he answered:

> For this we declare to you by the word of the Lord, that we who are alive, who are left until the coming of the Lord, will by no means precede those who have died. For the Lord himself, with a cry of command, with the archangel's call and with the sound of God's trumpet, will descend from heaven, and the dead in Christ will rise first. Then we who are alive, who are left, will be caught up in the clouds together with them to meet the Lord in the air; and so we will be with the Lord forever. Therefore, encourage one another with these words.
>
> Now concerning the times and the seasons, brothers and sisters, you do not need to have anything written to you. For you yourselves know very well that the day of the Lord will come like a *thief in the night* (1 Thess 4:15–5:2).

The striking expression will be found again in the Gospel of Luke, where the evangelist places it in the mouth of Jesus: "If the owner of the house had known at what hour the thief was coming, he would not have let his house be broken into. You also must be ready, for the Son of Man is coming at an unexpected hour" (12:39–40). Matthew will present Jesus as giving an almost identical discourse: "If the owner of the house had known in what part of the night the thief was coming, he would have stayed awake and would not have let his house be broken into. Therefore you also must be ready, for the Son of Man is coming at an unexpected hour" (24:43–44). The same allusion can be read in the Second Letter of Peter and in the Apocalypse of John.

It's not farfetched to imagine these converts listening expectantly for the least alteration that could affect the silence of the night, and, each time, growing disappointed because the trumpets, which they were sure would accompany the return of the Son of God, had not sounded.

No one letter of Paul is *a priori* a masterly account of his doctrine, but each one transmits one or many aspects of the tradition that he intended to establish. The whole contains *in fine* the exhaustive exposition of his teaching. From the First Letter to the Thessalonians, Paul formulated—probably with his own hand—a veritable solemn oath: "Beloved, pray for us. Greet all the brothers and sisters with a holy kiss. I solemnly

command you by the Lord that this letter be read to all of them. The
grace of our Lord Jesus Christ be with you" (5:25–28).

We must not doubt that the Letters of Paul aimed at establishing an
oral preaching that in essence risked being poorly understood, poorly
retained, and poorly transmitted. In the course of years, we would see the
Letters clarify the status of new churches and the responsibilities assigned
to their hierarchy. What also stands out vividly is that, everywhere and in
all times, the Letters affirmed Paul's unlimited faith.

In a Letter to the Corinthians—the first that he addressed to them—
Paul evokes the timidity that accompanied his first sermons in the city:
"When I came to you, brothers and sisters, I did not come proclaiming
the mystery of God to you in lofty words or wisdom. For I decided to
know nothing among you except Jesus Christ, and him crucified. And I
came to you in weakness and in fear and in much trembling" (2:1–3).
Certain people have wanted to explain this sort of "nervousness" as a
renewed outburst of the "thorn in the flesh." Perhaps that is to neglect the
psychological crisis born of his failure in Athens.

Philo of Alexandria affirms the existence of an important Jewish
community in Corinth. So from his arrival, Paul spoke in synagogues.
The first moments of surprise having passed, the Jews opposed this
preaching with a systematic and growing hostility. Paul persisted. Soon
the Jews used insults he found insupportable. One day, during the
Sabbath, his anger joined with the frenzy of a short time before to the
point that he began to tear his clothes, howling; "Your blood be on your
own heads! I am innocent. From now on I will go to the Gentiles."

Leaving the synagogue, he acted on his threat. He went to the home
of a certain Titius Justus, a Roman, whose "house was next door to the
synagogue" (Acts 18:6–7).

Everything shows that Paul progressively moved away from his Jewish
rites. But that he broke with Judaism itself, everything points to the contrary. The letters he will never cease to address to different Christian communities or to friends like Timothy are full of biblical citations or allusions.
With regard to the Jewish religion, the event that profoundly marked the
Corinthian stage was not—as many Jewish contemporaries have repeated—the desertion of a renegade but the extinction of a great hope: to make

the Jews understand that the Jew Jesus was the Messiah incarnate. Let us recall the behavior of the first Christians: none gave up praying in the Temple. Peter and John frequented it almost every day. For Paul, Christianity was not only imbued with Judaism; it *was* Jewish. In the Letter to the Romans, written in the last part of his life, he persisted: "I ask, then, has God rejected his people? By no means!" (11:1). He would go so far as to declare himself ready to renounce his own salvation for "the sake of my own people, my kindred according to the flesh. They are Israelites, and to them belong the adoption, the glory, the covenants, the giving of the law, the worship, and the promises; to them belong the patriarchs, and from them, according to the flesh, comes the Messiah, who is over all, God blessed forever" (9:3–5).

One of the most surprising analyses of Paul's duality after his break with the synagogue was given by Schalom Ben-Chorin, a Jewish pioneer of Jewish-Christian dialogue. He discovers alongside Paul's attachment to the religion of Abraham, never denied, a sort of "hatred of the Jewish self." Underscoring this coexistence, Ben-Chorin describes the "heart-rending ordeal" to which he sees the man from Damascus submit. It brings him sometimes to defend the right of Jews to consider themselves as children of God, and sometimes to claim that "they are not pleasing to God." Ben-Chorin speculates that Paul's rapport with Israel "is characteristic of a Jew of the Diaspora. His Jewish identity never ceases to be a problem for him." This author believes that such was never the case with Jesus of Nazareth: "This one was Jewish, totally Jewish, nothing but Jewish."

In the twenty-first century, in Catholic churches, we are obliged to read three texts at each Sunday Mass: the first is a passage from the Hebrew Bible, hence Jewish; the second is an excerpt from a Letter of Paul or, more rarely, from another apostle, Jewish in every way; the third, an episode drawn from the Gospels of Mark, Matthew, Luke, or John, all Jews. The psalms that we sing are those of the Bible. Many Christians ask themselves today why Paul was not understood by the Jews of his day. No one would undo history, but there is no doubt that the divorce between two Jewish currents was itself the source of great misfortunes.

LISTENING TO PAUL, many Corinthians became believers and received Baptism (Acts 18:8). In explaining to the Corinthians themselves the meaning of the teaching he gave, he enlightens us at the same time:

My speech and my proclamation were not with plausible words of wisdom, but with a demonstration of the Spirit and of power, so that your faith might rest not on human wisdom but on the power of God. Yet among the mature we do speak wisdom, though it is not a wisdom of this age or of the rulers of this age, who are doomed to perish. But we speak God's wisdom, secret and hidden, which God decreed before the ages for our glory. None of the rulers of this age understood this; for if they had they would not have crucified the Lord of glory. These things [the wisdom of God] God has revealed to us through the Spirit; for the Spirit searches everything, even the depths of God. For what human being knows what is truly human except the human spirit that is within? So also no one comprehends what is truly God's except the Spirit of God. Now we have received not the spirit of the world, but the Spirit that is from God, so that we may understand the gifts bestowed on us by God. And we speak of these things in words not taught by human wisdom but taught by the Spirit, interpreting spiritual things to those who are spiritual. Those who are unspiritual do not receive the gifts of God's Spirit, for they are foolishness to them, and they are unable to understand them because they are spiritually discerned. Those who are spiritual discern all things, and they are themselves subject to no one else's scrutiny.
"For who has known the mind of the Lord so as to instruct him?"
But we have the mind of Christ (1 Cor 2:4–16).

The unwarned reader has just encountered the language of Paul. With him we soar high above ordinary reasoning ("carnal," as he would say). The Letters maintain this level, this point that must be read with sustained attention in order to grasp all the subtleties. When a person becomes familiar with Paul's Letters, this question invariably crosses one's mind: if such language was maintained before the little people of Corinth, how did they understand it? In truth, these texts must have been addressed to personalities at the heart of the community, chosen for their spiritual qualities and their ability to assimilate the apostle's developments. I like to think that these persons knew how to translate Paul's theology into a more accessible language.

Nothing could have been more disparate than the assembly of Paul's converts. Greeks and Romans mingled with Jews, the circumcised with the uncircumcised. They gathered in particular houses where they took their meals in common. In conformity with the attitude that he had defined in Antioch, Paul did not prevent any of the new Christians from attending the numerous feasts, Jewish or pagan, that were celebrated in the city. To those who showed themselves reticent, especially Jews, Paul explained that one must not draw attention to oneself. Assisting at the feasts permitted one to form relationships useful for spreading the divine message. One lucid sentence sums up the essential point:

"All things are lawful," but not all things are beneficial. "All things are lawful," but not all things build up. So:

> eat whatever is sold in the meat market without raising any question on the ground of conscience, for *"the earth and its fullness are the Lord's."*[3] If an unbeliever invites you to a meal and you are disposed to go, eat whatever is set before you without raising any question on the ground of conscience. But if someone says to you, "This has been offered in sacrifice," then do not eat it, out of consideration for the one who informed you, and for the sake of conscience—I mean the other's conscience, not your own. For why should my liberty be subject to the judgment of someone else's conscience?

Paul goes so far as to offer himself as an example: "just as I try to please everyone in everything I do, not seeking my own advantage, but that of many, so that they may be saved." He concludes with a phrase superbly and proudly Pauline: "Be imitators of me, as I am of Christ" (1 Cor 10:23–29, 33; 11:1).

AT THE SAME TIME Corinth saw the arrival of the new proconsul of Achaia, Lucius Junius Gallio. The texts of the New Testament call him Gallio. An inscription on a commemorative stone unearthed at Delphi refers to a conflict the proconsul concerned himself with, and on which the Emperor Claudius delivered a verdict.

Of course it has no bearing on Paul's history, but its value lies in the fact that it marked a precise date in his biography. We deduce that Gallio—his traditional name—took his post in Corinth at the end of April 51. This was not a matter of a personage of second rank. His brother, the illustrious Seneca, was at the time tutor of the young Nero. Gallio should have remained an entire year in Corinth—the term of his mandate—but he would not finish it, having taken an intense dislike to the city, according to his brother.

Sitting at regular dates under the portico to render judgment, Gallio must have been greatly astonished when he saw a group of Jews appear. They were led by a certain Sosthenes, the leader of the synagogue, who was bringing before him—by force?—a stranger by the name of Paul. These Jews swore that "this individual" preached an "illegal cult of God" to which he wanted to "bring the people."

Roman law recognized the Jewish religion, which gave it certain advantages. What could be the "illegal cult" of which the Jews accused the little man brought before him? It is improbable that the proconsul thought anything of Christians for, even if we know that some lived in Rome, they were so few that he had probably never heard about them. Gallio saw that these Jews were so sure of themselves that he let the accusation unfold; after which, being a man of integrity, he allowed Paul to speak. Then he announced his verdict: he concurred that announcing a new religion would in fact be illegal. But if it were a matter of a new opinion preached within Judaism, that would be an entirely different thing. Gallio was aware of the differences that existed between the Sadducees and the Pharisees. If another now emerged, what could he do about it? Nothing could be clearer than his response: "If it were a matter of crime or serious villainy, I would be justified in accepting the complaint of you Jews; but since it is a matter of questions about words and names and your own law, see to it yourselves; I do not wish to be a judge of these matters."

Consequently, Paul was sent away from the tribunal a free man. If Acts is to be believed, the enraged Jews turned against this Sosthenes who made them lose face. Under the eyes of the proconsul, they beat him, "but Gallio paid no attention to any of these things" (Acts 18:14–17).

THE DAY WOULD COME when Paul would conclude that he had nothing more to expect from Corinth. He had sown and could be proud of the harvest. Even if the church he had established there did not number more than a few hundred faithful, including the slaves, the result surpassed by far his previous preaching. In the First Letter to the Corinthians, Paul returned to the happiness that, "in the name of Christ," he had received from the Corinthians and to the precious memories he had kept from his sojourn among them:

> I give thanks to my God always for you because of the grace of God that has been given you in Christ Jesus, for in every way you have been enriched in him, in speech and knowledge of every kind—just as the testimony of Christ has been strengthened among you—so that you are not lacking in any spiritual gift as you wait for the revealing of our Lord Jesus Christ. He will also strengthen you to the end, so that you may be blameless on the day of our Lord Jesus Christ. God is faithful: by him you were called into the fellowship of his Son, Jesus Christ our Lord (1:4–9).

Did he embark at Cenchreae in the fall of 51, before the prohibition of sea travel was pronounced? We lean rather to the spring of 52. First of all, we know that he had his head shaved to obey a vow. Reading the Book of Numbers enlightens us on the character of such a gesture; whoever decided to do this had to abstain from wine as well as strong drink and let his hair grow for at least thirty days. After that, in a room in the Jerusalem Temple, his head would be shaved and his hair burned as a sign of offering. By having what was left of his hair shaved at Cenchreae, Paul marked once again his duality: he who came from building the foundations of a new Christian church strictly observed the rite of the Jewish Law.

He embarked in the company of Priscilla and Aquila: on his part, fidelity in friendship; on theirs, confirmation of an ardent faith. Timothy accompanied them.

Their destination: Antioch.

10

SUFFERINGS AND STRUGGLES IN EPHESUS

The winter ban on sea travel having been lifted, everything that could sail was taken by force. At the beginning of the spring of 52, no one wanted to think about the heat of the coming summer. The powerful aroma rising from the hills of Megara and from Attica, the light breeze blowing on the waves—all inclined passengers to relaxation and enjoyment.

Paul, Priscilla, Aquila, and Timothy,[1] a small group bound by their faith, hardly ever left the bridge. Their worries were miles away! Their journey was paid for and provisions of food swelled their bags—a bit of normal peace for a Paul never free from his obsession with Christ, lived day-to-day. At the port of call of Ephesus, Aquila and Prisca would leave the ship to bring help to the small Christian community that had begun to take hold there with hardly a trace. As they approached their destination, anguish overcame the couple. As for Paul, I imagine him squatting on the bridge, pensive and grave. He would divest himself for the first time of the privilege that he had jealously and exclusively reserved. If the cult of Jesus continued to spread—and who could doubt it would?—he would have to get used to delegating, even if it tore his heart out....

THEY TACKED THROUGH the Cyclades—Kithnos, Siros, Tinos, and Mikonos—the famous Greek islands that have become the privileged

magnet of cruise tourism two thousand years later. The navigator's rule
was never to lose sight of land, as much as possible. Here was the sacred
island of Delos, whose name meant "brilliant." Legend had it that the
Cyclades—*o kuklos*, the circle—was sown by the gods around Delos like a
halo. Near the coast of Asia Paul and his friends got one look at Samos,
famous for its syrupy wine, and then the mountains of Ionia arose beyond
the prow that danced on the waves. In the music of this single word all of
ancient Hellade stood out: the never-forgotten dream of the adolescent
Saul. A few hours more, and they would discover Ephesus at the bottom
of the gulf.

When the ship dropped anchor in the first port of Panormus, Paul
and his friends descended into a boat. By way of a canal of about a mile
long, it brought them to the interior port of the city, face to face with the
marble of monuments, that of the amphitheater, and that of the agora. By
setting foot on the ground, Paul must have exhumed from his own mind
images arising from the readings or the teachings of revered masters: it
was there that blind Homer directed his hesitant steps; that Heraclitus
sounded being and the universe; that Pythagoras opened his school of
asceticism; that Thales laid the foundation of Western philosophy; that
Herodotus expressed the rules of history, which were immediately put
into practice.

The stopover had to be brief. It was impossible for Paul to linger in
this too rich city, whose inhabitants swore was "one of the capitals of the
world." The cult of the goddess Artemis drew enormous crowds, making
of the city a sort of duty-free port on the threshold of Asia. They imported, they exported, they sold, they bought. The expenses that the pilgrims
incurred were added to all this. From these crowds came a general prosperity lined with dreadful corollaries: flaunted money, a profusion of
monuments more lavish than inspired, and a vain multiplication of the-
aters, gymnasiums, stadiums, and porticoes.

Did he take all this in with one look? Paul had to limit himself to running to the synagogue to speak and introduce Prisca and Aquila to the
Jewish community. Did he speak about Jesus? Lacking the necessary
time, this would have been uselessly provoking. We can be sure that he
showed himself in full possession of his gifts: the Jews at this point were
so enchanted by his visit that they asked him to prolong his stay. He
refused: "I will return to you, if God wills" (Acts 18:21).2 He returned to
the shore.

The ship went southwest along the jagged coast of Anatolia. A stop at Cyprus brought back such memories! From the Palestinian port of Caesarea, where he disembarked, Paul would reach Jerusalem. The texts offer very little information about the reasons for this visit. They tell us only that Paul went to Jerusalem and "greeted the church" (Acts 18:22). We can deduce that he must have met James, from that time recognized as the official embodiment of Christianity. Moreover, that fact seemed not to have displeased James; the letter attributed to him is written in very solemn, even emphatic, language. His prestige became such that the Jewish-Christians circulated the absurd legend according to which—following the example of the high priest who alone was invested with this right—James had permission to enter the sanctuary of the Temple once a year. They went so far as to affirm that James was of the priestly race, to proclaim that his merits alone suspended the wrath "about to burst upon the people." Did Paul, straightforward man that he was, appreciate this?

As for Peter, apostle to the circumcised as Paul was to the Gentiles, we see him constantly on the road. Accompanied by his wife, he covered Syria in order to evangelize the Jews—and them alone. Mark, whom we saw following Paul a short time ago, now no longer left Peter's side. During the long years to come, he would hear the first of the apostles tell about Jesus. The words of the Lord would pass from Peter's memory into Mark's. After Peter's death the faithful would ask this unrivalled disciple to put those words down in writing. Thus the first Gospel would be born.

Antioch. No one, not even Paul, informs us of what he must have experienced on returning to this city where his destiny had been decided. How can we not believe that a surge of bitterness rose to his throat at the memory of his confrontation with Peter, which turned out so badly? Luke indicates that Paul remained "for a time" in Antioch, which seems to mean he did not linger there. One cannot imagine Paul remaining inactive in a city where an interminable, exasperating debate continued between Jewish and pagan Christians. The student of Gamaliel—as he reminds us unceasingly—was not the model of patience.

What satisfaction when news from Ephesus reached him! Yet what worry when he learned that Priscilla and Aquila were finding real difficulties there! A certain Apollos, a Jewish native of Alexandria, had just arrived in the city. He was said to be scholarly, an orator versed in the Scriptures, gifted with an assurance nothing could shake. Welcomed in the synagogue, he too presented himself as informed about Jesus by "the way of the Lord." Our tentmakers had heard him pour out torrents of eloquence on the mission of Jesus, even though he clearly knew nothing but questionable bits and pieces about him. They would have to instruct Apollos immediately. Would he consent to it? If he shrank from their teaching, would they allow him to spread a fallacious version of the story of the Messiah? Aquila and Priscilla put the question to Paul. He accorded such importance to their appeal that he immediately made it his duty to join them. This would be his third voyage.

PAUL'S PERSISTENT DESIRE to verify that "his" churches were staying the course explains why he decided to reach Ephesus by land. We should realize that such an enterprise represented, in the middle of the summer of 52, the trifle of 700 miles. Paul would confront mountains, plains, and valleys in temperatures that would reach and sometimes exceed 122 degrees Farenheit.

He again required the services of Timothy, who accepted to accompany him. They stopped in Tarsus, Paul's veritable home port. Were his parents still living? We know nothing about them at this point. He tore himself away from his native city.

When he passed through the doors of Cilicia and crossed the Taurus River, Paul was almost forty-five years old. At the time, that age marked a certain slide toward old age. Panting in the burning air, trying to protect their eyes from the blazing sun, bodies drenched with sweat, feet on fire, the two men took a little rest only in Lycaonia. Paul met the faithful of Lystra, went up to Iconium, and stopped at Pisidian Antioch. Did he not detect some uncertainty in the behavior of his dear Galatians? What we know of the grave conflict that would later arise among them leads us to think that, from that time, discord began to trouble them.

To reach Ephesus—he was so anxious to reach it—Paul chose the high valley of Lycos. The two men took the route on the side of the mountain that Strabo described. Did they linger to admire the flocks of black sheep so sought after for their wool? From Strabo again but also from Pliny, we are aware of the trade of tunics and mantles made on location, of the capital put in play and the prosperity of the banks of Laodicea: all subjects reminiscent of the childhood of Paul, who grew up in the textile industry. We see him pass through Magnesium and Tralles. Ignatius would attest to the existence of Christian communities in these two cities; their foundation would be attributed to Paul.

He and Timothy entered the valley of Meander, then that of the Cestrus to arrive at their goal toward the end of the summer of 52.

PAUL DID NOT HESITATE; he found accommodation at the home of Prisca and Aquila. Their workshop could count on one more worker. We know from Plutarch and Athenaeus that the city was famous for its tents.

He would not meet this Apollos who had so worried Priscilla and Aquila. Sure of having put the troublemaker back on the right track and knowing that he wanted to go to Achaia, they had dispatched Apollos to Corinth. They felt that his oratorical talent, which was superior to Paul's, would do marvels there. Apollos' teaching seems to have left traces in the high country; at the time of his passage, Paul must have put order in the beliefs of a dozen of the faithful. Their dialogue merits repetition.

"Did you receive the Holy Spirit when you became believers?" Paul asks.

Answer: "We have not even heard that there is a Holy Spirit."

"Into what then were you baptized?"

"Into John's baptism."

We can almost hear Paul hammer out each word of his reply: "John baptized with the baptism of repentance, telling the people to believe in the one who was to come after him, that is, in Jesus."

Convinced, these brave men asked to receive a new baptism, this time "in the name of the Lord Jesus" (Acts 19:2–5).

If Ephesus was one of the cities most extensively mentioned in ancient texts, it was because of the temple of Artemis—the Artemision. Can we doubt that Paul, who made himself an Ephesian during three years, did not once slip in among the crowds who, amid screams and shoving, pressed forward to find the most famous pagan temple in Asia? By consulting the plans and the texts, we can imagine the shock that the hundreds of thousands of visitors felt at the sight of the matchless building. It was four times the surface of the Parthenon, with one hundred twenty-seven Ionic columns aligned on a length of 200 yards. In the sixth century B.C., it required the fortune of Croesus, king of Lydia, to complete the construction of the prodigious whole. Praxiteles and Phidias took charge of the decoration. Faced with such a success, all antiquity delighted to the point of placing the Artemision among the seven wonders of the world.

What remains of such magnificence in the twenty-first century? In the middle of the scattered debris that time has eaten away, only one white marble column endures.

EVERY DAY FROM NOW on the apostle would have to force his way in the midst of fortune-tellers, flute players, and mimes who crowded the streets, mingling among jewelers and sellers of medals leaping out of their stores to harangue the shoppers. We have recovered some of these souvenirs, the same kind that are sold in places of pilgrimage throughout the world: clay replicas of the statue of the goddess, silver replicas of the temple, pendants, medallions. When the pilgrims did not themselves enter the shops, the merchants tried to press things into their hands by force. We can imagine Paul's reaction when this happened to him—and it must have happened a hundred times. From the irritation betrayed in his letters he must have moved on to abhorrence.

At the end of the day, most of the inhabitants, eager for coolness, climbed as far as the upper agora that overlooked the sea. I see Paul, finally calm, glance over the harmonious gulf that spread at his feet. It would have been impossible to offer to fleets from all origins and of all tonnage a port better defended by nature; two steep masses, the mounts of Pion and Coressus, flanked it on both sides. By connecting them with a wall five miles long, Lysimachus, Alexander's lieutenant, effectively sheltered the city from looting.

I hope the reader will permit me to stop here a moment to speak about a man who is very dear to us.

Throughout this book Luke has accompanied us. Even if at times we have called into question the information he offered, how could we not recognize that the Acts of the Apostles contains irreplaceable documentation? Armed with the Letters alone, we would only be able to penetrate Saint Paul's thought. Without Luke, what would we know of the details of his journeys, of his battles, of victories won, of trials suffered, of people met, of places crossed? Thank you, Luke.

Here, at Ephesus, near the colonnade of the upper agora, Luke's martyred body would one day be buried.

AT THE TIME PAUL returned to it, the city numbered around 225,000 inhabitants. The Roman proconsul resided there. The unavoidable Strabo tells us that the city had always had a bad reputation, corrupted by effeminate morals imported from Ionia, distracted from serious pursuits by the softness of the climate, abandoning study through laziness, taking only dance and music seriously, making "a bacchanalia of public life."

It seems astounding that Paul chose such a city to be the epicenter of his churches. We note, however, that the city was located at an equal distance from Galatia and Thessalonica (310 miles); it was 250 miles from Corinth, 275 from Philippi, and 205 from Pisidian Antioch. Provided that one was patient, one could send and receive messages to the churches without too much difficulty.

Had Paul forgotten he had torn his garments in the synagogue of Corinth? This apparently final gesture did not prevent him from entering the synagogue of Ephesus—where none had forgotten him—to preach with all assurance the Kingdom of God by revealing the earthly existence of his Son. The Jews of Ephesus listened to him for three months. After this, as usual, they could not bear any more: "Some...spoke evil of the Way before the congregation" (Acts 19:9). Paul made a clean break; *adieu* to the synagogue of Ephesus.

Some of the faithful—"God-fearers"?—followed him to the house of Tyrannus, who ran one of those schools, numerous in ancient cities, where they taught and debated. From that time on Paul would preach there every day, heard by a public as attentive as it was cosmopolitan. For some time Ephesus had no longer been an exclusively Greek city; each year the Asian influence made itself felt more and more, and ships unloaded cargoes there of immigrants of all origins. Paul would accomplish his conversions primarily among these people. Must we acknowledge the opinion of Renan, according to whom "Christianity will sprout in what we call the corruption of large cities"?

The three years of Paul's stay in Ephesus would be sown with hopes and successes but also with struggles and failures. At no time in the course of his apostolate had he remained so long in the same place and sustained efforts so trying. He confided that he often worked "in tears and in the midst of trials."

Paul kept the community on alert, multiplied conversions, and confronted dangers coming from every corner of the horizon. As he could not often get away, he acted like an admiral in the middle of a tempest, refusing to leave his post; he innovated by sending the most ardent of his faithful to evangelize cities that had not yet received the message of Jesus. We see him unceasingly in contact with the churches of Colossae, Laodicea and Hieropolis. We note that relations increased with Macedonia, where Timothy and Erastus had been sent. Paul said, "A wide door for effective work has opened to me" (1 Cor 16:9). He preached [effectively] "so that all the residents of Asia, both Jews and Greeks, heard the word of the Lord" (Acts 19:10).

We see Apollos, returned from Corinth, so totally reconciled with Paul that we can deduce the possibility of an exceptional common mission in Asia. And though Timothy showed himself to be Paul's most subtle agent—"I have no one like him who will be genuinely concerned for your welfare" (Phil 2:20)—it would be unjust to omit the work of Titus, Erastus, and Aristarchus.

We find many images illustrating this buzz of activity. Acts shows us a Paul suddenly assaulted by sick persons begging him to heal them, and "God did extraordinary miracles through Paul" (19:11). The impatient went so far as to apply to those who were sick cloths that had touched his skin! Did Paul really allow such behavior, bordering on hysteria and corresponding so little to his character? We have to ask ourselves here whether Luke did not let his imagination run away with him. Perhaps the episode can only be explained by the climate of occultism present at that time in Ephesus and whose origin was due to natural disasters such as pestilence, famine, and earthquakes that ravaged the region. Around the temple of Artemis, peddlers sold small bronze plaques supposed to bring relief from sickness. The great local families, the Greco-Romans themselves, appealed to miracle workers who, with the help of mysterious formulae, pretended to cast out the spirits that were blamed for all evils. Astrologers ran shops. People spoke about exorcists traveling the region and practicing healings by using this formula: "I adjure you by the Jesus whom Paul proclaims." The seven sons of Sceva, a Jewish high priest, were tempted to try their hand at this; the "evil spirit," having taken hold of a stranger, leaped on them with such force that they were saved only by escaping "naked and wounded" (19:16). The temple of Artemis was decidedly very far from the Parthenon.

It was too much. Some Christians reacted by coming to Paul and begging him to forgive them such bad habits. Better still, they threw at his feet the books of magic that they had acquired—the number fifty thousand is cited—and they burned them (19:19).

IN THE EARLY DAYS, Paul's sermons hardly troubled the pagans. To the extent that the number of conversions grew, rumors began to circulate; simple gossip soon grew into full-blown reports. In their temple, the priests of Artemis became alarmed—and even more so the silversmiths who sold, at the doors of the Artemision, the "souvenirs" that we are all familiar with. These brought in a great deal of income. One of the silversmiths, a certain Demetrius, was the first to become upset. Having entered into "rivalry" with the goddess, wouldn't this new god take away from these respected shop keepers the best of their profit? Demetrius presented his concerns to his colleagues. We know from Acts the speech he addressed to them:

> "Men, you know that we get our wealth from this business. You also see and hear that not only in Ephesus but in almost the whole of Asia this Paul has persuaded and drawn away a considerable number of people by saying that gods made with hands are not gods. And there is danger not only that this trade of ours may come into disrepute but also that the temple of the great goddess Artemis will be scorned, and she will be deprived of her majesty that brought all Asia and the world to worship her" (Acts 19:25–27).

A guild of silversmiths existed in Ephesus. These words spread, stirring up the craftsmen. Demetrius convinced his colleagues to gather at the theater. The procession swelled, and as it proceeded it picked up two Macedonians, Gaius and Aristarchus, known as Paul's friends. Everyone squeezed into the theater. The insults were aimed at Paul's Christians but also at the Jews. In order to calm the turmoil, it was necessary that a magistrate from the city speak. Pointing to Aristarchus and Gaius, he cried out: "You have brought these men here who are neither temple robbers nor blasphemers of our goddess. If therefore Demetrius and the artisans with him have a complaint against anyone, the courts are open, and there are proconsuls; let them bring charges there against one another" (Acts 19:37–38).

Warned, Paul himself wanted to go to the theater immediately; he was dissuaded. A silent anxiety arose among the converts. "Paul sent for the disciples" and encouraged them (Acts 20:1).

The next day he began to preach again. He had no illusions, knowing that those who had a grudge against him would not let go until they succeeded in throwing him into prison.

The prison in Ephesus was formidable. Tradition situated it in an enormous square tower, still visible today at one of the corners of the ancient ramparts erected in the third century B.C. It threatens ruin but is still standing. In the city where so many nations, religions, and races met and mingled, where dangerous areas were more common than anywhere else, where the nights were far from being safe, and where knife fights often broke out, a police force with a strong arm was needed. Thus it was a prison that inspired fear.

The little bald man, growing old, who had just been led to his cell could not but astonish his jailers: sometimes he became lost in prayer, sometimes he spoke and wrote. He was known only by his name, *Paul,* and his place of origin, *Tarsus*. There was nothing given as to the reason for his imprisonment.

Of what was this Christian accused? Who had sworn to get rid of him? The Acts of the Apostles is absolutely silent. The only light shed on Paul's imprisonment comes to us from the Letters. From many of these it is necessary to isolate and juxtapose phrases, to draw out the "sap." The letter Paul addressed to Philemon, one of his converts and an eminent member of the community of Colossae, begins this way: "Paul, a prisoner of Christ Jesus, and Timothy our brother, to Philemon our dear friend and coworker, to Apphia our sister, to Archippus our fellow soldier, and to the church in your house." Then follows this phrase that grips the heart: "I, Paul, do this as an old man, and now also as a prisoner of Christ Jesus." The issue with which the letter dealt was a Christian slave named Onesimus who, belonging to Philemon, had fled and placed himself in Paul's service. The latter had decided to send Onesimus back to his master so that he might avoid the punishment that was reserved for runaway slaves, which could go so far as death. Paul pleaded his correspondent's indulgence: "I wanted to keep him with me, so that he might be of service to me in your place *during my imprisonment for the gospel;* but I preferred to do nothing without your consent, in order that your good deed might be voluntary and not something forced"

(Philem 1–2, 9, 13). Here we see that it was because he preached the Christian faith that Paul had been imprisoned, and not for any other reason.

From his cell the letters multiplied. From it the Letter to the Colossians, a Christian community located in Phrygia, some 124 miles from Ephesus, was dated. It was founded by Epaphras, his disciple, who would rejoin Paul in his prison at the same time as Aristarchus: "Aristarchus my fellow prisoner greets you...." The letter ends thus: "I, Paul, write this greeting with my own hand. Remember my chains" (Col 4:10, 18).

Paul referred to this prison in the Letter to the Philippians as well. He wrote about his captivity as a fact they had already been informed of: "You hold me in your heart, for all of you share in God's grace with me, both in my imprisonment and in the defense and confirmation of the gospel." To this he added a commentary in his own style:

> I want you to know, beloved, that what has happened to me has actually helped to spread the gospel, so that it has become known throughout the whole imperial guard and to everyone else that my imprisonment is for Christ: and most of the brothers and sisters, having been made confident in the Lord by my imprisonment, dare to speak the word with greater boldness and without fear (Phil 1:7, 12–14).

In the same letter, Paul conveyed the greetings of those from "the emperor's household," a formula that seems to designate converts from the barracks of the praetorian guard of Ephesus (Phil 4:22).[3]

Evidence of a conflict that endangered Paul's life is underlined in a letter written several years later, that to the Romans, and is confirmed by a phrase in the First Letter to the Corinthians that alludes to a battle of the apostle "with wild animals" (15:32). Immediately we think of the first Christians thrown to the lions in the circus. Strangely, the redactor of *The Acts of Paul* will take up again the same words to evoke a confrontation between the prisoner Paul and a lion. Yet, as a Roman citizen, Paul could not be subjected to such torment. The expression must be considered a metaphor, but the words *wild animal* confirm that Paul's life was in danger. Wildcats existed not only in an animal state.

Who was responsible for this imprisonment? The Roman authorities, particular interest groups, or the Jewish community? I would exclude the representatives of the emperor; for the imperial power, a Jew having become Christian retained the rights accorded to a Jew. A resurgence of anger on the part of the merchants, silversmiths, and others is not credible in the face of Paul's repeated affirmations that he is in prison for having served the Christ.

Because Paul is the hero of our story, we grant to each of his acts and deeds, to each of his adventures, the importance they carry in our eyes, forgetting to relativize them. In this case, we have the tendency to consider the apostle's stay in prison as an event of first priority that the whole city must have discussed or worried about. If there had been newspapers at that time, we would almost imagine a veritable chronicle of his life in prison. This would begin with headlines on the first page: *The Christian Paul in Prison.* And later: *Crisis in Corinth. Paul receives envoys from the city in his prison cell.* Or again: *Confrontations between Christians. The religious leader Paul confers in his prison cell.*

In actuality, the vast majority of Ephesians ignored all Christians, including Paul. Paganism was an integral part of daily life. Each one implored Artemis in his or her prayers as, much later, Christians would pray to Mary.[4] Each month of May was consecrated to the goddess. Every four years her cult took on extraordinary proportions. Innumerable pilgrims descended upon the city, which was entirely decorated with flowers. The smallest room was rented several months in advance. All day joyous processions crossed the city, crying out and singing: "Great is Artemis of the Ephesians!" Tens of thousands of animals were sacrificed. At crossroads and in town squares wrestling matches were organized. At night, under the stars, people sang and danced. The prostitutes were not left out; quite the contrary.

This veneration of the goddess required an organization confided to ten of the wealthiest citizens of the city who, for its success and out of piety, paid considerable sums. An inscription found in excavations confirms:

> Considering that the entire month that bears the divine name [of Artemis] must be kept as holy and celebrated worthily, the inhabitants of Ephesus have decided to regulate her cult by the following decree: The whole month of Artemision will be holy, along with each day of the month. During the entire month we will celebrate feasts, panegyrics, and sacred solemnities. Our city will receive from this a new reputation and will be prosperous at all times.

Who in these surging masses would have taken an interest in a dissident Jew in prison? How can one doubt that Paul himself did not totally feel the imbalance, close to being laughable, of his situation? Never do we see him waver. Perhaps his most evident greatness lay therein: to feel oneself to be a needle in a haystack and never for an instant to deviate from one's course. Could this perhaps be holiness?

The explanation for his captivity lies elsewhere. Everywhere in Asia Judaizers who opposed Paul's doctrine with that of Peter and James began to spread. What unexpected reinforcement, however paradoxical, for the Jewish community of Ephesus! The irritation they felt concerning Paul changed little by little into hostility. Because of the conversions of Jews that Paul obtained, his brothers in YHWH became exasperated, and to this was added the equally furious intervention of Judaizers. Confrontations then took place, bringing together against Paul orthodox Jews and Judaizers. In the name of the *Pax Romana* they threw Paul into prison, for through him scandal had come.

HOWEVER THICK THE WALLS of his cell, news penetrated them. That same year, 54, the Emperor Claudius met his death; Agrippina, his second wife, had him poisoned. The praetorian guard then proclaimed the seventeen-year-old Nero emperor. He was Agrippina's son from her first marriage, whom Claudius had adopted.

But Claudius had a legitimate son, Britannicus. So began in lawlessness the reign of one of the bloodiest despots in history. No psychic in Ephesus would have dared to predict that Nero would have Britannicus poisoned, then have his own mother put to death before establishing himself, in an episode that would sicken the pagans themselves, as one who massacred Christians. A breach was about to open in the grandeur of Rome.

The correspondence Paul exchanged in the course of his captivity shows that he could often receive visitors and even have some of his friends stay with him. He needed a scribe for the letters that he wrote, and his guards provided one without difficulty. When, in the spring of 54, Christians traveling on business for Phoebe—a merchant from Corinth whom we have already met—arrived in Ephesus, Paul received them in prison. They brought very bad news: the community of Corinth was gradually abandoning the precepts that the apostle believed he had firmly inculcated in them. Some time later, three other Christians from Corinth—Stephanas, Fortunatus, and Achaicus—would come to confirm the disaster.

I see Paul at first incredulous; Corinth evoked for him a Christian church so closely bound, so coherent, so solid! Worry followed; he had to get to the bottom of it. He sent for Timothy—faithful among the faithful: let him leave, let him leave immediately. The disciple obeyed. He embarked for Corinth, but Paul no longer insisted on an immediate departure; he must respond to the questions and criticisms that had been put before him. So he dictated the First Letter to the Corinthians. It would reflect all that he felt: his praise, his reproaches, his anger. The corpus of the Letters had been born.

What had happened in Corinth? The affair can be summed up in four words: the Judaizers had struck. Judaizers, we recall, is the word adopted to designate the Jewish-Christians—otherwise known as Jewish converts to Christianity—who had remained faithful to the Hebrew Law. We may ask with astonishment: was not a commitment of non-belligerence ratified in Jerusalem? Were not zones of influence assigned to the majority attached to circumcision, and others to the minority embodied by Paul? The arrival in Corinth of Judaizing missionaries determined to thwart Paul's evangelization showed that the men of Jerusalem repudiated this pact.

In truth, James and his followers never believed in it. We find a reflection of this refusal in texts that will spread during almost a century and longer after their deaths: in Irenaeus, Eusebius, Saint Jerome, Papias, and many others. In the Letter to the Galatians, Paul would denounce this desire to annihilate his own churches. His enemies made him out to be a false prophet, a false apostle, a new Balaam, a heretic, a rogue who served as a prelude to the destruction of the Temple, a Simon the Magician, an intruder, an imposter.[5] His visions were pointed to as "the depths of Satan," and his churches became "the synagogues of Satan." They reprised his role as persecutor. They pretended that he was not even Jewish, but that he had had himself circumcised in order to marry the daughter of the high priest who, inspired by God, had rejected him.

We see these Judaizers arise throughout all of Asia. They spoke in the name of Peter, which never failed to impress new converts. They were not the only ones to take it out on Paul; every day a great many voyagers arrived at the port of Cenchreae, many of whom were already Christians but of another school than Paul's. With the authority of people who thought they knew it all, they questioned his integrity, they denied him the title of apostle, they repeated untiringly that he did not know Jesus. How prove himself right against the Twelve—they who had followed Christ during his public life, in Galilee as in Judea?

The Judaizers talked, and this talk found ears too willing among the Corinthian converts: for so long they had adopted relaxed morals! Having become Christians, they had vowed to put an end to the habits Paul condemned; they now relapsed. Worse still, Jews who, a short time ago, had scrupulously observed the laws of their religion now violated them under the pretext of having become Christians!

Everything mingled and intermingled. Although Apollos had since rallied to Paul, his teaching had wreaked havoc. We sense suspicion hanging over the First Letter to the Corinthians. Apollos was more inspired by Platonic philosophy than by Pauline teaching. For Plato, "the body is a tomb"; from there the Corinthians rejected the resurrection of the body that Paul advocated in favor of the resurrection of the soul.

Can we imagine what Paul must have felt? He could only give free rein to his indignation, and we know something about Paul's anger. An unspeakable suffering must have accompanied him. Knowing him, we can be sure he collected himself very quickly. Against the dangers he mobilized all his forces: an uncompromising energy and will.

It was the spring of 54. He would fight.

THE TEXT OF THE First Letter to the Corinthians blazes:

> What I mean is that each of you says, "I belong to Paul," or "I belong to Apollos," or "I belong to Cephas," or "I belong to Christ." Has Christ been divided? Was Paul crucified for you? Or were you baptized in the name of Paul? I thank God that I baptized none of you except Crispus and Gaius, so that no one can say that you were baptized in my name. (I did baptize also the household of Stephanas; beyond that I do not know whether I baptized anyone else.) For Christ did not send me to baptize but to proclaim the gospel, and not with eloquent wisdom, so that the cross of Christ might not be emptied of its power (1:12–17).

This passage not only confirms Paul's persuasive talent but it enlightens us on how he wrote the Letters. We cannot doubt that Paul dictated them and that a disciple transcribed his speech. Several times, the writer let himself be known by signing his name, and sometimes he even confirmed his identity with a personal message. In the text just read, we note that Paul corrected himself—"I did baptize also..."—with a spontaneity that manifests a remarkable freedom in the dictation, like this interruption. If the writer left such a passage, it was because the cost of parchment did not encourage him to begin the text again in its entirety.

Let us return to the disciples of Apollos whom Paul calls *psuchikoi*, the "psychics"—in other words, those who were left to their nature alone. Paul mocked them as "beautiful spirits" incapable of seeing what came from the Spirit of God. He contrasted them to the "spiritual" who were truly inspired by the Spirit (*pneumatikoi*): "Those who are unspiritual do not receive the gifts of God's Spirit, for they are foolishness to them, and they are unable to understand them.... Those who are spiritual discern all things, and they are themselves subject to no one else's scrutiny. 'For *who has known the mind of the Lord so as to instruct him?'* But we have the mind of Christ" (1 Cor 2:14–16).

Of the Judaizers and those Corinthians tempted by Platonism, Paul made just one statement: "For Jews demand signs and Greeks desire wisdom, but we proclaim Christ crucified, a stumbling block to Jews and foolishness to Gentiles, but to those who are called, both Jews and Greeks, Christ the power of God and the wisdom of God. For God's foolishness is wiser than human wisdom, and God's weakness is stronger than human strength" (1 Cor 1:22–25).

For Paul, the Corinthians must not deviate even an inch from his teaching. He agreed, however, to enlighten them. Nothing made sense apart from the certitude that obsessed both him and them: the Lord would soon reappear, without a doubt, any day now. Why in that case undertake whatever it was? Marriage, for example: was it necessary to bind oneself?

Paul's answer was striking:

> "It is well for a man not to touch a woman." But because of cases of sexual immorality, each man should have his own wife and each woman her own husband. The husband should give to his wife her conjugal rights, and likewise the wife to her husband. For the wife does not have authority over her own body, but the husband does; likewise the husband does not have authority over his own body, but the wife does. Do not deprive one another except perhaps by agreement for a set time, to devote yourselves to prayer, and then come together again, so that Satan may not tempt you because of your lack of self-control. This I say by way of concession, not of command. I wish that all were as I myself am. But each has a particular gift from God, one having one kind and another a different kind.

How should we understand *I wish that all were as I myself am?* We do not necessarily detect in it the asceticism of someone struggling to triumph over one's natural tendencies; if that were the case, Paul would say so clearly. The tone used leads us rather to see him having achieved a total indifference over sexual impulses, but knowing that most men and women are not like him: "To the unmarried and the widows I say that it is well for them to remain unmarried as I am. But if they are not practicing self-control, they should marry. For it is better to marry than to be aflame with passion" (1 Cor 7:19). Who has not read and reread these last words? They have the merit of posing the problem as clearly as possible.

Curiously, Paul indicated that he had not received on that point an order from the Lord: "I have no command of the Lord, but I give my opinion as one who by the Lord's mercy is trustworthy." He boldly confirmed that the return of Christ was near (*the time is shortened*), and from this he drew these deductions: "Are you bound to a wife? Do not seek to be free. Are you free from a wife? Do not seek a wife. But if you marry, you do not sin, and if a virgin marries, she does not sin. Yet those who marry will experience distress in this life, and I would spare you that." It is not certain that Paul attached much importance to these questions: "If anyone thinks that he is not behaving properly toward his fiancée, if his passions are strong, and so it has to be, let him marry as he wishes; it is no sin." He expresses the same latent indifference: "So then, he who marries his fiancée does well; and he who refrains from marriage will do better."

To formulate a rule in passing can do no harm: "A wife is bound as long as her husband lives. But if the husband dies, she is free to marry anyone she wishes, only in the Lord. But in my judgment she is more blessed if she remains as she is" (1 Cor 7:25, 27, 28, 36, 38, 39).

Did questions on the relationship of men and women fascinate the Corinthians? Then it was necessary to respond: "[Man] is the image and reflection of God; but woman is the reflection of man. Indeed man was not made from woman, but woman from man."[6] Yet another rule: "Nevertheless, in the Lord woman is not independent of man or man independent of woman" (1 Cor 11:7–8, 11).

Paul further said, "...women should be silent in the churches. For they are not permitted to speak, but should be subordinate, as the law[7] also says. If there is anything they desire to know, let them ask their husbands at home" (1 Cor 14:34–35).

We have before our eyes Paul's opinion on women, which is always brought up in discussions about the apostle. Let's not evade it: if for men and women of the twenty-first century such positions are inadmissible, the entire world at the time of Paul held them to be just. Paul was not being innovative; he only meant to echo, in toning it down, the Jewish Law. He placed himself very much beyond Roman law and far in advance of the laws of barbarians. The "dogma" of Paul's misogyny is based on a limited number of phrases—always the same ones—drawn from his Letters. Do they indicate a conviction on his part that women were inferior? Paul's accusers underline that he never spoke of his mother, but he did not say any more about his father, either.

Paul advised women to wear a veil on their heads, but this custom was almost universal. Must we hold a grudge against him, since we know that the prostitutes of Corinth and its bacchantes in their madness went bareheaded? For him to make of man the glory of God and of woman the glory of man is just a throwback to Genesis where, as we all know, God drew Eve from the body of Adam. It is said that Paul ordered women to be quiet in the assembly, but it was the same in the synagogues, where they were relegated far behind the men.

Of the bonds that united men and women in marriage, Paul wrote: "This is a great mystery, and I am applying it to Christ and the church" (Eph 5:32). "By this single phrase marriage enters on a level with the Christian mystery, and sexuality, far from being suspect, receives all its legitimacy."[8]

The biographer will also permit himself to remind the reader that, throughout the Letters of Paul, women appeared who fought alongside him, who held important posts in the Church, one of whom even became "minister" of a community. Within the limited circle of his Christian friends whom Paul mentioned explicitly, there were nine women for whom, on several occasions, he expressed the esteem and affection he had for them.

A simple concern for balance is in order.

Paul's references to Judaism were not limited to the status of women; they concerned the whole of Christian life. Let us open again the First Letter to the Corinthians: "I do not want you to be unaware, brothers and sisters, that our ancestors were all under the cloud, and all passed through the sea, and all were baptized into Moses in the cloud and in the sea" (10:1–2). Consider that Paul addressed pagans who had nothing in common with the Jews. Most had not even heard him speak of Moses. Now Paul invited them to consider as their "fathers" those who had passed dry-shod through the Red Sea—proof that, for him, Christianity was the direct and total heir of Judaism. He would return to this even more explicitly in the Letter to the Romans.

Paul was asked how Christians are to behave during worship; most important was that Christians from all origins, poor and rich, feel themselves to be brothers and equals. He considered it scandalous that at the time of the meals, where they ate in common while receiving the body of Christ, one could be hungry while another stuffed himself.

As many questions, as many answers. Gradually, Paul drew the frame of Christian life that, at the heart of growing communities, needed to be codified. The architect took on the hand of the theologian.

All of that made for many subjects in one letter. The First Letter to the Corinthians is long, of extreme density, and of surprising variety. For example, a "case of misconduct" put Paul beside himself: "A man is living with his father's wife" (5:1). He was asked what he would do to this sinner. Paul did not hesitate: "You are to hand this man over to Satan for the destruction of the flesh, so that his spirit may be saved in the day of the Lord" (5:5).

The case of those Corinthians who denied the resurrection of the dead appeared to him much more serious, a fundamental point in Paul's eyes. To overcome this unbearable error, he used the logic that he handled better than anyone: "If there is no resurrection of the dead, then Christ has not been raised; and if Christ has not been raised, then our proclamation has been in vain and your faith has been in vain." He pressed his advantage: "If for this life only we have hoped in Christ, we are of all people most to be pitied. But in fact Christ has been raised from the dead, the first fruits of those who have died." He prophesied:

> We will not all die, but we will all be changed, in a moment, in the twinkling of an eye, at the last trumpet. For the trumpet will sound, and the dead will be raised imperishable, and we will be changed. ...Then the saying that is written will be fulfilled: *Death has been swallowed up in victory. Where, O death, is your victory? Where, O death, is your sting? The sting of death is sin, and the power of sin is the law* (15:13–14, 19–20, 51, 52, 54, 55).

WOULD THE FIRST LETTER to the Corinthians deserve the importance that we attribute to it if it did not contain the magnificent text that gave meaning to all Christianity? It needs no commentary; in this litany that reaches the summit, we rediscover Jesus in every verse:

> If I speak in the tongues of mortals and of angels, but do not have love, I am a noisy gong or a clanging cymbal.
>
> And if I have prophetic powers, and understand all mysteries and all knowledge, and if I have all faith, so as to remove mountains, but do not have love, I am nothing.
>
> And if I give away all my possessions, and if I hand over my body so that I may boast, but do not have love, I gain nothing.
>
> Love is patient; love is kind; love is not envious or boastful or arrogant or rude. It does not insist on its own way; it is not irritable or resentful; it does not rejoice in wrongdoing, but rejoices in the truth.
>
> It bears all things, believes all things, hopes all things, endures all things.
>
> Love never ends.
>
> But as for prophecies, they will come to an end;
>
> as for tongues, they will cease;
>
> as for knowledge, it will come to an end.
>
> ...And now faith, hope, and love abide, these three; and the greatest of these is love (13:1–8, 13).

The letter was sent. Paul waited. The speed of letter exchange depended at that time on one single agent: the wind. Whether it blew or not over the Aegean Sea changed everything. Paul exuded an air of confidence: how could such a cry on his part—so unforeseen, let's admit it—not rally the hesitant Christians of Corinth around the Truth? Whether the answer came sooner or later, it knocked Paul from his high horse: the Corinthians had not wavered in rallying around the Judaizers. Even more, their position had been reinforced.

That was what struck directly at the reasoning Paul sustained victoriously in Jerusalem and Antioch: there he had affirmed that, for adult pagans, circumcision would be an obstacle prohibitive to conversion; the success of the Judaizing missionaries in Corinth proved the contrary. The pagans who submitted to the rabbi's knife demonstrated that the Christianity of James was more compelling than that of Paul.

In the summer of 54, when Timothy returned to Ephesus, he reported that he had been very badly received in Corinth. Anyone but Paul would have collapsed. He held up well. Didn't we realize that he never gave up? Is it here that we should locate the episode of an unexpected journey to Corinth? Would he have been given a prison furlough? Acts does not mention a second journey to the city. It is from Paul himself that we know of it. In the Second Letter to the Corinthians he promised them a third visit, and this one would take place, which confirms the existence of the second one (cf. 2 Cor 12:14; 13:1).

For the first time Paul would see his authority publicly called into question. An anti-establishment brother attacked him in front of everyone, and it appears that the community did not support the apostle. He did not insist. Deeply humiliated, Paul left the city.

Must we situate the mission confided to Titus within this moment? There is no doubt of it. Paul would have begged him to undertake everything in order to attempt to convince the Christians of Corinth to return to him. He would have handed Titus a letter that he said was written "with many tears" (2 Cor 2:4). There is no doubt that this letter was sent; unfortunately it has disappeared. It is probably the case of other correspondence that the exegetes came to situate in the context we have here, in which Paul learned that grave disorders threatened the church in Corinth. So he wrote a letter that was lost. Following Timothy's visit, questions were put to him in writing. Paul responded to them in our First Letter to the Corinthians. It did not achieve the result he had counted on. There took place the hasty voyage to Corinth. On returning to Ephesus, he wrote his third letter, now lost, "written in tears."

Thus is posed the problem of the Second Letter to the Corinthians as we have it. We hesitate to assign a definite date when it was written. More difficult still, the layout that has long been given to it is today under discussion. According to present teaching, after Paul's death it would have been cut into five pieces, certain ones of which would have been inserted in the First Letter in order to make it more coherent.

Simple logic, which I would agree with, leads to the belief that the Second Letter was composed after Paul had left Ephesus. In the following chapter we will find him again at Troas, waiting with extreme anxiety precisely for Titus' return. In the second letter, he attested that this return did take place. This is the phrase that should dispel all hesitation: "He [Titus] told us of your longing, your mourning, your zeal for me, so that I rejoiced still more.... I rejoice, because I have complete confidence in you" (7:7, 16).

IN THE COURSE OF the year 54, Paul was still in prison. Even though pressures against the Christian community became more pronounced, his captivity was as liberal as always. This allows us to recognize that he could have been freed in order to make the second visit to Corinth, and then put in prison again. Toward the end of winter 54–55, his prison regimen seems to have hardened. Was this because messages had come from Galatia diminishing his prestige?

It is easy to reconstruct the unfolding of events. Coming from Antioch, the emissaries of James seem to have arrived among the Galatians. They knew very well of the existence of Christian communities Paul had established. He himself had told them that one of the bastions of his authority was to be found there.

Desire seizes this biographer—which is what happened to certain of his predecessors—to depict the troublemakers who came into central Anatolia to take over Paul's churches as traitors in a melodrama: in dark dress, heads low, creeping at night between houses to undertake their evil task. The historian naturally grows attached to Paul; fatally one is led to think that all Paul's enemies were wrong. The error here is patent. Those sent from Jerusalem were men of good faith, persuaded that they held the truth. Jews like Paul, they were not his enemies but were convinced that he had thrown the church onto a path that would lead to disaster. Their duty was to enlighten those unfortunate ones led astray by Paul.

They told the Galatians—simple people, easy to convince, who had listened to Paul and who believed him to be right—that they were not good Christians. The proof: they were not circumcised. Jesus was circumcised. The apostles were circumcised. What was more, circumcision was excellent for one's health: it prevented illness, etc. The Judaizers declared themselves proud of their circumcision and proclaimed that one was only a real man if he was circumcised. The decisive blow was struck when they declared that this obligation was confirmed by the apostles, among them their chief, Peter, and James, the brother of the Lord.

At first the Galatians protested. They had met Paul three times; they loved him. Why would he have wanted to mislead them? A restatement followed on the part of the Judaizers: We too love him well. But did he not tell you that he never saw Jesus?

The Galatians were astonished; he had spoken so well of Jesus! They were given proof. This time they were moved. The Judaizers asked other questions: Did he admit to you that, in his youth, he persecuted Christians, that he had hundreds thrown into prison, that he tortured some and still worse? Staggering, horrified, the Galatians were struck dumb: Paul had told them nothing of this. Would they have to repudiate all that the man from Tarsus had taught them?

The Judaizers hastened to reassure them that the essential of what they had learned remained valid. The only fault of Paul, too anxious to convince, was not to have taught them respect for the Law given by God. The Creator of all things had spoken to Abraham. He had even entered into a covenant with him. We, the Jews, received it after him and we have never ceased to respect it. We have never forgotten what God said to Abraham: "This is my covenant, which you shall keep, between me and you and your offspring after you: Every male among you shall be circumcised. You shall circumcise the flesh of your foreskins, and it shall be a sign of the covenant between me and you" (Gen 17:10–11).

The Judaizers insisted with an infectious force and certitude: It was the same God who sent us Jesus, the Messiah, who is his Son. We have recognized him; you have recognized him. If we did not accept the whole Law, it would be God himself whom we wronged.

THIS CONFRONTATION—briefly summed up, surely—reached Paul's ears. How could we not imagine him immediately flying into a rage? He abhorred these cowards—I believe I can hear him say the word—who attacked those defenseless people in order to destroy their faith.

Furious, he summoned a scribe and, on the spot, dictated the most impassioned of his letters. The reader already knows many excerpts from the text. To justify himself, to show that he alone was right, Paul felt the need to narrate many passages from his life. These constitute an invaluable source for the historian. I insist here on taking the measure of Paul's anger:

> Paul, an apostle—sent neither by human commission nor from human authorities, but through Jesus Christ and God the Father, who raised him from the dead—and all the members of God's family who are with me, to the churches of Galatia: Grace to you and peace from God our Father and the Lord Jesus Christ, who gave himself for our sins to set us free from the present evil age, according to the will of our God and Father, to whom be the glory forever and ever. Amen (Gal 1:1–5).

If he wanted to begin strongly, he succeeded perfectly. From the first line, Paul displayed the title of "apostle" like a banner when, until then, he had used it but timidly. It sounded like a challenge: I, an apostle—I hold the truth! When he spoke of the *brothers* who were with him, he manifested his union with *all of those* whom he had converted. This was but the beginning:

> I am astonished that you are so quickly deserting the one who called you in the grace of Christ and are turning to a different gospel—not that there is another gospel, but there are some who are confusing you and want to pervert the gospel of Christ. But even if we or an angel from heaven should proclaim to you a gospel contrary to what we proclaimed to you, let that one be accursed! (Gal 1:6–8)

He, Paul, would not compromise. And he explained: "For I want you to know, brothers and sisters, that the gospel that was proclaimed by me is not of human origin; for I did not receive it from a human source, nor was I taught it, but I received it through a revelation of Jesus Christ" (Gal 1:11–12). He did not evoke the road to Damascus at random. Paul insisted on vividly remarking that if the Twelve, for the most part, had followed and heard Jesus, if certain members among them had the distinguished privilege of having seen him risen, he, Paul, enjoyed a unique exception: Jesus had manifested himself personally for him alone.

Paul struck as he knew how to strike:

> You foolish Galatians! Who has bewitched you? It was before your eyes that Jesus Christ was publicly exhibited as crucified! The only thing I want to learn from you is this: Did you receive the Spirit by doing works of the law or by believing what you heard? Are you so foolish? Having started with the Spirit, are you now ending with the flesh? Did you experience so much for nothing?—if it really was for nothing. Well then, does God supply you with the Spirit and work miracles among you by your doing the works of the law, or by your believing what you have heard? (3:1–5)

He threw this at the Judaizers who identified with the heritage of Abraham:

"The scripture, foreseeing that God would justify the Gentiles by faith, declared the gospel beforehand to Abraham, saying, *'All the Gentiles shall be blessed in you.'*[9] For this reason, those who believe are blessed with Abraham who believed" (3:8–9)—which, let us acknowledge, cut short his competitors' argument. He confirmed his advantage:

Christ redeemed us from the curse of the law by becoming a curse for us—for it is written, *"Cursed is everyone who hangs on a tree"*[10]—in order that in Christ Jesus the blessing of Abraham might come to the Gentiles, so that we might receive the promise of the Spirit through faith (3:13–14).

A solemn warning followed:

Formerly, when you did not know God, you were enslaved to beings that by nature are not gods. Now, however, that you have come to know God, or rather to be known by God, how can you turn back again to the weak and beggarly elemental spirits? How can you want to be enslaved to them again? You are observing special days, and months, and seasons, and years. I am afraid that my work for you may have been wasted!

Friends, I beg you, become as I am, for I also have become as you are. You have done me no wrong.... [You] welcomed me as an angel of God, as Christ Jesus. What has become of the good will you felt? For I testify that, had it been possible, you would have torn out your eyes and given them to me. Have I now become your enemy by telling you the truth?

They make much of you, but for no good purpose; they want to exclude you, so that you may make much of them. It is good to be made much of for a good purpose at all times, and not only when I am present with you. My little children, for whom I am again in the pain of childbirth until Christ is formed in you, I wish I were present with you now and could change my tone, for I am perplexed about you (4:8–20).

We could almost cite this entire letter. How he moves us, this unyielding Paul, who, in dictating, humbled himself by recognizing the inadequacy of his style! How he begrudged those who had come to sow anguish among them! "You were running well; who prevented you from obeying the truth? Such persuasion does not come from the one who calls you. A little yeast leavens the whole batch of dough. I am confident about you in the Lord that you will not think otherwise. But whoever it is that is confusing you will pay the penalty" (5:7–10).

Here I pose a question: to which Galatia does Paul address a letter of this kind, where invective adjoins the declaration of love? Galatia extended over a vast territory. It is obvious that a great majority of the population never knew this famous text. The churches established at Iconium, Lystra, Derbe, and Pisidian Antioch remained too small to be privileged addressees. The most likely hypothesis is that Paul had the text carried by one of his disciples to the different overseers who themselves broadcasted it verbally. Jurgen Becker indicates that it is a matter of "the only *encycli-*

cal letter from the hands of Paul" and also "the earliest witness presenting in the most explicit way the message of the apostle relative to justification."

It would be unforgivable not to cite certain formulas from the Letter to the Galatians:

"It is no longer I who live, but it is Christ who lives in me" (2:20). "For you were called to freedom, brothers and sisters" (5:13). "For the whole law is summed up in a single commandment, *'You shall love your neighbor as yourself'*" (5:14).[11]

It is impossible to read the Letter to the Galatians and not be carried away by Paul's torrent or take his side in his rage to be heard. It was a matter of life and death for the Galatians, but as much for him. How could the scribe follow the vehemence of Paul's thought? We can't seem to catch our breath until the moment of its conclusion. We see Paul practically tearing the pen from the scribe's hand:

> See what large letters I make when I am writing in my own hand! It is those who want to make a good showing in the flesh that try to compel you to be circumcised—only that they may not be persecuted for the cross of Christ. Even the circumcised do not themselves obey the law, but they want you to be circumcised so that they may boast about your flesh. May I never boast of anything except the cross of our Lord Jesus Christ, by which the world has been crucified to me, and I do the world. For neither circumcision or uncircumcision is anything, but a new creation is everything! As for those who will follow this rule—peace among them, and mercy, and upon the Israel of God.
>
> From now on, let no one make trouble for me, for I carry the marks of Jesus branded on my body. May the grace of our Lord Jesus Christ be with your spirit, brothers and sisters. Amen (6:11–17).

He is harsh, merciless, admirable. We cannot but find ourselves in agreement with Renan, when he writes of this letter that we can "compare it, save for the art of writing, to the most beautiful of classical works," and that in it "[Paul's] impetuous nature is painted in letters of fire."

WHO WON, PAUL or the Judaizers? In this matter, each one can go with his or her preference. Most believe that Paul's victory was complete, searching for proof in the fact that his relations with the Galatians were never interrupted. Meanwhile, Simon Legasse, one of the most recent and most expert commentators on Paul, remains in doubt: "The First Letter of Peter includes among its recipients the pagan Christians of Galatia." Until the fall of Jerusalem in 70, the Judaizing church would retain over the region a sort of jealous authority. We must wait until the end of the first century for the Judaizers and the pagan Christians to risk a reconciliation. But this—we remain astonished by it—would work to the detriment of Paul, who would be thrown back into the shadows for an entire century. Similarly in Corinth, with unbelievable cynicism the church would swear that it owed its origin to Peter, as well as to Paul.

When the Church later became concerned about sorting out the authentic texts of its history and the apocrypha, it gave back to Paul his importance by recognizing the value of his writings as foundational for Christian theology.

In prison Paul waged his final battle—and what a battle! Many indications lead us to believe that at the very moment he was dictating the Letter to the Galatians, his life was in danger. He himself would recall the crucial role his fellow tentmakers played: "Greet Prisca and Aquila, who work with me in Christ Jesus, and who risked their necks for my life, to whom not only I give thanks but also all the churches of the Gentiles" (Rom 16:3–4). Did they try to help him escape? Some scholars think so.

It was not a leader of the church surrounded by the veneration of the faithful who left Ephesus, but a man hunted down.

11

THE ROAD TO JERUSALEM

Surrounding the man from Tarsus, now almost fifty years old, a handful of the faithful walked alongside the sea. The coastal route passed through Smyrna, avoiding Pergamum, and stretched around the Gulf of Edremit. They were going toward Troas. The little man had decided to return to Macedonia and then to Achaia, this sort of false island attached to southern Greece by the isthmus of Corinth.

He had made no secret that his next goal was Jerusalem. And they had heard him murmur, "After I have gone there, I must also see Rome."[1]

Did he have a presentiment that Rome would one day be the rallying point of Christians? His apostolate had always expressed itself as an eternal march forward. The Damascus road had sent him on the roads of the world. He saw as awaiting his coming all those countries that had not yet heard about Christ.

He would write to the Romans: "But now, with no further place for me in these regions, I desire, as I have for many years, to come to you..." (15:23).

A new obsession occupied the man who walked. Since the conference of Jerusalem an idea had germinated to take up a great collection for the mother church. Paul and Barnabas had offered to collect funds for it in the name of the community of Antioch. Whatever was said about it, the promise did not figure among the conditions of the peace agreement. Personally Paul considered himself committed. In Ephesus he had decided to act; the collection would concern the churches of Asia Minor and Greece. Paul wanted to forget that the church of Jerusalem might be at the root of his recent troubles. This collection would concretize Isaiah's prophecy on the unity of believers.

To whom would it go? Paul specified it himself: to the saints—that is to say, the Christians—"the poor among the saints at Jerusalem" (Rom 15:26). Formerly in Jewish society, few people were very rich and few were very poor. From century to century, the gap had widened. At the time of Paul, Jerusalem swarmed with beggars, including those Galileans who had come to follow Jesus and who, after his crucifixion, had remained obstinately in the city of David. They were still there, their families dying of hunger. The mother church did her best to help them, but her resources remained very few. Paul repeated that the other churches, wherever they were, had the duty to help the mother church: "They were pleased to do this, and indeed they owe it to them; for if the Gentiles have come to share in their spiritual blessings, they ought also to be of service to them in material things" (Rom 15:27).

Throwing himself body and soul into this mission, Paul proposed to the Corinthians the example of the Macedonians, who "during a severe ordeal of affliction" and despite "extreme poverty" had "overflowed in a wealth of generosity." Let the Corinthians imitate them! (2 Cor 8:2)

But the Corinthians were not ready for this. Far from it. In each community Paul gave instructions so threatening they resembled the orders of a military chief. The Corinthians were to economize week after week and to hoard the money while they waited for him to come in person—he alone, Paul—to supervise the operation and to choose those who would make up the escort that he himself would lead to Jerusalem. Such a way of acting was totally at odds with the custom the synagogues had practiced until then for the transfer of annual contributions destined for the Temple: the notables of each city themselves took charge and, until the moment of their expedition, managed the sums collected. To the extent that a person showed himself favorable in principle to the collection, he challenged the apostle's pretension in considering himself solely responsible for the project. Even more serious, this criticism came as much from converts of Jewish origin as from "God-fearers."

To tell the truth, this new crisis masked another bitterness, older and moreover contradictory. Paul had never until then accepted financial help from the Christians of Corinth. Instead of admiring him for this, they appeared offended. With what right did he refuse a spontaneous gift that could have permitted him to live only for his mission? He wanted to live from the work of his hands? Was this not pride? In spite of Paul's forceful response—"Am I not free? Am I not an apostle?" (1 Cor 9:1)—this attitude had unleashed a hostility that was never extinguished. The ultimate irony was that the messengers he dispatched regularly to Corinth, after he was away from the Corinthians, would themselves be brought to solicit financial help, and it would not be given to them. The Corinthians understood none of this—let's try to put ourselves in their place—and their wrath grew accordingly.

Paul was now reproached for having fixed for the Christians of Corinth, without consulting them, an amount disproportionate to their means. That the communities saw themselves denied all control scandalized and soon raised the suspicion of possible embezzlement. Briefly, a harmful climate settled in Corinth and Paul was soon informed of it. We see him misunderstood, deceived. As he did each time he found himself in difficulty, he tried to persuade them by writing. He reminded the Corinthians that they had been the first to accept the project. Would they now go back on their commitment? Here the strategist got the better of the combatant. He claimed that he wished only to give an opinion. The Corinthians themselves would decide the amount of their contribution. Other escorts would be chosen, one of them by the churches of Asia, of whom everyone spoke highly:

> Now as you excel in everything—in faith, in speech, in knowledge, in utmost eagerness, and in our love for you—so we want you to excel also in this generous undertaking. I do not say this as a command, but I am testing the genuineness of your love against the earnestness of others. For you know the generous act of our Lord Jesus Christ, that though he was rich, yet for your sakes he became poor, so that by his poverty you might become rich (2 Cor 8:7–9).

Would this letter be enough? Titus, always in Corinth, was charged with defending its content.

PAUL WAS ALWAYS on the move. All the landscapes he crossed evoke some part of his passing. Before the site of the Troade took shape, was it possible that Hellespont, the Aegean Sea, the Gulf of Edremit, or Mount Ida did not stir anything within him? No matter, he was especially preoccupied about finding Titus at Troas.

Now Titus was conspicuous by his absence. Paul's anxiety grew: "When I came to Troas to proclaim the good news of Christ, a door was opened for me in the Lord; but my mind could not rest because I did not find my brother Titus there" (2 Cor 2:12–13).

Why was Titus not at the meeting place?

Instead of Titus, Luke arrived unexpectedly. It was thus with the physician, always faithful but too absorbed by his other occupations to be predictable. Arriving from Philippi, he had crossed the Aegean Sea to rejoin a small group who were already in Troas and whose names he gave us: Sopater from Beroea; Aristarchus and Secundus from Thessalonica; Gaius from Derbe; Timothy, Tychicus, and Trophimus from Asia (cf. Acts 20:4–5): evidently a gathering of "escorts" for the funds of the collection.

Luke would remember having stopped for a week in Troas. During that time he witnessed an incident that he would never forget:

> On the first day of the week, when we met to break bread, Paul was holding a discussion with them; since he intended to leave the next day, he continued speaking until midnight. There were many lamps in the room upstairs where we were meeting. A young man named Eutychus, who was sitting in the window, began to sink off into a deep sleep while Paul talked still longer.

Luke, we see, has lost nothing of his qualities as a chronicler, not excepting the irony. In the eighteenth century, Jonathan Swift, famous author of *Gulliver's Travels,* but also most senior member of Saint Patrick's in Dublin, chose as a theme for one of his sermons: "On sleeping in church." In it he referred to Eutychus' accident to show that even Saint Paul put his listeners to sleep.

Another detail survives: under the influence of the soporific sermon, the unfortunate Eutychus fell from three stories. He was believed to be dead. Paul ran down the stairs and, taking him in his arms, cried out to reassure those who were despairing: "Do not be alarmed, for his life is in him."

"Then Paul went upstairs," Luke continues, "and after he had broken bread and eaten, he continued to converse with them until dawn; then he left. Meanwhile they had taken the boy away alive and were not a little comforted" (Acts 20:7–12).

AND STILL TITUS never came! Unable to wait any longer, Paul set sail before the expected moment. Passing anew through Europe, he disembarked in Neapolis as he had done before. He couldn't wait for Titus, but Paul hated missing him.

We have no indication of the itinerary he would follow. We must believe that he went first to Philippi where, after so many obstacles, he could finally hope to find some comfort. Dear Philippians! Even for these exemplary faithful Paul showed the anxiety that from now on would trouble him. "Beware of the dogs, beware of the evil workers, beware of those who mutilate the flesh!" (Phil 3:2)

He left, resuming contact with the communities of Thessalonica and Beroea. Did he advance up to the coast of the Adriatic? "...So that from Jerusalem and as far around as Illyricum I have fully proclaimed the good news of Christ" (Rom 15:19).

Without our being able really to follow his exact steps, he went, came, stopped, preached, exhorted, debated. Anxiety consumed him: where was Titus? What was Titus doing? In the Second Letter to the Corinthians, Paul would come back to this difficult period: "For even when we came into Macedonia, our bodies had no rest, but we were afflicted in every way—disputes without and fears within" (7:5).

Finally Titus arrived! And the news was good! The faithful among the faithful had negotiated new rules for the collection. Titus had put an end to the rebellion while making them recognize Paul's exclusive authority—a remarkable success! He had even succeeded in making the faithful he had won back publicly disavow the Judaizers.

Paul did not delay in showing his joy and his gratitude to the Corinthians: "But God who consoles the downcast, consoled us by the arrival of Titus, and not only by his coming, but also by the consolation with which he was consoled about you." Because they were ashamed, the converts of Corinth had wept!

> Now I rejoice, not because you were grieved, but because your grief led to repentance.... For godly grief produces a repentance that leads to salvation and leaves no regret, but worldly grief produces death. For see what earnestness this godly grief has produced in you, what eagerness to clear yourselves, what indignation, what alarm, what longing, what zeal, what punishment!

The conclusion was laconic in the apostle's perfect style: "At every point you have proved yourselves guiltless in the matter" (2 Cor 7:6–11).

In rereading the same letter, it is impossible not to be struck by this unshakable man letting himself go, even as the crisis lessened, to confide that his heart remained heavy and his soul disenchanted.

I wish you would bear with me in a little foolishness. Do bear with me! I feel a divine jealousy for you, for I promised you in marriage to one husband, to present you as a chaste virgin to Christ. But I am afraid that as the serpent deceived Eve by its cunning, your thoughts will be led astray from a sincere and pure devotion to Christ. For if someone comes and proclaims another Jesus than the one we proclaimed, or if you receive a different spirit from the one you received, or a different gospel from the one you accepted, you submit to it readily enough.

To moan a long time was not like him. He shook himself to return to himself. "I think that I am not in the least inferior to these super-apostles.[2] I may be untrained in speech, but not in knowledge" (2 Cor 11:1–6).

PAUL PASSED THE WINTER of 55–56 in Macedonia. His resolution was unrelenting: he would himself bring the amount of the collection to Jerusalem. Was it to supervise the gathering of funds or to test the level of his popularity that he decided to pass through Corinth?

Undoubtedly the season again prohibited navigation, so he chose a land route. He crossed Thessalonica from north to south and went along the coast of Attica, necessarily taking the narrow pass of Thermopylae. Would he continue toward Athens? Never! Without being able to escape the great shadow of Oedipus, Paul cut through Thebes. After the fortress of Eleutherae, the route descended toward Eleusis. And, behold, the isthmus that no longer held a secret for him.

At Cenchraea, which he reached at the beginning of the summer, how could he not be struck by the dear memory of Prisca and Aquila? The friendly couple had returned to Rome. Naturally his steps found the road of the upper city, so often covered since his first stay there. Nothing of the great city had changed. The heat turned it into a furnace in the middle of the day. The summit of the Acrocorinth was as haunting as always . The erotic temple perched on it was as irritating.

What welcome would they reserve for him? He wondered.

Gaius opened his arms to him. Paul would say that he was his host and that of "the whole church" (Rom 16:23). The man was attached to him by sacred ties: Paul had baptized him with his hand. Comforted by the disavowal of the Judaizers, the apostle no longer thought about a general reconciliation. The summer would be dedicated to it. Paul intended to use an ancient practice already mentioned in Deuteronomy: if two elders were in open conflict, they could demand arbitration. Was this on Paul's part the beginning of a capitulation? Not at all. He was always Paul; he announced baldly that he did not envisage arbitration except in defending himself tooth and nail. This position of the apostle who they believed had quieted down would produce the worst of effects: the Judaizers would retake the advantage.

Paul had lost the game. Corinth was no longer his city. When, in the fall, he packed his bags and returned to the port of Cenchraea, how else can we imagine him but in despair? He would need long weeks to recover his peace of soul. Winter was beginning, but he couldn't travel. He felt the need to write a new letter that would reorder his certainties. Until then he had always acted out of a sense of urgency. Sometimes he had to encourage the faith of the flock; sometimes he had to battle his adversaries. Each time he went to the essential, striking blow for blow, driving in the nail of his doctrine. The form? Without importance. At Cenchraea he had time. He would construct an account as Gamaliel his master had taught him to compose one. Everything he believed would be said there.

Before beginning to work, he summoned the scribe Tertius to his side. He dictated. Little by little he would forge, according to Luther, "the heart and the marrow of all the books." Paul wrote the Letter to the Romans, the indisputable monument of his correspondence.

What inspiration already in his first lines:

> Paul, a servant of Jesus Christ, called to be an apostle, set apart for the gospel of God, which he promised beforehand through his prophets in the holy scriptures, the gospel concerning his Son, who was descended from David according to the flesh and was declared to be Son of God with power according to the spirit of holiness by resurrection from the dead, Jesus Christ our Lord, through whom we have received grace and apostleship to bring about the obedience of faith among all the Gentiles for the sake of his name, including yourselves who are called to belong to Jesus Christ, To all God's beloved in Rome, who are called to be saints: Grace to you and peace from God our Father and the Lord Jesus Christ (1:1–7).

From the great—the very great—Saint Paul. What is missing here is the equivalent of what could be found at the head of all the other Letters: the address, *praescriptio,* to one church. The reason is again very simple: the church of Rome did not yet exist.

Who brought Christianity to Rome? Let us not forget the great movement that, many times a year, attracted the Jews of the Diaspora to Jerusalem, why would those of Rome have absented themselves from it?

Having left to pray at the Temple, they returned talking only about Jesus, the Messiah finally incarnate. They hastened to inform the nearest synagogue of this, troubling some, irritating others. No apparent organization was put in place. Today we believe in the development of small independent groups, at the heart of which currents of faith would have been established, somewhat disparate, which, lacking any hierarchy, is not surprising.

Who informed Paul of the existence of Christians in Rome? One passage in the letter explained that, wanting to reach Spain, he would need help, probably financial. Another passage—the comparison between the weak and the strong—seemed to indicate a knowledge of the religious specifics of the *Urbs*. Would Aquila and Priscilla have informed him of these? Yet none of this reveals the identity of the addressees. To whom was Paul writing?

Dieter Hildebrandt, whose power of analysis and originality I like, has formulated in this respect a hypothesis that summarizes a single phrase: this "mountain," this "massif of inaccessible heights" would never have been meant for the Romans alone. And here Hildebrandt strikes his readers with one of his shortcuts that I find enchanting: "By its title it is one of the greatest bluffs in the literature of its time."

He explains. It was necessary in the Pauline work to have a writing intended for the city *par excellence,* center of the world, quintessence of power, home of civilization. Since the letter was not addressed to some group in Rome—*ad Romanos*—it was necessary that the title acknowledge its grandeur and its glitz. Moreover, such was the primacy that posterity gave to it. That the Fathers of the Church put it in the first place, when it should have been in the last, reinforces this reasoning.

Even so we push the paradox too far. The Romans were concerned with the same issues that the Philippians, the Corinthians, or the Galatians were. The difference was that Paul knew each of these correspondents—but not the Romans. So he felt no need whatsoever, according to his old habit, to engage in controversy with them, nor even to seek to impose his authority upon them. Hence an extremely new tone of which one could say, in comparing it to that of the Letter to the

IN THE
FOOTSTEPS OF
PAUL

The well in Tarsus from which, according to tradition, Paul drank.

The Damascus Gate in the city of Jerusalem.

A panoramic view of the Old City of Jerusalem.

Roman arches in the city of Caesaria.

Antioch in Pisidia: the remains of the Church of St. Peter, on the site of the synagogue where Paul preached (Acts 13:13–52).

Excavations at the city of Philippi.

The Lechaion Road leading into the city of Corinth.

The theater at Ephesus where a riot broke out because Paul's preaching disturbed the merchants who sold statues of the goddess Diana (Acts 19:21–41).

The marketplace of the city of Ephesus.

The city of Colossae once stood on this location. The site was later abandoned.

The ruins of the city of Miletus, where Paul took leave of his flock
(Acts 20:17–21).

Ruins of ancient Rome.

The Mamertine prison in Rome where Paul awaited his execution.

The interior of the Mamertine prison.

PAUL

IN ART
&
ICONOGRAPHY

Fourth-century fresco of St. Paul from the Catacombs
of the Via Dino Compagni, Rome.

Detail of St. Paul from a sixth-century mosaic
in the Church of St. Vitalis, Ravenna, Italy.

Painting of St. Paul by Giotto (1267–1337), located in the upper church
of the Basilica of St. Francis, Assisi, Italy.

Thirteenth-century painting of St. Paul by Meliore di Jacopo
in the Church of St. Leonino Panzano, Montefalcone, Italy.

St. Paul Visiting St. Peter in Prison, fresco by Masaccio (1424–1428), in the
Church of Santa Maria del Carmine, Brancacci Chapel, Florence, Italy.

Fifteenth-century painting of St. Paul by Girolamo da Salerno
in the Cava dei Tirreni, Salerno, Italy.

St. Paul in prison by Rembrandt (1608–1669), Stuttgart, Germany.

Saints Peter and Paul by El Greco (1541–1614),
in the National Museum of Stockholm, Sweden.

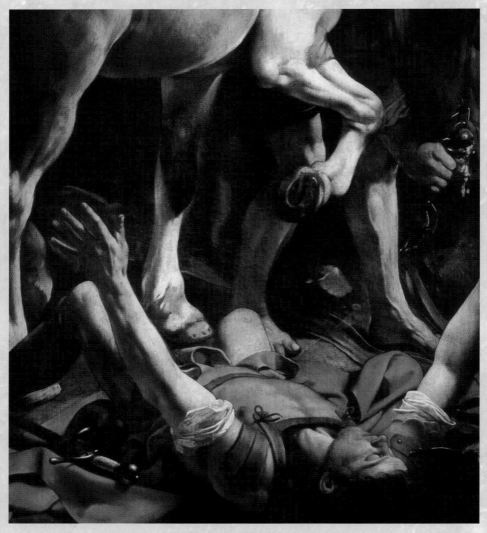

The Conversion of St. Paul by Caravaggio (1571–1610),
in the Church of Santa Maria del Popolo, Rome.

St. Paul on a journey by Trento Longaretti (b. 1916),
in the Collection of Modern Religious Art, the Vatican.

St. Paul: Light of Christ, by Fratel Venzo (1977),
in the Collection of Modern Religious Art, the Vatican.

The Conversion of St. Paul by Armando Bandinelli (1977),
in the Collection of Modern Religious Art, the Vatican.

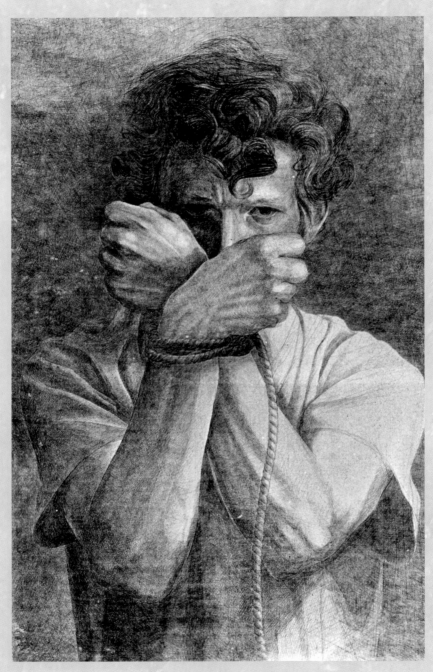

St. Paul in Chains by Robert Baxter (1977),
in the Collection of Modern Religious Art, the Vatican.

Twentieth-century icon of St. Paul's Martyrdom,
Monastery of Cerrnica, Bucharest, Romania.

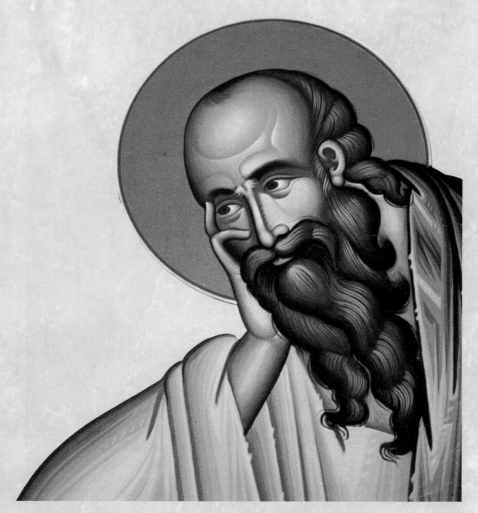

Icon of St. Paul in the Church of St. Demetrius, Thessalonica.

Galatians, that the latter "was the Rhone before Lake Lemanus; the Epistle to the Romans, the same river after Geneva."[3]

Given the impossibility of giving a face to those who would read him, Paul addressed himself to several publics at the same time. One exegete sees him with "one eye trained on Jewish Christians, the other on the believers from among the pagans." It is uncertain that these two groups were the sole addressees. Paul spoke alternately to pagans and to Christians, but we sense that the traditional Jews, so numerous in Rome, were always in the back of his mind. Even more, we see the Judaizers suddenly appearing, a constant danger that he would dread. As in the past, they preceded him to Rome. To whom was the letter addressed? To all of these groups.

Paul naturally gave priority to the Christians: "First, I thank my God through Jesus Christ for all of you, because your faith is proclaimed throughout the world." We find again his taste for emphasis: "Without ceasing I remember you always in my prayers, asking that by God's will I may somehow at last succeed in coming to you." He expands his intention. "I want you to know, brothers and sisters, that I have often intended to come to you (but thus far have been prevented), in order that I may reap some harvest among you as I have among the rest of the Gentiles. I am a debtor both to Greeks and to barbarians, both to the wise and to the foolish—hence my eagerness to proclaim the gospel to you also who are in Rome" (Rom 1:8, 9–10, 13–15).

At first glance, it is hard to understand why, speaking to pagans, Paul gave so much space to Jewish questions. In truth, he was faithful to himself: he could not announce the message that would regenerate humanity except by presenting its initiator Jesus as a Jew, the Son of the God of the Jews. In other words, in accepting Jesus the pagans had to accept Judaism at the same time—with the exception, certainly, of the restricting rules that we know of.

Contrary to the criticism of the nineteenth century, which saw in the Letter to the Romans a doctrinal writing, that of the twentieth century discerned in it a plan for reconciliation. Did the dreadful conflicts tearing Christianity apart threaten the converts of Rome? Paul may have feared so. Hence this distressing plea: "Welcome one another, therefore, just as Christ has welcomed you, for the glory of God" (Rom 15:7).

The Letter to the Romans wielded immense historic influence, not so much when it was written but in the time to come. In the fifth century, when the serious controversies on the free nature of salvation began, theologians would draw from it to put an end to them. In the sixteenth century, it would be the epicenter of Luther's reform. Calvin would discover in it themes for his doctrine: "Whoever achieves its true understanding has like an open door to enter as far as the most secret treasure of the Scriptures."[4]

ALL READERS OF the Letter to the Romans are struck by its particularly rigorous framework. That does not mean, however, that it contains a theological overview, a veritable "summary of Christian doctrine," as has often been maintained. Today's exegetes would say it has too many gaps.

It is impossible to adequately cover the details of the Pauline argumentation contained in the letter; it would be necessary to cite it in its entirety. In fact, it can be divided into two parts: the first (chapters 1–9) proposes to the Christian the means of gaining salvation; the second (chapters 9–15) looks for the reasons why the Jewish contemporaries of Jesus rejected this salvation as it was offered to them.

The first four chapters illustrate the will of God not to impose himself on men and women but to let them find him. If certain people had recognized his goodness, many others had ignored him, which had offended him and provoked his wrath:

> For the wrath of God is revealed from heaven against all ungodliness and wickedness of those who by their wickedness suppress the truth. For what can be known about God is plain to them.... Ever since the creation of the world his eternal power and divine nature, invisible though they are, have been understood and seen through the things he has made. So they are without excuse; for though they knew God, they did not honor him as God or give thanks to him (1:18–21).

Paul acknowledged that the pagans had been able to feel the presence of God. But he judged that, not having drawn any salutary consequence from it, they deserved the wrath of God. The Jews? They had received so many favors from the Creator that, since they transgressed the Law, all indulgence must be denied them:

> You, then, that teach others, will you not teach yourself? While you preach against stealing, do you steal? You that forbid adultery, do you commit adultery? You that abhor idols, do you rob temples? You that boast in the law, do you dishonor God by breaking the law? For as it is written, *The name of God is blasphemed among the Gentiles because of you.* Circumcision indeed is of value if you obey the law; but if you break the law, your circumcision has become uncircumcision (2:21–25).

With true obstinacy, Paul returned to the case of his Jewish brothers: "What then? Are we any better off? No, not at all; for we have already charged that all, both Jews and Greeks, are under the power of sin" (3:9). This leads to Paul's key point:

> Now we know that whatever the law says, it speaks to those who are under the law, so that every mouth may be silenced, and the whole world may be held accountable to God. For *no human being will be justified in his sight* by deeds prescribed by the law, for through the law comes the knowledge of sin. But now...the righteousness of God has been disclosed...the righteousness of God through faith in Jesus Christ for all who believe. For there is no distinction, since all have sinned and fall short of the glory of God; they are now justified by his grace as a gift, through the redemption that is in Christ Jesus (3:19–24).

Paul leaned on the case of Abraham whose *faith was reckoned to him as righteousness:* "How then was it reckoned to him? Was it before or after he had been circumcised? It was not after, but before he was circumcised" (4:10). Always this paradox of proposing to pagans a new religion through an ancient religion they did not know, unless it proves that those commentators are right who hold that the Letter to the Romans was only written to reconcile Judaizers and pagan Christians in Rome.

In the same Chapter 3, a few words seemingly without brilliance would suddenly reveal themselves as the Everest of Paul's thought: "For we hold that a person is justified by faith apart from works prescribed by law" (3:28).

Here we have come to what theologians have called "justification by faith." By substituting faith for the law as the source of salvation, Paul invited the human race to a revolution. Now, fifteen centuries of Christianity would put this major position in brackets.

Why? Because justification by faith was too radical to be followed. Because human nature was so made that a person who was not taken up totally by divine grace would always believe that, if he or she lived a life conformed to the commandments, that person would be saved. The church in Rome applied itself to drawing up a catalog of the narrow rules that Christians must obey. These "commandments" were inscribed in the same line as those Moses had promulgated.

A German monk named Luther, furious at the sale of indulgences, had only to read attentively the Letter to the Romans to be persuaded that he had found the answer: faith was essential, works were merely secondary.

Yet perhaps the affair was not as clear as he had supposed it. Paul had added: "Do we then overthrow the law by this faith? By no means! On the contrary, we uphold the law" (3:31). Luther would oppose this apparent contradiction with the verdict: "Faith fulfills all the laws. Works do not fulfill the law in any way."

Around this theme, people would go further and further. In the twentieth century, militant revolutionaries would identify with Saint Paul. Others would not hesitate to compare him to Lenin. We must always return to Talleyrand: "Everything that is exaggerated is insignificant."

CHAPTERS 5 THROUGH 8 of Paul's letter plunge directly into what a convert or a pagan ready to convert must know. Baptism allowed the believer to escape from sin, since Jesus, in offering himself on the cross, had erased Adam's fault and granted eternal life to Jews as well as to pagans. Chapter 9 returns to the pagans who, not seeking faith, had received it, while "Israel, who did strive for the righteousness that is based on the law, did not succeed in fulfilling that law. Why not? Because they did not strive for it on the basis of faith, but as if it were based on works" (9:31–32).

Chapters 10 and 11 suggest other reflections on what brought pagans and Jews together and apart. Chapter 12 returns to the obligations to which Christians must submit in order to please God:

> Let love be genuine; hate what is evil, hold fast to what is good; love one another with mutual affection; outdo one another in showing honor. Do not lag in zeal, be ardent in spirit, serve the Lord. Rejoice in hope, be patient in suffering, persevere in prayer. Contribute to the needs of the saints; extend hospitality to strangers. Bless those who persecute you; bless and do not curse them. Rejoice with those who rejoice, weep with those who weep. Live in harmony with one another; do not be haughty, but associate with the lowly; *do not claim to be wiser than you are.* Do not repay anyone evil for evil, *but take thought for what is noble in the sight of all.* If it is possible, so far as it depends on you, live peaceably with all (12:9–18).

Chapter 13 invites Christians to be subject to authority, "for there is no authority except from God." It is necessary to render to each one what is his due: "taxes, revenue, respect, honor" (13:1, 7). The Christian must be filled with certitude that the return of Christ is very near: on this Paul never changes. Chapter 14 recommends welcoming "those who are weak in faith, but not for the purpose of quarreling over opinions," and prescribes not judging one's brother: "Blessed are those who have no reason to condemn themselves because of what they approve" (14:1, 22). Chapter 15 recommends love among Christians, the source of spiritual happiness: "May the God of hope fill you with all joy and peace in believing, so that you may abound in hope by the power of the Holy Spirit" (15:13).

Paul then reverts to his immediate plan, the journey to Jerusalem, and does not conceal in any way that he fears its dangers:

> I appeal to you, brothers and sisters, by our Lord Jesus Christ and by the love of the Spirit, to join me in earnest prayer to God on my behalf, that I may be rescued from the unbelievers in Judea, and that my ministry to Jerusalem may be acceptable to the saints, so that by God's will I may come to you with joy and be refreshed in your company. The God of peace be with all of you. Amen (15:30–31).

To consider the Letter to the Romans as Paul's last will and testament is by no means a flight of fancy; never again would he compose a text of this magnitude.

After soaring so high, it is difficult for us to return to the collection; to tear oneself away from such sublime ideas to listen to the jingle of gold or silver pieces! But he, Paul, insisted on his collection. From now on it would overtake everything. The closer he came to departure, the more anguish rose in him, of which Luke would report so many signs. Paul knew perfectly that the Judaizers hated him and that they wielded great power in Jerusalem. And he was going to Jerusalem.

Then did no one advise him against such a journey, so provocative and perilous? The answer resounds: it was said ten times, twenty times. True to himself, Paul did not want to hear any of it.

SURPRISINGLY, HE DID not put to sea at Cenchreae. A study on the climatology of the Aegean Sea has shown that winds from the north, which blew in the eastern Mediterranean during the heatwave, would have made the crossing unbearable.[5] Hardly anyone today believes the "plot" reported by Luke: "He was about to set sail for Syria when a plot was made against him by the Jews, and so he decided to return through Macedonia" (Acts 20:3).[6] We know he must have traveled 441 miles northward. Didn't all this walking begin to exhaust him? Several of his escort had left ahead of him and awaited Paul in Asia.

In the episode that follows, Luke passes from "he" to "we"; once again we are dealing with an eyewitness. I may have so analyzed, so discussed, and so contradicted this narrative that I have ended up totally disconcerting the reader. I believe absolutely that Luke has erected here a sort of production, classic in antiquity, suitable for adapting the events described to the portrait he wants to impose on Paul. He seems to ignore the whole collection, his opponents say, and makes only one passing allusion to it. Could Luke have participated in this journey and not seen that remitting funds to the church in Jerusalem was the apostle's only goal? He devoted himself to showing Paul celebrating Passover and desiring above all to be in Jerusalem for Pentecost. But in the Letter to the Galatians, Paul strongly condemned the calendar of Jewish feasts that the Judaizers wanted to introduce in Galatia. This only means that Luke was not infallible. Writing a long time after Paul's death, he wanted to show the apostle going deliberately to meet the danger, in order to offer an example to future generations. Because of this must we doubt everything Luke has proposed?

I frankly admit to finding in Luke a truth that satisfies me. The series of events, the precision unceasingly delivered, and the small details that sound right encourage me to take him as a principal guide—even if it naturally means attempting to keep his words in check.

IN ASSOS, ON tHE NORTHERN COAST of the Bay of Edremit, the distribution of the collection would take place. We know from Flavius Josephus the rules that were followed in this situation: the different moneys were reduced to gold, and it was shared out among the different members of the escort. The pieces were sewn into the garments of each person, taking care that it would not jangle at the least gesture. All untimely noise must be excluded.

We know the stages of the journey: from Assos the ship headed toward Mytilene, port of the great island of Lesbos, where it reached, in one stop, the island of Chio, the homeland of Homer. One stop to Samos, facing the mount Mycale, one port of call at Trogyllion, and arrival at Milet.

The expansion of this large city situated a few leagues from Ephesus, formerly metropolis of Ionia, dated from the time of Alexander. The export of products from the naturally rich hinterland and the pilgrimages to the sanctuary of Apollo of Didyma made its four ports wealthy. It is useless to look for them today, because the deposits of the Meander Valley have gradually pushed back the city to the land's interior. Only the tiers of the theater, built in the second and third centuries, bear witness to a grandeur that has since disappeared.

"Paul," says Luke, "had decided to sail past Ephesus, so that he might not have to [waste] time in Asia" (Acts 20:16). Waste time? The truth was that Paul had no desire to throw himself into the wolf's mouth. He wished to meet with certain of his faithful and he called them to join him; nothing could be more natural than that. Luke applies himself to reconstructing once more the intentions Paul would have kept before them:

"You yourselves know how I lived among you the entire time from the first day that I set foot in Asia, serving the Lord with all humility and with tears, enduring the trials that came to me through the plots of the Jews. I did not shrink from doing anything helpful, proclaiming the message to you and teaching you publicly and from house to house, as I testified to both Jews and Greeks about repentance toward God and faith toward our Lord Jesus.

"And now, as a captive of the Spirit,[7] I am on my way to Jerusalem, not knowing what will happen to me there, except that the Holy Spirit testifies to me in every city that imprisonment and persecutions are waiting for me. But I do not count my life of any value to myself, if only I may finish my course and the ministry that I received from the Lord Jesus, to testify to the good news of God's grace.

"And now I know that none of you, among whom I have gone about proclaiming the kingdom, will ever see my face again. Therefore I declare to you this day that I am not responsible for the blood of any of you, for I did not shrink from declaring to you the whole purpose of God. Keep watch over yourselves and over all the flock, of which the Holy Spirit has made you overseers, to shepherd the church of God that he obtained with the blood of his own Son.

"I know that after I have gone, savage wolves will come in among you, not sparing the flock. Some even from your own group will come distorting the truth in order to entice the disciples to follow them. Therefore be alert, remembering that for three years I did not cease night or day to warn everyone with tears. And now I commend you to God and to the message of his grace, a message that is able to build you up and to give you the inheritance among all who are sanctified.

"I coveted no one's silver or gold or clothing. You know for yourselves that I worked with my own hands to support myself and my companions. In all this I have given you an example that by such work we must support the weak, remembering the words of the Lord Jesus, for he himself said, 'It is more blessed to give than to receive'" (Acts 20:18–35).

Paul fell silent. His emotion was intense: "There was much weeping among them all; they embraced Paul and kissed him, grieving especially because of what he had said, that they would not see him again. Then they brought him to the ship" (Acts 20:37–38).

Favorable winds blew until Cos. The next day they reached Rhodes and came to Patara on the third day, on the coast of Lycia. Since their ship was continuing its voyage to another destination, they found another that was loading for Tyre, where they disembarked after a voyage of six to seven days. A Christian church already existed there and, in welcoming Paul, they showed a concern about his fate almost equal to that of his companions. Each person attempted to divert him from going to Jerusalem. Throughout a whole week he seemed not to hear. At the end of the seven days, he took his leave and rented a small boat that landed in Ptolemais, where Saint Joan of Arc of the crusaders would rise. The next day Paul and his companions set off again for Caesarea, walking thirty-four miles. They would stay there several days with the deacon Philip, one of Stephen's seven: here, then, implacable foes reconciled.

A certain Agabus, described as "a prophet of Judea," appeared suddenly one morning in a state of extreme excitement. He theatrically brandished a belt, with which he tied Paul's feet and hands, and swore that the Jews of Jerusalem would use the same to deliver him into the hands of the pagans; the Holy Spirit had announced this to him. Seeing their fears confirmed, Luke and his companions begged Paul to retrace his steps. He confined himself to answering, "What are you doing, weeping and breaking my heart? For I am ready not only to be bound but even to die in Jerusalem for the name of the Lord Jesus" (Acts 21:13).

It was impossible to convince him. "The Lord's will be done" (Acts 21:13–14). Paul took his leave. The small group set out on the road to Jerusalem.

Going up to Jerusalem is not only an image. Covering sixty-two miles, they sustained a difference in altitude of 2,625 feet. While Paul did not easily become alarmed, as the reader knows well, it is difficult to believe that, as he passed one more time through the gate of the holy city, he was completely unmoved. His escort followed without hurrying: each found himself weighed down by belts filled with gold. They would lodge at the home of a certain Mnason of Cyprus, "an early disciple" (Acts 21:16).

Paul had hardly arrived in Jerusalem when James, the brother of the Lord, invited him to his home. The man from Tarsus complied the next day. For a few minutes a true cordiality reigned. The elders listened eagerly as Paul related what he had accomplished in God's service among the pagans.

Meanwhile, those who had read Paul's letters—it would have been strange if at least snippets had not found their way to Jerusalem—hadn't failed to feel shocked because the "thirteenth apostle" did not seem to consider the practice of the Law as fundamental. Also, where circumcision was concerned, he had set as a rule the simple tolerance that had been granted to him. Had not the head of the church in Jerusalem committed to the Judaizing offensive? Paul admitted that he was no longer subject to the Law (1 Cor 9:20–21; Phil 3:8–9). For the sake of the Gentiles, he favored Christ over the Law. Just one of these behaviors would have been enough for them to denounce him as a renegade.

James seems not to have wanted to draw all the consequences from such a serious report. The indulgence of his welcome, as Luke signaled, gave proof of this. In his eyes Paul must have been an eccentric, one of those ungovernable people to whose errors one is tempted, perhaps more than for another, to turn a blind eye. Moreover, how could they minimize the work he had accomplished? The biographer of James appears stricken by Luke's silence on the matter of the collection: not a word about its organization, the problems that it posed, and now its remittance. Could it be that James did not even accept it? "Without a doubt Luke would not have failed to mention its acceptance, which would have constituted an additional witness in favor of the unity of the church. It is possible, however, that James, before making a decision concerning the collection, asked Paul to demonstrate his fidelity to the Law."[8] Luke, on the other hand, shows that the first congratulations were followed by the expression of a worry born of Paul's ignorance about himself: he did not understand that his reputation was detestable not only among the Christians of Jerusalem, almost unanimously Judaizers, but among all Jews. The unfortunate thing, he was told, was that most everyone knew perfectly well the doctrine he recommended: "They have been told about you that you teach all the Jews living among the Gentiles to forsake Moses, and that you tell them not to circumcise their children or observe the customs. What then is to be done? They will certainly hear that you have come" (Acts 21:21–22).

Someone—James—found the solution: Paul must carry out a purification. Fortunately, it happened that four men were preparing as well to purify themselves, a rite that required that they pray in the Temple for seven days and that they shave their heads. Let Paul join them and take care of their expenses during the coming week.

"Thus all will know that there is nothing in what they have been told about you, but that you yourself observe and guard the law" (Acts 21:24).

Paul came around to accepting their advice. When he left James, did he wonder whether he was seeing him for the last time? In the company of the four designated men, Paul went to the Temple to fix the date on which the offering could be presented and the purification obtained.

The seven days came to an end. Then, in the Temple—a stroke of bad luck!—the Jews of Asia recognized him. Anger stirred within them. Paul! They seized him and incited the crowd, crying, "Fellow Israelites, help! This is the man who is teaching everyone everywhere against our people, our law, and this place; more than that, he has actually brought Greeks into the temple and has defiled this holy place" (Acts 21:28).

In the city Paul had been accompanied by Trophimus from Ephesus, one of his eight travel companions. Certain people hurried to deduce from this that Paul had led him into the Temple and even shown him into the court, where only the Jews could enter.

Until now we have seen Judaizers take it out on Paul, a "pagan Christian." In Jerusalem, it is now the Jews faithful to the tradition of Moses who are taking it out on a "renegade."

It is necessary to know the framework in which this confrontation occurred. The reader already knows that the Temple of Jerusalem was composed of two parts: the court of the Gentiles, where anyone could go, and the sacred enclosure where only Jews could enter. This was surrounded by a low wall made of stones, the *soreg,* marking the limit beyond which one could not cross if one was not a Jew. Here and there, this warning was posted in Greek and Latin: "It is forbidden to strangers to cross the barrier and enter the enclosure of the sanctuary. Whoever is caught will himself be responsible for the death that will follow." Note that the warning was categorical. So Paul was not only accused of treason toward his religion but, more serious still, of having deliberately violated the sacred enclosure by bringing a pagan there.

It is impossible that Paul could have shown himself capable of such a provocation, because for him the Temple remained a sacred place. We can only suppose that he inadvertently led his companion too close to the low wall, after which the rumor could have arisen from those whom the crowds accepted with much more eagerness because they were false.

Luke, who loves to amplify numbers, tells us that "all the city was aroused and the people rushed together" (Acts 21:30). We translate this to mean that many people were in the Temple that day and they reacted vigorously.

They seized Paul and dragged him out of the Temple, immediately closing its doors. They beat him. Would they drive him to a city gate to stone him outside the walls? It was Paul's luck that the entire scene unfolded two steps away from the Fortress Antonia: the news reached the tribune of the cohort that "all Jerusalem was in an uproar" (Acts 21:31).

We know the name of the tribune, Claudius Lysias. Commander of the cohort whose barracks were in the Fortress Antonia—around six hundred men—he immediately ordered one of the centurions to assemble the strength of one company to hold the demonstrators at bay. Always the *Pax Romana,* the order that no one had the right to infringe. For Paul the outcome was positive, because the crowd stopped hitting him. Having rushed up, the tribune ordered that the object of so much noise be chained. The questions he asked showed him to be at least perplexed: "Who is this man? What has he done?" (cf. Acts 21:33)

The answers rang out, clashed, and contradicted themselves. It was impossible to understand anything in the middle of such an uproar. For the sake of peace, the tribune ordered that Paul be led into the fortress.

When the detachment began dutifully to climb the stairs, the crowd attempted to tear the prisoner away to lynch him. Making a barricade for him with their bodies, the soldiers took hold of Paul, lifted him over their heads, and threw him into the fortress, after which they closed the doors. Then a furious clamor rang out:

"Away with him!" (Acts 21:34–36)

12

THE MAN IN CHAINS

Adjoining the Temple at its northwest corner, the Fortress Antonia, or the *Antonia* as it was known in Jerusalem, overwhelmed the quarter with its enormous walls and towers, the highest of which measured forty yards. From the top of the confines of the Temple, pilgrims could see therein the barracks, offices, residence of the tribune, and the interior courts. The Roman cohort practiced there each day along with a contingent of cavalry, totaling a thousand men. As in all the provinces administered by a procurator, most auxiliary troops were recruited on site. Only non-Jews need apply here.

It was clear that the large staircase that permitted one to pass directly from the Antonia to the esplanade of the Temple was conceived as a guarantee against disorder. The riot that had just erupted was the best proof of this. Lysias, the tribune, did not know what to think; why had this little bald man provoked such trouble?

For one moment, he thought he was dealing with that Jew from Egypt who, proclaiming on his part the kingdom of God, had stirred up against the Romans thousands of zealots, implacably opposed to the occupiers. No one could say what happened to this imposter after his defeat. At the least sign of a riot he seemed to have reappeared.

"May I say something to you?"

Thus the man now addressed him. In Greek.

"Do you know Greek?"

Paul confirmed he did and, giving his name, formulated a demand that added to the tribune's perplexity. He said, "I beg you, let me speak to the people" (Acts 21:37–39).

Contrary to all expectations, the tribune agreed. The doors were reopened. It was an astounding image: this prisoner weighted with chains who stood to harangue the furious crowd that the Roman legionnaires contained only with difficulty. Their great surprise at the prisoner's reappearance made them fall silent. "There was a great hush," says Luke (Acts 21:40).

"Brothers and fathers, listen to the defense that I now make before you.... I am a Jew, born in Tarsus in Cilicia, but brought up in this city..." (Acts 22:1, 3).

A long discourse followed, in which Paul exposed the principal phases of his life, the story of his conversion and of his call, including his encounter with the risen Jesus on the road to Damascus. He then came to his return to Jerusalem:

> "After I had returned to Jerusalem and while I was praying in the temple, I fell into a trance and saw Jesus saying to me, 'Hurry and get out of Jerusalem quickly, because they will not accept your testimony about me.' And I said, 'Lord, they themselves know that in every synagogue I imprisoned and beat those who believed in you. And while the blood of your witness Stephen was shed, I myself was standing by, approving and keeping the coats of those who killed him.' Then he said to me, 'Go, for I will send you far away to the Gentiles.'"

He would not go further. The crowd cut him off, insulting him and crying for his death, "'Away with such a fellow from the earth! For he should not be allowed to live.' And...they were shouting, throwing off their cloaks, and tossing dust into the air..." (Acts 22:17–23).

Exasperated, the tribune cut them short. He ordered the troops to bring Paul back into the fortress.

Both of them stood there, face to face in the moistness of four stone walls. Divided between disdain and disbelief, the tribune struggled to clarify things in his own mind: he had to tear this man's secret from him, if he had one. Before withdrawing, the tribune ordered the soldiers to make the troublemaker ready; scourging almost always preceded the interrogation of a suspect. This time, things happened quickly: the prisoner was stripped and tied, and a legionnaire had already grabbed hold of the handle of the whip when Paul—we can picture him expressing himself with deliberate calm—asked a question of the centurion on duty, "Is it legal for you to flog a Roman citizen who is uncondemned?"

Instantly the centurion stopped the arm of the soldier who was ready to strike, and hurried to inform the tribune, "What are you about to do? This man is a Roman citizen!"

A Roman citizen! The tribune immediately weighed the risk he had almost taken. What a way to compromise his advancement! He hastened back to the prisoner and asked him, "Tell me, are you a Roman citizen?"

"Yes."

"It cost me a large sum of money to get my citizenship."

"But I was born a citizen."

Flogging was now out of the question. Paul would pass the night in a fortress cell (Acts 22:24–29).

THE TRIBUNE, FOR his part, must not have slept well. He could not of his own initiative release a man who had aroused the hatred of the people, but did he have the right to keep Paul in prison without judging him? Since the man was Jewish, why not hand him over to the authority that appeared most competent, the Sanhedrin?

The highest judicial and religious authority of the country was no longer seated in the Temple but outside its walls, very near to the tower of Herod, an obvious calculation of Roman power. In case of difficulty, public force could more easily gain access to this place.

Paul's chains were removed. He was dragged before seventy-one persons full of their right to "speak" the Torah. The high priest Ananias had held his position for ten years, and enjoyed a genuine consideration.

The accused was informed that he had to mount his own defense. Luke describes Paul "looking intently at the council." The image is a beautiful one. It evokes the picture of an unarmed man confronting a pack who want his ruin, yet whom he keeps at bay by the sheer force of his look. Paul raised his voice and said, "Brothers, up to this day I have lived my life with a clear conscience before God...."

Ananias reacted brutally: *This man is lying!* Tradition required that a liar be struck on the mouth. Ananias ordered that such be done. By the strength of his voice Paul caused the man who approached him to recoil. He thundered, "God will strike you, you whitewashed wall! Are you sitting there to judge me according to the law, and yet in violation of the law you order me to be struck?"

From the heart of the seventy-one present there rose a horrified protest: "Do you dare to insult God's high priest?"

Paul's voice softened: "I did not realize, brothers, that he was high priest; for it is written, 'You shall not speak evil of a leader of your people.'"

The Sanhedrin seemed reassured: at least the man knew the Scriptures. However, it was clear that not everyone had the same reaction. The assembly was divided between Sadducees and Pharisees. Paul had noticed this since his arrival. "The Sadducees," Luke notes, "say that there is no resurrection, or angel, or spirit; but the Pharisees acknowledge all three." The moment had come to make good use of this knowledge: "Brothers, I am a Pharisee, a son of Pharisees. I am on trial concerning the hope of the resurrection of the dead."

"Then a great clamor arose," Luke summarizes. The Sadducees were scandalized, but the Pharisees' reply was no less vehement: "We find nothing wrong with this man. What if a spirit or an angel has spoken to him?" (Acts 23:1–9)

The two factions seemed ready to come to blows. We can imagine the tribune on the verge of alarm. What if his prisoner should be a victim of the confrontation? One brief command and the legionnaires threw Paul outside the hall. We can almost hear the tribune's shamed voice: "Let him return to the fortress!"

Would the account of the hearing that we have just read contain as many details if Luke had not witnessed it? Questions can be raised, and they have certainly not been lacking: did the chief of a Roman garrison have the power to convoke the Sanhedrin? Was it possible that Paul really did not recognize the high priest who was presiding? Would Ananias have consented to having a tribune present while Paul was being interrogated? Yet these objections do not prevent the whole account, beginning with the dialogue, from sounding right.

Having spread immediately, the affair of the Sanhedrin would rekindle the anger of the Judaizers. Forty from among them would meet at dawn and swear to make Paul, the Jewish traitor, pass from life to death. They committed themselves by an oath "to taste no food until we have killed Paul." The tactic they imagined was as old as history: they would intercept Paul, bring him to a safe place, and finish him off once and for all. These conspirators were ingenious. A delegation of "defenders of the Law" got a hearing with a Sanhedrin badly set back by what had happened to it. The delegation strongly urged it to request of Claudius Lysias a new appearance of the man from Tarsus. The tribune had confided to the Sanhedrin the mission of judging the renegade, and the scandalous behavior of the accused had prevented the assembly from managing its task well. This plan delighted some priests. How could the tribune refuse a new appearance? For the Judaizers, Paul's fate was settled.

They were mistaken. In this story full of new developments, a young man suddenly appears whom we only glimpsed in the first pages of Acts: Paul's nephew, who lived in Jerusalem. How did he get wind of this plot? The only thing we know for certain is that he managed to enter the fortress and warn his uncle. Paul reacted immediately. He ordered one of the centurions, "Take this young man to the tribune, for he has something to report to him."

By the tone used, the centurion understood that he must not argue. He accompanied the prisoner's nephew to the tribune's home. In a few moments the entire matter was exposed. It was punctuated with a warning: "But do not be persuaded by them, for more than forty of their men are lying in ambush for him.... They are ready now and are waiting for your consent."

This Lysias was a man of decision. Realizing that a threat could compromise the security of the Empire, he would have Paul transferred to Caesarea into the hands of the procurator of Judaea, who held supreme judicial power in the province. He summoned two centurions in an instant and commanded, "Get ready to leave by nine o'clock tonight for Caesarea with two hundred soldiers, seventy horsemen, and two hundred spearmen. Also provide mounts for Paul to ride, and take him safely to Felix the governor" (Acts 23:12–24).

The importance of such an escort, not very credible *a priori*, can be explained by the number of the declared conspirators. Without a doubt, they would have to be broken up by force. Lysias took the time to write to the procurator Felix in order to put the whole affair before him. Thus he gave to Paul an *elogium* that, until his arrival in Caesarea, could be shown to each Roman in a position of responsibility.

Paul was astride the entire night. Dawn was breaking when, at the halfway point on the road that separated Jerusalem from Caesarea, they stopped at Antipatris, another foundation of Herod the Great. Paul could rest there a few hours.

All danger having disappeared, the major part of the escort was sent back to Jerusalem. Only the cavalry detachment accompanied the apostle all the way to Caesarea (Acts 23:26–32).

In the fourth century B.C., the king of Sidon founded a modest port. A village gradually grew up around it and took the name the Tower of Strabo. In 63, Pompey granted it autonomy and, seven years later, the emperor Augustus gave it to Herod the Great, who discovered there a building site worthy of him. Through immense labors a jetty rose from the sea and behind it a port was dug, 100 feet in depth, "more spacious than Pireas," which sheltered ships from the most powerful storms. It took twelve years to finish the city. The royal palace was built of white marble. Herod made it the capital of his kingdom and, in honor of Caesar Augustus, baptized it Caesarea. Its splendors filled the people of that time with awe.

When Paul in chains entered the city, Herod's palace had become the official residence of the Roman procurators of Judea. Antonius Felix now occupied it.

Freed by the emperor Claudius, Felix was brother of this Pallas who had pushed Agrippina and Nero to the highest rank. Without nuance Tacitus depicted Felix as being "cruel and debauched, exercising the royal power with the soul of a slave." He had became the procurator of Judea in 53 at the request of the ex-high priest Jonathan. Felix's brutality to the people gave rise to serious trouble on several occasions. His only feat was to crush the incredible "army" gathered in the desert by this "Jew from Egypt," with whom Ananias had oddly enough confused Paul. What a film we could make from this unlikely odyssey! The "Jew from Egypt" in question had presented himself as another Joshua, predicting that he would cause the walls of Jerusalem to fall; the procurator had massacred four hundred of his supporters and captured two hundred others, who were immediately sold as slaves. The rest, fleeing to the desert, had beaten records set at Olympus.

The procurator's reputation was so bad that Tacitus accused him of having committed robbery for his own sake by recruiting several of the *sicarii*. These Illyrian pirates armed themselves with small daggers (*sica*) and sold themselves to the highest bidder. Flavius Josephus dedicated several pages to the affair. As for Suetonius, he described Felix as "husband to three queens": the first without importance; the second being nothing less than the granddaughter of Antony and Cleopatra; and the third, the young and ravishing Drusilla, daughter of Agrippa I and sister of Agrippa II. The procurator took her away from her first husband, the king of Emesa, with the help of a magician named Simon. Without the least concern about her legitimate husband, Felix hastened to make her his wife.

WHEN THE APOSTLE tendered his *elogium* to the procurator, we can well imagine Felix read it without joy. Why had Lysias inflicted such a chore upon him? He eventually admitted that the tribune could not have acted otherwise. He said to Paul, "I will give you a hearing when your accusers arrive" (Acts 23:35).

As proof that he understood the prisoner's uniqueness, Felix would keep Paul in his own palace, chained but able to move. Several of Paul's disciples would catch up with him and install themselves in the city.

Five days later, a delegation of Jews from Jerusalem arrived, headed by the high priest Ananias. An attorney named Tertullus accompanied them. Most likely certain disciples of the apostle were authorized to attend the audience, again allowing Luke to retrace the scene like a professional journalist. Tertullus opened fire by brazenly scorning Paul and only addressing Felix:

> "Your Excellency, because of you we have long enjoyed peace, and reforms have been made for this people because of your foresight. We welcome this in every way and everywhere with utmost gratitude. But, to detain you no further, I beg you to hear us briefly with your customary graciousness. We have, in fact, found this man a pestilent fellow, an agitator among all the Jews throughout the world, and a ringleader of the sect of the Nazarenes.[1] He even tried to profane the temple, and so we seized him. By examining him yourself you will be able to learn from him concerning everything of which we accuse him" (Acts 24:2b–8).

Unanimously the Jewish delegation affirmed that those were exactly the charges against Paul. At the procurator's signal, Paul began his difficult task and started to speak. As the attorney had done, Paul addressed Felix only:

> "I cheerfully make my defense, knowing that for many years you have been a judge over this nation. As you can find out, it is not more than twelve days since I went up to worship in Jerusalem. They did not find me disputing with anyone in the temple or stirring up a crowd either in the synagogues or throughout the city. Neither can they prove to you the charge that they now bring against me. But this I admit to you, that according to the Way, which they call a sect, I worship the God of our ancestors, believing everything laid down according to the law or written in the prophets. I have a hope in God—a hope that they themselves also accept—that there will be a resurrection of both the righteous and the unrighteous. Therefore I do my best always to have a clear conscience toward God and all people. Now after some years I came to bring alms to my nation and to offer sacrifices. While I was doing this, they found me in the temple, completing the rite of purification, without any crowd or disturbance. But there were some Jews from Asia—they ought to be here before you to make an accusation, if they have anything against me. Or let these men here tell what crime they had found when I stood before the council, unless it was this one sentence that I called out while standing before them, 'It is about the resurrection of the dead that I am on trial before you today'" (Acts 24:10–21).

Paul had finished. Did he convince Felix? Other arguments would be exchanged, supporting either the prosecution or the defense. The procurator gleaned from it that Paul was a Christian, and not among the least of them. Finding that the proceeding was dragging on, Felix swiftly put an end to the debates by declaring to the Jewish delegation, "When Lysias the tribune comes down, I will decide your case" (Acts 24:22).

He ordered the centurion to keep Paul in the palace prison. But, notwithstanding the chains that would remain, the regimen of his captivity would have no unnecessary harshness. His faithful followers would be allowed to look after him.

The centuries and the sand have engulfed the city of Caesarea. After the Second World War, the remains of Herod's jetty were eroded gradually under the assault of the waves. In 1946, excavations were undertaken that the state of Israel has actively pursued since its creation. The result is obvious. A juxtaposed past spreads before our eyes: the ramparts Saint Louis erected blend into what is left of Herod's wall; Herodian foundations support the remains of the Christian cathedral; traces of a Byzantine road flank what remains of the Roman hippodrome. In excavating the Roman theater in 1961, an inscription specifying that the building was dedicated to Tiberius by the *prefaectus* Pontius Pilate was found. This is the oldest existing epigraphic documentation about Pilate.

In the depths of sea and sky, haloed with a dazzling light, the whole place suggests a sort of thirst for life heralding from the beginning of time. Paul lived his imprisonment in this setting. The beauty of the countryside never compensated for his lack of freedom. Only rare occurrences broke the monotony of this captivity.

Shortly after the delegation from Jerusalem departed, Felix summoned Paul to his apartment, and for the first time Paul discovered the beautiful Drusilla. A Jewess, she seemed to have totally ignored the Christians. That she was now determined to interrogate one of them was understandable. That the ever amorous Felix agreed to it would astonish no one. That Paul voluntarily answered her questions—about justice, mastery of instincts, and the judgment that each human being must await from God—was not surprising. Interested at first sight, Felix and Drusilla slowly demurred. Continence especially did not agree with them by any means. Felix cut Paul short, saying, "Go away for the present; when I have an opportunity, I will send for you" (Acts 24:25).

Would a guilty ulterior motive have been tormenting Felix? At the time of Paul's confrontation with his accusers the collection was mentioned. Did the procurator believe that Paul had concealed part of it? Or else did he imagine that Paul's friends had kept it in their possession? If that were the case, they could "ransom" the prisoner. "He hoped that money would be given him by Paul," says Luke, "and for that reason he used to send for him very often and converse with him" (Acts 24:26).

A YEAR PASSED. I see Paul practicing first to control his impatience. As far as colonization was concerned, the basic rule was never modified: to make one's strength felt, but to avoid provoking others head-on. Paul must have hoped that the pressure coming from Jerusalem would eventually end. He was far from everything, weighted with chains, so what could they fear from him? Surely they would forget him, and the procurator would set him free.

Yet all the information that reached Felix proved to him that Paul's situation preoccupied not only the honest and harsh Jews of the Sanhedrin, but also the Judaizing Christians. An unbelievable alliance took shape between the Jews for whom Jesus was nothing and these others who considered the Nazarene as the Messiah announced by God. The already close connections that we see growing stronger between the high priest and James convince us of this. Felix could not have failed to recognize this kind of holy union against Paul. All he could do was open wide his palace to the disciples of the man from Tarsus, who came and went as though they were at home.

In the course of the second year, we can imagine a Paul who was unable to stay still, calling upon the Lord and furious that he received no answer. Paul's life had been sown with visions, yet neither Acts nor the Letters report any from this time.

We can picture Paul facing the sea, its beauty appearing to him now almost as an insult, no longer able to tolerate the white marble walls of Herod's palace; and dreaming perhaps of having at his disposal the strength of Samson to bring down the columns. We see him literally enraged, wandering from room to room, accusing everyone, his disciples as well as orthodox Jews, and then again the Judaizers. He probably found consolation only in the synagogue where, it seems, he was allowed to go. There, having suddenly become like a lamb under the *tallit* that he threw over his shoulders, he proclaimed with an anguished cry the word of God.

Paul only found comfort in the messages he addressed to the churches that he had founded—how could he refrain from writing to them?—and in the visits of the faithful who came at times from far away, such as Macedonia and Asia. Felix's yoke on Palestine proved to be increasingly unbearable. In his *Antiquities,* Flavius Josephus would later denounce Felix's bad administration as much as his anti-Semitism. The authorities in Jerusalem increased their complaints to Rome, where they had a great deal of influence. Felix had gone too far. He risked much. Although Pallas had practically lost his credibility, he managed to save the life of his brother who, in 59 or 60—the date is debated—was replaced by Porcius Festus.

JUST THREE DAYS after his arrival in the province, the new procurator went to Jerusalem. As proof that the hatred directed against Paul had in no way subsided, the chief priests and other notables descended upon Festus to denounce the unbelievable leniency that the prisoner had enjoyed from Felix: "They appealed to him and requested, as a favor to them against Paul, to have him transferred to Jerusalem. They were, in fact, planning an ambush to kill him along the way" (Acts 25:2–3). Festus, who detected the trap, reminded them that Paul's place of detention must remain Caesarea, where Festus himself was preparing to go. Why not accompany him?

"If there is anything wrong about the man, let them accuse him."

The Jewish notables took him at his word. Many of them set out at the same time as Festus. The day after their arrival at Caesarea, the new procurator gave the order to bring Paul to him. Luke describes the scene perfectly: "The Jews who had gone down from Jerusalem surrounded him, bringing many serious charges against him, which they could not prove." Appearing very calm, Paul changed nothing in his defense: "I have in no way committed an offense against the law of the Jews, or against the temple, or against the emperor."

Festus asked him: "Do you wish to go up to Jerusalem and be tried there before me on these charges?"

With impressive swiftness, Paul frustrated the trap, responding, "I am appealing to the emperor's tribunal; this is where I should be tried. I have done no wrong to the Jews, as you very well know. Now if I am in the wrong and have committed something for which I deserve to die, I am not trying to escape death; but if there is nothing to their charges against me, no one can turn me over to them. I appeal to the emperor."

A veritable theatrical coup ensued. We know nothing about the deliberations that followed, but we can guess they were stormy. When the council reconvened, the procurator settled the matter: "You have appealed to the emperor; to the emperor you will go" (Acts 25:5–12)

Some exegetes have doubted the story of the trial that we owe to Luke. They claim that an appeal to the emperor was rarely effective; if it had been practiced often, the Roman tribunes would not have been able to face the upsurge. To this we can respond that such an appeal was an acknowledged right and that the *lex Valeria*, the laws *Porcia* and *Julia*, guaranteed the fate of Roman citizens. Had not Felix himself sent the bandit Eleazar to Rome to be judged there? The fact that Luke searched unceasingly for ways to enlarge Paul's stature does not annul this reality; an appeal to the emperor could legitimately be invoked, and it was.

Sometime later, the Jewish king Agrippa II announced his arrival at Caesarea, where he wanted to stay with his sister Bernice. She would soon meet Titus, son of Vespasian, and the passion that would carry them one to the other would immortalize them both. Festus at once explained to the king Paul's case and the decision that he had made. Interested, Agrippa wished to hear this extraordinary prisoner. "So on the next day Agrippa and Bernice came with great pomp, and they entered the audience hall with the military tribunes and the prominent men of the city. Then...Paul was brought in" (Acts 25:23). Immediately the king demanded that the prisoner make his case. We know the discourse of the man from Tarsus, very long and naturally coming out of Luke's pen. Who would be surprised that he should begin with a recital of the apostle's mission among the pagans and the recollection of his exhortations to "turn toward God by living in a manner that responded to this conversion"? He went on: "To this day I have had help from God, and so I stand here, testifying to both small and great, saying nothing but what the prophets and Moses said would take place: that the Messiah must suffer, and that, by being the first to rise from the dead, he would proclaim light both to our people and to the Gentiles."

This was too much for Festus. He raised his voice and said, "You are out of your mind, Paul! Too much learning is driving you insane!"

Paul ignored Festus. He turned to Agrippa: "Indeed the king knows about these things, and to him I speak freely; for I am certain that none of these things has escaped his notice, for this was not done in a corner. King Agrippa, do you believe the prophets? I know that you believe."

Agrippa preferred to joke. "Are you so quickly persuading me to become a Christian?" he asked.

Paul grew excited: "Whether quickly or not, I pray to God that not only you but also all who are listening to me today might become such as I am—except for these chains."

The audience ended. Agrippa did not conceal the fact that Paul had convinced him of his innocence. "This man is doing nothing to deserve death or imprisonment.... This man could have been set free if he had not appealed to the emperor" (Acts 26:22–32).

THE SUMMER OF 60 ended, and navigation would soon be forbidden. Festus wanted to hurry. They would take advantage of a ship based in Adramyttium, a port of Asia Minor, bound for Lycia. Here Luke again uses the famous "we." He will remain an eyewitness until they arrive in Rome. His account of the voyage contains so many details about ancient navigation that Admiral Nelson, himself familiar with the Mediterranean, would one day go so far as to claim that he had learned his trade from Acts.

When Paul embarked, always in chains, he found on board the ship other prisoners brought there for unstated reasons, who must also have been on their way to Rome. Several soldiers were charged with their surveillance. A centurion named Julius, from the Augustan cohort, commanded them. Aristarchus, a Macedonian from Thessalonica, and certainly Luke received permission to follow their master.

The first port of call was Sidon, modern-day Saida, a Lebanese city. Julius allowed Paul and his companions to go ashore to meet Christians who lived there. They met with happiness and fervor. When they headed for Cyprus, contrary winds forced them to bypass the island toward the west. They had to struggle against them all along the coasts of Cilicia and Pamphylia. It took fifteen days to finally reach the port of Myra, the ship's final destination.

What did the centurion do with his human cargo? By chance, a ship from Alexandria heading for Italy was in port; it was probably one of the ships from Egypt loaded with wheat to feed Rome and Italy. The ship that took on Julius and his prisoners gauged about five hundred tons and, with a tail wind, could cover about six thousand nautical miles (around seven miles) per hour.[2] On embarking, the crew, passengers, prisoners, and soldiers numbered 276 persons on board.

Contrary winds always arose: "We sailed slowly for a number of days and arrived with difficulty off Cnidus" (Acts 27:7). They chose to sail toward the south of Peloponnesus, to the north of Crete. Having only just passed the cape of Salmone at the eastern end of the island, they hugged the southern coast. Near the city of Lasea, they found shelter in a cove called "Fair Havens," known today as Kali Limene. Those whose memory is filled with images from the Acts of the Apostles and who might search for these places today to find the ports—believing them to be well named—set themselves up for a cruel deception: enormous tanks filled with oil now line the coast.

According to the sailing plan conceived at Caesarea, they were very late. Taking into account the bad weather, it was becoming dangerous not to obey the rule—*mare clausum*—which forbade navigation. A debate arose among those who wanted to take to the sea and those who thought it prudent to wait until the month of March. To the surprise of the crew and the soldiers, Paul intervened and said, "Sirs, I can see that the voyage will be with danger and much heavy loss, not only of the cargo and the ship, but also of our lives" (Acts 27:10).

A well-meant warning! In the Second Letter to the Corinthians Paul refers to three shipwrecks that he barely escaped, however, we cannot identify their place or time. It must have been during one of these that he swam "for a night and a day...adrift at sea" (11:25). The captain was not far from sharing this opinion, as did also the cargo overseer, who represented the interests of the ship's owner (let's not forget that rich cargo of wheat). Reckoning that the port was ill-suited for wintering, which was true, the majority decided to seek another mooring. It seemed possible to reach Phoenix on the south of Crete. They would spend the winter there sheltered from the most dangerous winds, those from the north. They lifted anchor.

A small breeze blowing from the south filled the sail and delighted the optimists. But everything changed when they reached open sea. A gigantic storm descended, the kind that sailors call a northeaster. It carried the ship southward with terrifying swiftness. It was impossible to move with the wind; they could barely take in the sail. "We gave way to it," says Luke, "and were driven" (Acts 27:15). This lasted until they came to a small rocky island by the name of Cauda, twenty-five miles south of Crete. Under its lee, the wind lost some of its force. The crew took advantage of the situation to hoist overboard the dinghy attached to the rear; its violent pounding risked breaking the cable. Another part of the crew secured the ship with rigging to protect it from the heavy seas repeatedly striking the hull.

No sooner had they moved away from the island than the violence of the winds once again pushed the ship south. Would they be driven to the coast of Africa? "We were being pounded by the storm so violently," Luke continues, "that on the next day they began to throw the cargo overboard, and on the third day with their own hands they threw the ship's tackle overboard." Clearly the ship had become a kind of wreck. This condition lasted fourteen days and fourteen nights: "...Neither sun nor stars appeared for many days" (Acts 27:18, 20). In the midst of a hundred oppressive tasks, no one ate anything but what they had at hand.

On a bridge swept by furious waters, one can picture Paul suddenly standing up. In the roar of the wind, we can almost him howl:

> "I urge you now to keep up your courage, for there will be no loss of life among you, but only of the ship. For last night there stood by me an angel of the God to whom I belong and whom I worship, and he said to me, 'Do not be afraid, Paul; you must stand before the emperor; and indeed, God has granted safety to all those who are sailing with you.' So keep up your courage, men, for I have faith in God that it will be exactly as I have been told" (Acts 27:22–25).

By the fourteenth day they were still adrift. It was impossible to guide themselves by the stars, for the sky was totally opaque. What to do? "...About midnight the sailors suspected that they were nearing land. So they took soundings and found twenty fathoms; a little farther on they took soundings again and found fifteen fathoms. Fearing that we might run on the rocks, they let down four anchors from the stern and prayed for day to come." At the first light of dawn, Julius' soldiers noticed that the sailors had lowered the dinghy into the sea, evidently with the intention of deserting ship. Promoted to the rank of expert, Paul implored the centurion and his soldiers to stop them: "Unless these men stay in the ship, you cannot be saved."

The soldiers pounced, pushed back the sailors, and adopted a radical solution: they cut the ropes of the dinghy which rapidly disappeared from view (Acts 27:27b–32).

On that miserable wreck, drifting at the mercy of blasts of wind and currents, they swung between hope and anguish. Paul spoke again, "Today is the fourteenth day that you have been in suspense and remaining without food, having eaten nothing. Therefore I urge you to take some food, for it will help you survive."

"After he had said this," Luke attests, "he took bread; and giving thanks to God in the presence of all, he broke it and began to eat. Then all of them were encouraged and took food for themselves. After they had satisfied their hunger, they lightened the ship by throwing the wheat into the sea" (Acts 27:33–36, 38). The poor cargo overseer!

It was day. A land was in sight that the most experienced among the sailors did not recognize. They made out a bay at the end of which they guessed lay a beach. The captain resolved to run the ship aground. They abandoned the anchors in the sea, dropped the rear oars that served as a rudder, hoisted the small front sail, and headed for the beach. Well before they reached it, a terrible shock caused the hull to shake: they had bumped into a sandbank! The prow had sunk deeply into it. Under the heavy sea, the stern fell apart. If they did not jump overboard into the water, they risked remaining captives of a ship that would cave in on them. On the question of the fate reserved for the prisoners, the soldiers reacted furiously: "We must kill them all! Or else they will escape by swimming away!"

Although the ship was literally breaking apart, Julius vehemently opposed this. He ordered those who knew how to swim to jump into the water and make for land. The others had only to hang on to the wreck. "And so it was that all were brought safely to land" (Acts 27:44). Of the 276 people aboard, not one was lost.

THIS ISLAND THAT NO ONE had recognized was Malta. The ship had covered nearly 470 miles since it left Crete. The Maltese welcomed them warmly. The village inhabitants threw themselves into the waters and helped the swimmers reach shore. A freezing rain had begun to fall. The Maltese ran to get wood and managed to light a fire so that the survivors could warm themselves. Paul gathered a stick of dead wood without noticing that a viper was wrapping itself around his arm. He contented himself with shaking the creature into the fire without its biting him. A cry full of astonishment and admiration rose from these Maltese, who were pagans: "He is a god!"

A certain man whom Acts designates as "the leading man of the island" (28:7), and who lived nearby, presented himself in his turn. Roman since 218 B.C., Malta came under the province of Sicily. This man named Publius must have been the administrator delegated by the praetor; inscriptions attest that he was indeed a "leading man of Malta." Publius was distressed and busied himself with bringing the shipwreck survivors into his home, where they could change their clothes, dry off, and recover their strength. He would put them up for three days.

We do not know much about how all these people were accommodated after that: in the "grotto of Saint Paul" what is shown today? The crew, the prisoners, and their guards had to await the arrival of spring, three months away.

In the twenty-first century, Malta remains entirely filled with reminders of Saint Paul. The place where he is supposed to have landed was given the name *Saint Paul's Bay,* and the tourist never ceases to meet churches, chapels, and statues of the saint along the way.

Who found the ship needed to repatriate 276 persons? Probably the centurion Julius whom, oddly enough, Luke no longer mentions by name. He seems to have faded from the chronicler's horizon, as have the Roman soldiers and their prisoners. Let the reader be assured: there exist several versions of the New Testament of which Acts is an integral part. There is an "Antiochene" text, an "Alexandrian" text, and a text called "Western." It is in this last text that we rediscover the centurion lost from sight. We even see him escort Paul all the way to Rome and, having arrived at his destination, hand him over to "the prefect of the praetorium."

Paul was fifty-three years old when, at the beginning of March 61, he boarded a ship placed under the sign of *Dioscures,* also known as Castor and Pollux. Being from the homeport of Alexandria, it was a cereal cargo ship that, probably following a mishap or an unexpected delay, had been forced to winter in Malta without being able to deliver its cargo in Italy. We would have to imagine a ship literally loaded with merchandise and passengers beyond what was reasonable. They sailed toward Sicily.

To reach Syracuse—sixty thousand nautical miles—would not have required more than twenty-four hours. They stopped there three days. The trees were in bloom, the air was light, the crowd pressed at the agora or at the doors of the theater. Would Paul have enjoyed this sight—"the most beautiful of all the Greek cities"—that aroused the enthusiasm of Cicero? His interest certainly must have carried him especially to the Christian community, founded by a disciple of Peter. Paul must have found the vitality of this community irresistible.

Having taken to the sea again, they sailed alongside the coast to arrive at Rhegium, known today as Reggio di Calabria, in Italy's southwest. Not far from there, toward the north, the sailors located the famous whirlpool containing small boats that let themselves be trapped between Charybdis and Scylla. The port of call required just one day. The next day, when entering the Gulf of Naples, did Paul remember the *Georgics* of Virgil, composed on these very shores?

Carried by a good wind from the south, the travelers would cover in less than two days the 217 miles that separated them from Puteoli, otherwise known as Pozzuoli. Paul's contemporaries praised this port as "the first warehouse of Rome and of Italy, the most important of Egypt and the Orient"; two hundred thousand tons of grain, mainly Egyptian, were unloaded there each year. Even more cosmopolitan than its counterparts in the Mediterranean, the city had long welcomed all the peoples of the East—among them many Jews—who gradually had established their trading posts and introduced their gods.

They were surprised to find a small Christian community in Pozzuoli.[3] "There we found believers," Luke says, "and were invited to stay with them for seven days" (Acts 28:14). Taking advantage of the rest that the centurion wanted to obtain for his prisoners, Paul was thus able to remain several days with his brothers in Christ. After this, prisoners and guards would have to start in the direction of this *Urbs* that Paul had hoped so ardently to find when, three years earlier, he had written to the Romans the letter in which he had put so much of himself.

The best way to follow Paul's footsteps on these trails is to take the poet Horace as a guide. Arriving in Brinidisi, he denounced the "wily innkeepers" along the *Via Appia:* at the stopping places, he confronted their crudeness, the beds where vermin swarmed, and the disgusting food. To find sleep required a miracle. And that was the case for a prestigious and wealthy traveler. We hardly dare think of the fate that awaited prisoners.

Paul moved toward Rome, closely guarded and in chains. How could we not remember the Letter to Philemon, written not that long before, in which we could almost discern his moan: "And I, Paul, do this as an old man..." (v. 9). How long had it been since he had walked jauntily toward those he wanted to convert? Then he had felt himself capable of confronting all obstacles, whether from Satan or from men. Three years later, he was sure of winning over the Romans to the true Light and of confronting victoriously, on their turf, these Judaizers who created problems for him everywhere. Where was he now on this route along which he dragged himself?

To reach Rome by way of Capua the group had to cover 155 miles on foot—as always. We can hardly go astray as to the stages of Paul's journey: first he took the *Via Campana*, then left it in Capua for the *Via Appia*. Opened in 312 B.C. at the initiative of the censor Appius Claudius, it aroused the enthusiasm—or the irony?—of Titus Livy: "The name of Appius will be celebrated by future generations because he built a road."

Not everything was cause for gloom throughout this forced march: spring covered the cherry and apple trees with flowers, turning the air fragrant. Paul had all the leisure to count the famous *milliariae*, these boundary markers erected at every Roman mile. Enormous stone cylinders, each one measured close to six feet in height and weighed at least two tons. What traveler would not count these milestones—first of all to calculate the road left behind, and even more to estimate the road that remained to be covered?

By way of a bridge called Tirenus—which Cicero alluded to in one of his letters—the *Via* crossed the Garigliano, which the French troops of General Juin would make famous much later, in the Second World War. Along the riverbank stretched the city of Minturna, whose forum, aqueduct, baths, and theater have survived. Under the ever vigilant guard of the centurion, the group reached Formiae, where Cicero was assassinated, then Itria. Squeezed into a narrow pass and separated by a ravine, two parallel routes ran over several miles. Paul walked on.

Beyond Fundi, the *Via Appia* avoided the large neighboring lake. Enormous blocks of stone protected it from the mischief of this particularly capricious length of water. When the *Via* climbed the hill of Anxur where, on the heights dominating Terracina, a famous temple was dedicated to Jupiter, Paul ignored the image of the king of Olympus.

They walked along the Gulf of Gaeta. How many milestones still to come before Rome? From the moment of their entrance into Latium, each man in the group feared the test of crossing the famous Pontinus swamp, from which myriads of mosquitoes arose. Before Emperor Augustus had had the canal dug, the swamp was almost insurmountable. Since then, travelers—Paul and his companions like others before them—were installed on a barge drawn by mules. Finally a little rest?

At the Forum of Appius, who were the strangers who advanced before Paul and his companions? They introduced themselves as being sent by the church of Rome. Here exegetes again criticize Luke, who relates the episode: how would these Roman Christians have been informed of a prisoner's arrival? Why would they in his honor run forty-five miles going and another coming back? I answer these skeptics with great simplicity: And why not? At Three Taverns, thirty miles from Rome, a new delegation arrived: "On seeing them, Paul thanked God and took courage" (Acts 28:15). After Albano, the *Via* widened to thirteen feet. The slabs became enormous. If Paul was thirsty, he could slake his thirst at the fountains raised here and there along the route. As for the admirable marble statues that lined the road from then on, I would tend to think Paul looked away from their nudity.

Through the Porta Capena, near the Circus Maximus and the imperial palace, Paul of Tarsus, a man in chains among other men in chains, entered Rome.

13

PAUL AND NERO

Enter Lucius Domitius Ahenobarbus, having become by adoption Tiberius Claudius Nero, whom we call Nero. He had just turned twenty years old. Later, Suetonius would portray him for posterity: of average size, with "blue eyes, a thick neck, prominent stomach, spindly legs." "Naturally red complexion," according to Lucian of Samosata. "Golden-haired," according to his fans; "redheaded" according to others.

Incapable of selecting from among his disorganized ambitions, this young man really did not know whether he should aspire to the empire of the world or seek to make himself admired as the greatest artist of his time. He was not yet one of the most hateful men of history. But he was not far from it.

LIMPING AMONG THE other prisoners, Paul was surely not wondering about such a dilemma. His ordeal concerned his end. How old he felt!

The others devoured the Seven Hills with their eyes. From there, since the she-wolf had suckled Remus and Romulus, the legend of Rome had taken off. Paul must have only turned a sad and vague look at the marvels that surrounded him. Since the end of the Republic, the *Urbs* had changed profoundly. As an aedile charged by Augustus, Agrippa had multiplied the fountains, constructed the first thermal baths, and erected the Pantheon. The temple of Apollo dominated the Palatine Hill. In the field of Mars the altar of Peace (*Ara pacis augustae*) and the mausoleum of

Augustus told of the magnificence of the first emperor. To win the favor of the citizens and that of the common people, a theater and a library had been built. At his arrival, Augustus had found a city of stone and brick; to his successors, he bequeathed a city of marble.[1]

And yet, surprisingly these superb monuments were lost, hidden in an insane labyrinth: an anarchy of "narrow roads, winding, rambling, as though drawn without a ruler."[2] The rapidity with which the fire of 64 would spread would be due essentially to this pile-up, as Tacitus confirms.

The guards doubled their vigilance. Nothing could facilitate the escape of a prisoner more than these congested roads, where wagons, litters, sedans, knights, and pedestrians all mingled; it was a river that ran all day long, a din that never died, even when night fell.

An old man in chains soliloquized: to sleep, to sleep, to sleep.

Where were the Jews of Rome? Philo shows them at the beginning of the first century having chosen to take up residence beyond the Tiber, particularly in the quarter named the Trastevere. In the middle of the tanneries, the workshops, and the gut work rooms, laborers dressed in rags practiced all the small trades of the period: "hawkers or sellers of matches," as the learned Charles Perrot portrays them; "beggars and popular storytellers, such as the woman who sold dreams and taught her children to beg in a good location, and charlatans or swindlers." Rare were those who escaped this subproletariat and these shantytowns before their time: tentmakers, but also schoolteachers, actors, even a poet named Menophilos whom Martial would accuse of having stolen his verses.

Most of the Jews were freedmen. "Brought to Italy as prisoners of war," Philo of Alexandria explains, "they had been freed by their masters, without being made to change any of their traditions."[3] For this abundance, Flavius Josephus draws the following explanation: the Jews arrived as slaves and were redeemed by free Jews.[4] There were hardly any Jews among the higher classes, although Nero's wife Poppaea was considered to have been "sympathetic," and Fulvia, the wife of a senator, was attached to the Jewish cause. Ovid makes fun of these women who pretended to gather on the Sabbath.[5] Research confirms that the vast majority of the Jews of Rome were "financially and culturally poor."

THE CENTURION KNEW where he was going; he had to lead all his people to the imperial Forum, more precisely to the general quarter of the praetorian guard. At the moment of separation, we can imagine jeering as well as effusiveness from prisoners to guards. There is every indication that the praetorium prefect in charge of the strangers closely examined Paul's case. The prisoner's status as a Roman citizen would have protected him from incarceration in a city jail, a prospect justifiably feared. "When we came into Rome," says Luke, "Paul was allowed to live by himself, with the soldier who was guarding him" (Acts 28:16). Was this the result of the special status he enjoyed in appealing to the emperor?

Even though he was exempt from prison, Paul remained in chains. They would never again be removed from him.[6] We must refer here once more to *The Acts of Paul,* which makes up for the silence of other sources of information. It also evokes the particular residence made available to Paul in Rome: "He hired a barn outside Rome, where with the brethren he taught the word of truth."[7]

People have often been astonished that, preferring them to the Christians, Paul had always insisted first and foremost on meeting the Jewish community of Rome. He had acted thus from the beginning of his mission. Why would he change now? Three days after having occupied his house, he invited the "local leaders of the Jews" to meet with him. It is necessary to read attentively the strange clarification that he addressed to them:

> "Brothers, though I had done nothing against our people or the customs of our ancestors, yet I was arrested in Jerusalem and handed over to the Romans. When they had examined me, the Romans wanted to release me, because there was no reason for the death penalty in my case. But when the Jews objected, I was compelled to appeal to the emperor—even though I had no charge to bring against my nation.[8] For this reason therefore I have asked to see you and speak with you, since it is for the sake of the hope of Israel that I am bound with this chain."

The Jews' answer is very clear: "We have received no letters from Judea about you, and none of the brothers coming here has reported or spoken anything evil about you. But we would like to hear from you what you think, for with regard to this sect we know that everywhere it is spoken against" (Acts 28:17–22).

Other meetings would follow between Paul and those to whom he remained so close. He would so like to persuade these Jews! He felt so much in agreement with them! Their prayers were his, his love of God was theirs. Would they finally recognize that the God of the Jews had gone to the extreme of compassion for his people by sending them his own Son? Let them do so, and Judaism would conquer the world. "From morning until evening he [Paul] explained the matter to them, testifying to the kingdom of God and trying to convince them about Jesus both from the law of Moses and from the prophets. Some were convinced by what he had said, while others refused to believe. So they disagreed with each other" (Acts 28:23–25).

Paul's final response is heartrending. As his visitors left, he chanted a text from the prophet Isaiah (6:9–10; cf. Acts 28:26):

> *"Go and say to this people:*
> *'Keep listening, but do not comprehend;*
> *keep looking but do not understand.'*
> *Make the mind of this people dull,*
> *and stop their ears,*
> *and shut their eyes."*

The reader has so often met Luke that he or she will read with gratitude, I am sure, the last lines of the Acts of the Apostles that the chronicler has redacted: "[Paul] lived there two whole years at his own expense and welcomed all who came to him, proclaiming the kingdom of God and teaching about the Lord Jesus Christ with all boldness and without hindrance"[9] (Acts 28:30–31). Nothing more.

Luke leaves us with a huge question mark. If he is often accused of having improvised too much, here he ends his book without having finished it. The explanations offered for this are very naïve, that is, Luke stopped because he had run out of parchment or because he found his book too long. Some would argue that the ending was lost, which makes no sense since we know the care with which the Christians of this time preserved the writings of the first years of the apostolic period. Others imagine that Luke, having left for the East, ignored what happened to Paul. Really? How could the news of Paul's death, an event more significant for Luke than anyone else, not have reached him, thanks to the many comings and goings in the Mediterranean or to the large correspondence between East and West?

An explanation remains that we have no right to exclude. Those who defend it recall that the plan of the Acts of the Apostles, fixed according to the usage of the time, can be read in 1:8. Luke shows the apostles eating with the risen Jesus and asking him this question: "'Lord, is this the time when you will restore the kingdom to Israel?' He replied, 'It is not for you to know the times or periods that the Father has set by his own authority. *But you will receive power when the Holy Spirit has come upon you; and you will be my witnesses in Jerusalem, in all Judea and Samaria, and to the ends of the earth*'" (Acts 1:6–8). The presenters of the TOB[10] insist on explicating this passage: "From Jerusalem and the Jews of the whole world and the pagans, such must be the *space* of the apostolic witness and such is the plan of Acts." Luke in effect leads his hero from Jerusalem to Antioch, from Asia Minor to Greece, and finally as far as Rome. According to Francis Brossier, as soon as Paul arrived in Rome, "the limit of the route announced by Luke had been reached."

In Luke's eyes, his work was done.

IN THE YEAR 62, a message was brought to Rome, news capable of plunging the Christian population into affliction and terror: James, "the brother of the Lord," was dead in Jerusalem, having been stoned at the order of the high priest Ananus.

I envision Paul's grief nurtured by acute though conflicting feelings: the respect borne for this exceptional man in whose veins flowed the blood of Jesus, and the bitter rancor for which we have no right to blame Paul. Calling to mind the close connection with the high priest and the Sanhedrin that James had enjoyed, how do we explain such an unexpected development? Flavius Josephus provides a clear and convincing answer.

The death of the procurator Festus in Jerusalem appears to be at the origin of everything. As soon as Nero was informed of it, he designated a certain Albinus to replace him. Because of the slow means of transportation, several months elapsed between Festus' death and the arrival of Albinus in Judea.

Now during this time, Agrippa II, the king of Galilee and Perea, found himself obliged to appoint a new high priest. He chose a certain Ananus, whom Josephus describes as endowed "with a proud character and remarkable courage," but also "a follower of the doctrine of the Sadducees, who are inflexible in their point of view compared to other Jews." According to Ananus, the error of the Pharisaical high priests had to be put to an end. They believed it was possible to maintain cordial relations with James, but for Ananus this was to betray one's religion. And traitors received the only end they deserved: death.

We know that the Roman procurators did not tolerate any breach of a longstanding ban that decreed the Jews did not have the right to enact capital punishment. Here fate intervened, because there was no procurator in Jerusalem to remind them of this. Let us return to the words of Josephus: "Ananus, thinking to take advantage of a favorable time between the death of Festus and the arrival of Albinus, assembled a Sanhedrin and handed over to them James, the brother of Jesus called the Christ, and certain others, accusing them of having broken the Law, and had them stoned." But Ananus could not foresee the general outcry that James' execution would raise, not only among Jewish converts to Christianity but among those raised in the Law of Moses alone: "All of the inhabitants of the city who were the most moderate and who observed the Law most strictly were annoyed," says Josephus,

> and they sent to ask the king secretly to enjoin Ananus not to act thus again, for previously he had acted unjustly. Certain ones among them even went to meet Albinus, who was coming from Alexandria, and informed him that Ananus did not have the right to convoke the Sanhedrin without his [Albinus'] authorization. Persuaded by their words, Albinus wrote angrily to Ananus threatening to take vengeance on him. Because of this King Agrippa stripped him of the high priesthood that he had held for three months and conferred it upon Jesus, son of Damnaeus.

Paul's public life would thus unfold between two stonings: that of Stephen and that of James.

To discover the "ending" of which Luke deprives us, we must turn to a text whose redaction is situated in the 80s, and which we owe to Clement of Rome, the successor of Peter and considered as pope. "It is because of jealousy and of discord that Paul showed what the price of patience is: seven times in chains, exiled, stoned, he became the herald of the Lord in the East and West, and received as prize for his faith a shining glory." After having taught justice to the whole world to the farthest reaches of the West, he bore witness before the authorities [another translation: "he was the victim of torture before those who governed"], and thus he left this world to gain the holy place and became for us an illustrious model of patience."[11]

Reading Clement, we cannot doubt that Paul died in Rome. According to Jurgen Becker, "In all the ancient Church there does not exist testimony contradicting this location in Rome." It was necessary, however, to wait more than a century to find confirmation of it. Between 200 and 213, Tertullian of Carthage, founder of the first theology in the Latin language, relates the martyrdom of Peter and Paul under Nero, the first being crucified like Jesus, the second decapitated like John the Baptist. In 313 Eusebius of Caesarea will confirm it: "We tell that under the reign [of Nero], Paul had his head cut off in Rome, and that likewise Peter was crucified there, and this account is confirmed by the names of Peter and Paul that, to this day, are given to the cemetery of this city."[12]

Is there nothing more about the end of our hero? Let us again return to *The Acts of Paul*. According to the commentators Willy Rordorf and Rodolphe Kasser, "The author of *The Acts of Paul* has gathered the local traditions about the apostle and his collaborators."

This document relates in detail the apostle's end. He specifies that Paul received the faithful—along with the curious, no doubt—in a barn. The author did not choose the place lightly; no barn could be found in imperial Rome, but there were many in the outskirts of the city where vagabonds, owning nothing more than "a fistful of straw," made their way. Juvenal saw them as hardly more than "musicians, charlatans, and sorcerers." This leads us to the question: Would Paul not have appeared to the authorities as a marginal sort, and the disciples who joined him as suspects? Suetonius underlines the hostility that arose in Nero's eyes for those who came together for philosophical or religious reasons. Tacitus affirms that political figures were accused under the grievance of being philosophers. The Stoics themselves would be suspected of demonology. After having enjoyed an apparent tolerance for two years, was Paul finally arrested for this reason?

When Paul was brought before Nero, did Nero believe him to be in the service of a king who "overthrew all kingdoms," and who consequently threatened Nero's own power? Paul would have forcefully declared to the emperor that he was gravely mistaken: "For we do not march, as you suppose, with a king who comes from earth, but one from heaven, the living God, who comes as judge because of the lawless deeds that are done in this world. And blessed is that man who shall believe in him and live for ever."[13]

Paul would have been led to his death after discourses like this, judged by Nero to be intolerable. We find here an indication of a tradition that the Christian churches have ratified: Paul was executed, according to the right that citizenship accorded him, "by the sword." Eusebius of Caesarea situates Paul's execution between July 67 and June 68. Modern authors judge that the most probable time would have been the day after the burning of Rome.

THE MOST FAMOUS fire in history raged during the night of July 18 or 19, around midnight. The fire started at the foot of the Palatine Hill, in a quarter where shopkeepers had stored a quantity of merchandise and other flammable materials. The wind immediately stirred it up. The wooden structure of the neighboring Circus Maximus, the numerous dwellings also made of wood, all helped to make the blaze quickly become an ocean of flames. Private homes, public edifices, and buildings with many stories all burned and collapsed. Tacitus described seven thousand firefighters prevented from acting by the very violence with which the fire spread. He depicted women, the elderly, and small children "with heartrending cries, looking to save themselves from the flames or to save their neighbors," and colliding against other crowds rushing up from elsewhere: "The people who threw a last glance on the goods they were abandoning were assailed by the flames that came up to meet them. Often, having thought to have fled to shelter, one found oneself instead seized by the fire."

The suspicion persisted in all minds that giving free rein to his incipient madness and persuaded that a new urbanization had become indispensable for Rome, Nero would have wanted to raze and burn the city. Suetonius shows him, having just arrived from his villa in Antium—after three or four hours on horseback—rushing to the summit of the Tower of Maecenas and not bothering to conceal his joy: "Enthused by the beauty of the spectacle of the flames, putting on his theater costume," he began to recite famous verses that evoked the siege of Troy. Today scholars no longer believe in a premeditated will: the ravages of the fire made the emperor the principal victim of the catastrophe by destroying his collection of art works, the passion of his life, which disappeared at the same time as his palace.

Rome burned during six days and seven nights. The last flames were barely extinguished when accusations rang out spontaneously from the ranks of the people, "For," says Tacitus, "it was not possible to silence the defamatory opinion as to who had ordered the fire." They cried for vengeance and Nero feared that he would soon be accused. The emperor took the initiative and ordered Tigellinus, the prefect of the praetorium, to search for the guilty party. The answer was not delayed in coming: the Christians had started the fire. The episode is familiar to us, perhaps even more so because of *Quo Vadis,* the immense bestseller, where the memory of its cinematic adaptations made more of an impact than the reasoned consultation of the authors of antiquity. Tacitus describes the massive arrests of Christians and the implacable decision to make a spectacle of their agony. He depicts these unfortunates, sewn into the skins of animals and thrown to starving dogs in the circus, while Nero on his chariot sought cheers. Some were put on crosses in the Vatican gardens. The refinement was pushed to its height when, night having come, the atoning victims, coated with flammable material, were reduced to being human torches.

If one holds that Paul escaped the fire because of his house arrest outside of the capital, and if he was indeed executed shortly after, we can believe that his death came as a consequence of the abominable repression. Everything indicates that he was accused as a "troublemaker of disturbing novelties," a term too often used. If he had a regular trial—which we do not know—the condemnation could have been pronounced by virtue of the imperial law on the *maiestas** that Nero had reinstated in 62.

Respectable traditions associate the memory of Paul's martyrdom with that of Peter. The two men would have been executed at the same time or a few days apart: Paul decapitated, Peter crucified and, out of humility and at his request, nailed head down.

We would not know how to read without emotion the words that the first churches repeated faithfully on each anniversary of Paul's death: "Then Paul stood with his face to the east, and lifting up his hands to heaven prayed at length; and after communing in prayer in Hebrew with the fathers he stretched out his neck without speaking further."[14]

---

* A number of criminal offenses against the state (Ed.)

The Romans customarily buried the condemned not far from where he had been executed, but they did not refuse to give back the body to the family and friends. From the second century, the martyrdom of Paul was located at the gates of Rome, *ad Aquas Salvias,* on the Ostian road. In the nineteenth century, excavations in this area uncovered a small cemetery. The inscriptions on certain tombs went back to the Roman republic, confirming the antiquity of the site. A letter of the Roman priest Gaius written around the year 200 confirms that Paul's remains were carried there: "I can show you the trophies of the apostles. If you come to the Vatican or on the Ostian route, you will find the trophies of the founders of this church." The word trophy here designates a sarcophagus topped by a small chapel.

In the fourth century, when the Emperor Constantine, in his conversion to the religion of Christ, brought with him the whole Empire, Paul's tomb was sought. A basilica was erected on the site where it was believed to have been found. The successors of Constantine—Valentinian II, Theodosius the Great, and Honorius—would take to heart its enlargement and enrichment. The definitive basilica, designated as that of "the three emperors," measures four hundred feet long, two hundred feet wide. For fourteen centuries the memory of Saint Paul was celebrated there.

On July 16, 1823, two carpenters were working on the roof. In a rash act, fire broke out, spread, and the basilica burned. All that remained were ruins burned to a cinder. It was immediately decided to build a new one. In the course of the work, a broken marble plaque was discovered in the soil, bearing the words: PAULO APOSTOLO MART. It was dated from the fourth century and led us directly back to Constantine.

Less antique, alas, but infinitely more sumptuous, the new basilica counts eighty granite and alabaster columns, three hundred varieties of marble, and windows of onyx. Completed in 1854, it became Saint Paul Outside the Walls. From that time on it would be visited by all who venerate the memory of the "Apostle to the Nations."

It's striking how quickly Paul of Tarsus was forgotten. Reduced to inactivity in his last years, he could not sustain with his strength of old the ideas that had convinced so many people and horrified so many others. In his lifetime they had already lost their impact. After his death the

Christian community of Rome, cruelly stricken, had other worries to deal with. The Judaizing current, moreover, seems to have carried it away. The small group that had formed around Paul scattered. What remained of the Pauline position? The disciples whom we know best, such as Timothy and Titus, would no longer be mentioned. The churches that Paul founded in Macedonia and Galatia collapsed. Those in Corinth and Ephesus passed under the authority of those whom he fervently fought against. No legend was spun about him, while Peter became an inexhaustible subject of fabulous inspiration. "You are not the master of your legend," comments Renan.

We have had to feel our way into the years that followed Paul's death. The obstacles increased: belated documents, controverted texts. All that had survived was "the outcome of a long history of material transmission."[15]

An appalling episode covered over the tracks: the Romans' capture of Jerusalem. The latent rebellion of the Jews against their occupiers won all of Judea. In September 66—two years after Paul's death—an insurrectionary government was proclaimed in Jerusalem. Thus began the Jewish war, recounted with superb powers of evocation by Flavius Josephus. Vespasian would spend three years crushing the insurgents of Galilee, then those of Judea. After his accession as emperor, his son Titus undertook before Jerusalem a siege that lasted four months. In the summer of 70, only a ruined city remained, with the Temple burned and a forest of crucified men. Nothing was left of the archives.

What became of the Christians of Jerusalem? Eusebius of Caesarea affirms that they left the city before the war, "in such a way that the holy men abandoned completely the royal metropolis of the Jews and all the land of Judea." According to Flavius Josephus, all of the Jewish insurgents from Syria were massacred, in particular those from the cities. It is unlikely that a distinction was made between traditional Jews and Jewish Christians. From the second Jewish Revolt (132–135), led by Bar Kochba and crushed as cruelly as the first, "Christians, and they alone, were made to endure the ultimate torment if they would not deny and blaspheme the name of Christ."[16]

The last Christian communities that had maintained "constant, even conflictual" contact with Judaism disappeared in this region of the world. This would lead to the ultimate consequence of a worse separation of the two communities of the same origin that had been so close to one another—nearly twenty centuries of antagonistic development, generating hatred and tragedies even while claiming the same God and the same Word! It was only after the greatest massacre of Jews in history that a dialogue was established, at first "in a low voice"[17] and gradually made stronger by the will of some.

These tragedies did not prevent the appearance of writings that emerged from several regions of the Empire: from Rome (very few), from Syria, from Palestine, from the province of Asia. This happened toward the end of the first century and the beginning of the following. None came from Jerusalem—and for a reason—nor from Alexandria, which deprives us of all information on early Egyptian Christianity. The inventory of these writings, including the Gospels, would be long and difficult. Little by little the disciples of Paul regained confidence: they regrouped and published the Letters that we know.

There is no doubt that the communities to whom Paul addressed his letters kept them in their possession. We must admit that, in conformity to the will of Paul himself, they were copied many times over. Around 150, Justin, a Greek-speaking Christian apologist, defined the Gospels, to which he added the Letters of Paul, as the "memories of the apostles."[18] It is no surprise that extrapolations were detected, even the combining of different letters to compose just one. The same would happen to the Gospel texts. At the beginning of the third century, Origen notes, "It is an obvious fact that today a great diversity exists among manuscripts, whether it is due to the negligence of the scribes or to the perverse audacity of men who corrected the texts, or again to the fact that there were some who added to them or removed from them at their liking, thereby appointing themselves as proofreaders." We are indebted to Pierre Geoltrain for a very fine analysis of this transmission of foundational texts. Oral memory played a principal role. Let us not forget that the first preachers were sure that they would soon see Jesus again, a fact that logically lengthened the crossing from the oral to the written. The situation was complicated when "the collective oral memory slipped in the process." By referring to the constant memorization in antiquity and particularly in the Jewish world, the most optimistic exegetes want to convince themselves that "oral transmission did not alter the meaning or the form of the speech transmitted."

Besides the difficulties posed by the accuracy of the text, the problem of their dating arises. At times it would be necessary to wait until the twentieth century to arrive at a probable date, rarely at a sure one.

Modern historians believe that the Christian religion really took shape after 70. By then the ruin of the Jerusalem Temple was complete and reformers from among the Pharisees, from that time in charge of the religious destiny of Israel, "expelled" them from Judaism (to use Etienne Trocmé's term). That the Jewish Christians felt this rejection painfully and sought to escape it is evident. If in their Gospels Matthew and John multiplied the attacks against the Pharisees, it was not without reason. The critical revision of the Letters of Paul, forgotten by an entire generation, could perhaps as well be held as one of the marks of this resistance. By publishing the Acts of the Apostles ten years after the fall of Jerusalem, Luke appears as an active element in the "return" to Paul.

When the time of the great councils came, Paul's thought stood out. In 325 Nicea decided the central terms of the *Credo,* a task completed in 381 at Constantinople. Some have spoken of a "glorification" rather than a reconquest. It would again know eclipses. In the fourth century, Saint Augustine made Paul his teacher but, in the course of the Middle Ages, Latin Christianity exalted Saint Peter to the detriment of Saint Paul. Hardly any churches were then built in his name. The fisherman from the Lake of Tiberias, walking on the water, spoke more to the imagination of brave men than the apostle-philosopher demonstrating in Greek that justification was by faith and not by works. The Letters were no longer studied except in a few monasteries.

There was a new "return" at the time of the Renaissance. To a cultured society, Gutenberg gave access to the great books, and people rediscovered the range and the force of the Letters. In 1515, a German Catholic religious and teacher of philosophy at the university of Erfurt, belonging to the convent of the Augustinians in Wittenberg and a professor at the university of the same name, plunged into the Letter to the Romans to make a deeper exegesis of it. He stopped at 3:28, thus conceived: "For we hold that a person is justified by faith apart from works prescribed by the law. Or is God the God of Jews only? Is he not the God of Gentiles also? Yes, of Gentiles also, since God is one...." To verse 31: "Do we then overthrow the law by this faith? By no means! On the contrary, we uphold the law" (Rom 3:28–29a, 31).

Martin Luther had just discovered, as a dominant theological principle, the doctrine of salvation by faith: God did not require justice of man, but freely offered it to those who believed in Christ. "Then let us hold that man is justified without works of the Law. By faith alone."[19]

It would take only two years to spread his *Ninety-five Theses* throughout Wittenberg.

The Reformation was born. It placed itself under the sign of Paul.

By a kind of tactical reversal, Rome hoisted Paul to the rank of Peter, without nevertheless managing to make him a popular saint. In the eighteenth century, certain strong spirits would begin to affirm that the founder of Christianity was not Jesus, but Paul. This opened the field to a debate that is still with us. But was he?

To answer, it is necessary not only to wonder about the author of the Letters but about the repercussions of what he preached. It is necessary to confront Judaism and Christianity; *in fine*, Jesus and Paul. This is no small thing. Reimarus in the eighteenth century, and Nietzsche in the nineteenth, counted for nothing. In our own day liberal Protestants have sustained this thesis of Paul as founder. They did this not to glorify Paul but to reproach him for having erected a religion derived from the Torah, weighted by disheartening rules, and for having substituted for the man Jesus a reconstruction "that no longer has anything human about it." Jewish innovators, going back on the anathema decreed by their ancestors, today consider the condemned man of Golgotha as "an authentic Jewish prophet, whose message comes marvelously within the scope of the religion of their Fathers." This is what the Protestant Etienne Trocmé teaches us: "If Christianity later broke with Judaism, it was because Paul hellenized it and deprived it of its Jewish roots. The man from Tarsus was thus the true father of this new religion in which Jesus would not have been able to recognize himself." Michel Quesnel, director of the Department of Research at the Catholic Institute in Paris, agrees that Paul's speech is "built on philosophical and theological concepts borrowed from the Greek world, unknown to the historic preaching of Jesus and most often missing from the Gospel texts." Certainly, we look in vain in the Gospels for the words redemption, justification, conscience, and freedom. But should we reproach Paul for having introduced them into the vocabulary of the Church?

As soon as we pose the question of whether Paul is the founder of Christianity, we come back to the carpenter's son. Names of places that Paul never mentioned sing in our memories: Nazareth, Bethlehem, Capernaum, Jordan, Tiberias. So do images: fishermen, their boats and nets, the multiplication of the loaves, the healing of the blind man, the raising of Lazarus, the merchants in the Temple, the appearance before the Sanhedrin, the crucifixion. And the same goes for sayings missing from the Letters: "Love one another as I have loved you" (Jn 15:12); "Do not judge, and you will not be judged" (Lk 6:37); "Ask, and it will be given to you; search, and you will find; knock, and the door will be opened for you" (Mt 7:7); "Let anyone among you who is without sin be the first to cast a stone at her" (Jn 8:7); "Come to me, all you that are weary and are carrying heavy burdens" (Mt 11:28); "Blessed are the meek, for they will inherit the earth. Blessed are those who mourn, for they will be comforted. Blessed are the pure in heart, for they will see God" (Mt 5:5, 4, 8). Does Paul even know that Jesus prayed his Father to forgive his executioners: "For they do not know what they are doing" (Lk 23:34)? Does he know that the son of Mary showed himself to be a man among men: "My God, my God, why have you forsaken me?" (Mk 15:34)? Always we reread the parables inhabited by sheep, sowings, harvests, and the fruit of the vine. Even if we are led to conclude that Jesus and Paul did not have exactly the same religion, we mingle our tears with those of the daughters on Calvary.

Can there be a founder of Christianity other than the Christ?

I can hear the criticism and imagine the disdain: "Must one be satisfied with a sensible Christianity?" The words, the signs, the gestures that you love, do you deny to others the right to extend their meaning? Should Saint Augustine have kept silent?

If he had followed Jesus in Galilee, perhaps Saul would never have become Paul. Perhaps it was best that he did not know Jesus: had he met him like Mark, Matthew, Luke, and John, Paul might not have searched in his depths for the meaning of the message revealed on the road to Damascus. Christians would not recognize him today as one of the pillars of the Church. His thought would astonish fewer philosophers and would not enlighten those who seek. If the Letters of Saint Paul are read at each Catholic Mass, if Reformation churches identify with him so strongly, it is because he was what he was meant to be.

No one can deny that Paul contributed, more than anyone else, to spreading not the word of Jesus but the idea that he had of him.

It is impossible to dispute the initiative of his apostolate to the Gentiles or to deny him the courage that included heroism and an obstinacy that was confirmed at every stage by positive results. Without ceasing he exposed himself deliberately to prison, torture, and death. Pascal would only believe in "stories whose witnesses had their throats cut." Paul was one of those witnesses, which did not prevent him, at any moment, from contradicting the image held of the traditional saint. He who wanted to conquer the masses gave himself to doctoral exposition so arduous that only Greek philosophers or converted rabbis have been able to penetrate all their meanings. He was so anxious to convince, and he felt so much the certainty that he was right, that one of his best commentators sees him not taking the time to articulate his reasoning: "He vibrates, becomes heated, thinks of a thousand things at the same time, expands the meanings of words."[20] Wanting to go directly to the essential, he sometimes lost his way, "leaving the adversary disarmed if not convinced." Yet he opened the way, nevertheless, to endless perspectives. His personality was overwhelming. His letters remain as unique documents that demonstrate at once "an inner will, an impressive mysticism, a genius for synthesis."[21] In the Letter to the Romans, Paul wrote his message in eternity.

THE PAUL OF ACTS, speaking to the elders of Miletus before his last journey to Jerusalem, portrayed himself as the prophet of his own death. For the attention of his disciples, he added these gripping words, "Be alert, remembering that for three years I did not cease night or day to warn everyone with tears" (Acts 20:31).

With tears: could not the image of a Paul weeping in order to make his certainty accepted bring some nuance to the image of the inflexible and intolerant apostle that has imposed itself even on iconography? Some paintings have even shown him brandishing a sword. To explain this nonsense, we usually refer to the Letter to the Ephesians: "Take the helmet of salvation, and the sword of the Spirit, which is the *Word of God*" (6:17), a text reprised from the prophet Isaiah. There is nothing to prove that Paul sought to ensure the success of the implacable image of the blessed and the damned which, as we know, Dante used. In the same Letter to the Ephesians, Paul proclaimed that all people will be saved in Christ and that consequently only one Church must gather in its bosom Jews and Christians alike.

Paul always marched on the roads of our spirit.

We see him, God's eternal fool, announcing everywhere, throughout Asia and Europe, the One who reconciles men with men and each one with himself; pugnacious when he wrote; furious when his ideas, which he was sure he held from God, were attacked; tender with Philemon; driven to despair by the Galatians; anguished by the Corinthians. Whatever we say, whatever we think about him, he was certainly human.

At the moment of taking leave of Saint Paul, I ask myself: Did I treat him appropriately? He irritated me and I said so. He deceived me and I said so. Was it thus that I ought to have confronted him, not as the great saint—he is that only statutorily—but as the great man? Should I not have tried to heave myself up to his height rather than bring him down to my weakness?

His personality was crushing. Among Jews and Christians of his time, his thought was towering. To become a religion, the message of Jesus needed him. Paul was the apostle of his universalism. He said: "I have fought the good fight, I have finished the race, I have kept the faith" (2 Tim 4:7).

APPENDICES

Appendix I

The Martyrdom of Saint Paul
According to *The Acts of Paul*

It seemed to me that it would be useful to put before the reader's eyes the account of the death of Paul as it is presented in *The Acts of Paul*. Many fragments of this apocryphal text of the second ce ntury have survived. The most ancient were published in 1698 in Oxford. Today forty-eight manuscripts of it are known, eleven of which made possible the scholarly edition of the work *Ecrits apocryphes chretiens* (1997), under the direction of François Goyon and Pierre Geoltrain.

The historic importance of *The Acts of Paul* has often been emphasized; they were collected from oral traditions that allowed the image Christians had of Paul in the century after his death to become clear.

One could also consider why *The Acts of Paul* was excised from the collection of texts recognized as canonical. Alongside information that can be considered quite acceptable, the author succumbed to the temptation to include certain "marvels." These evidently put off the authors who made the definitive selection for the canon. No doubt the best example is the milk that flowed from the neck of the decapitated Paul, and even more the too-bold parallel drawn with the death and resurrection of Jesus.

The version of the "Martyrdom of the Holy Apostle Paul" that follows has been compiled from the *Acta apostolorum apocrypha* I, edited by Lipsius (1891), the Hamburg Papyrus, and the Heidelberg Coptic Papyrus. It can be found in volume two of *New Testament Apocyrpha: Writings Relating to the Apostles; Apocalypses and Related Subjects,* edited by Wilhelm Schneemelcher and translated into English by R. McL. Wilson (Louisville: Westminster John Knox Press, 2003), pp. 260–263.

Martyrdom of the Holy Apostle Paul

1.　There were awaiting Paul at Rome Luke from Gaul and Titus from Dalmatia (cf. 2 Tim 4:10). When Paul saw them he was glad, so that he hired a barn outside Rome, where with the brethren he taught the word of truth. The news was spread abroad, and many souls were added to the Lord (cf. Acts 2:41), so that there was a rumor throughout Rome, and a great number of believers came to him from the house of Caesar (cf. Phil 4:22), and there was great joy.

But a certain Patroclus, Caesar's cup-bearer, came late to the barn and, being unable because of the crowd to go in to Paul, sat at a high window and listened to him teaching the word of God. But since the wicked devil was envious of the love of the brethren, Patroclus fell from the window and died (cf. Acts 20:9ff.), and the news was quickly brought to Nero. But Paul, perceiving it in the spirit, said: "Brethren, the evil one has gained an opportunity to tempt you. Go out, and you will find a youth fallen from a height and already on the point of death. Lift him up, and bring him here to me!" So they went out and brought him. And when the crowd saw (him), they were troubled. Paul said to them: "Now, brethren, let your faith be manifest. Come, all of you, let us mourn to our Lord Jesus Christ, that this youth may live and we remain unmolested." But as they all lamented the youth drew breath again, and setting him upon a beast they sent him back alive with the others who were of Caesar's house.

2.　When Nero heard of Patroclus' death, he was greatly distressed, and when he came out from the bath he commanded that another be appointed for the wine. But his servants told him the news, saying: "Caesar, Patroclus is alive and standing at the table." And when Caesar heard that Patroclus was alive he was afraid, and did not want to go in. But when he had entered he saw Patroclus and, beside himself, cried out: "Patroclus, art thou alive?" And he said: "I am alive, Caesar." But he said: "Who is he who made thee to live?" And the youth, borne by the conviction of faith, said: "Christ Jesus, the king of the ages" (cf. 1 Tim 1:17). But Caesar in perplexity said: "So he is to be king of the ages, and destroy all the kingdoms?" Patroclus said to him: "Yes, all the kingdoms under heaven he destroys, and he alone shall be for ever, and there shall be no kingdom which shall escape him." But he struck him on the face and said: "Patroclus, dost thou also serve in that king's army?" And he said: "Yes, lord Caesar, for indeed he raised me up when I was dead." And Barsabas Justus of the flat feet, and Orion the Cappadocian, and Festus the Galatian, Nero's chief men, said: "We also are in the army (cf. 1 Tim 1:18, 2 Tim 2:4) of that king of the ages." But he shut them up in prison, after torturing dreadfully men whom he greatly loved, and commanded that the soldiers of the great king be sought out, and he issued a decree to this effect, that all who were found to be Christians and soldiers of Christ (cf. 2 Tim 2:3) should be put to death.

3.   And among the many Paul also was brought bound; to him all his fellow-prisoners gave heed, so that Caesar observed that he was the man in command. And he said to him:[1] "Man of the great king, but (now) my prisoner, why did it seem good to thee to come secretly into the Empire of the Romans and enlist soldiers from my province?" But Paul, filled with the Holy Spirit (cf. Acts 4:8), said before them all: "Caesar, not only from thy province do we enlist soldiers, but from the whole world. For this charge has been laid upon us, that no man be excluded who wishes to serve my king. If thou also think it good, do him service! for neither riches nor the splendor of this present life will save thee,[2] but if thou submit and entreat him, then shalt thou be saved. For in one day he will destroy the world with fire."

When Caesar heard this, he commanded all the prisoners to be burned with fire, but Paul to be beheaded according to the law of the Romans. But Paul did not keep silence concerning the word, but communicated it to the prefect Longus and the centurion Cestus.

In Rome, then, Nero was (raging) at the instigation of the evil one, many Christians being put to death without trial, so that the Romans took their stand at the palace and cried: "It is enough, Caesar! For these men are ours. Thou dost destroy the power of the Romans!" Then he made an end (of the persecution), whereupon none of the Christians was to be touched until he had himself investigated his case.

4.   Then Paul was brought before him in accordance with the decree, and he adhered to the decision that he should be beheaded. But Paul said: "Caesar, it is not for a short time that I live for my king. And if thou behead me, this will I do: I will arise and appear to thee (in proof) that I am not dead, but alive to my Lord Christ Jesus (cf. Rom 14:8), who is coming to judge the world" (cf. Acts 17:31).

But Longus and Cestus said to Paul: "Whence have you this king, that you believe in him without change of heart, even unto death?" Paul communicated the word to them and said: "Ye men who are in this ignorance and error, change your mind and be saved from the fire that is coming upon the whole world. For we do not march, as you suppose, with a king who comes from earth (cf. Jn 18:36), but one from heaven, the living God, who comes as judge because of the lawless deeds that are done in this world. And blessed is that man who shall believe in him, and live for ever (cf. Jn 11:25f.), when he comes to burn the world till it is pure." So they besought him and said: "We entreat thee, help us and we will let thee go." But he answered and said: "I am no deserter from Christ, but a lawful soldier of the living God. Had I known that I was to die, I would have done it, Longus and Cestus. But since I live to God and love myself, I go to the Lord that I may come (again) with him in the glory of his Father." They said to him: "How then shall we live, when thou art beheaded?"

5.   While they were still saying this, Nero sent a certain Parthenius and Pheretas to see if Paul had already been beheaded; and they found him still alive. But he called them to him and said: "Believe in the living God, who raises up from the dead both me and all who believe in him!" But they said: "We are going now to Nero; but when thou dost die and rise again, then will we believe in thy God." But when Longus and Cestus questioned him further about salvation, he said to them: "Come quickly here to my grave at dawn, and you will find two men praying, Titus and Luke. They will give you the seal in the Lord."

Then Paul stood with his face to the east, and lifting up his hands to heaven prayed at length;[3] and after communing in prayer in Hebrew with the fathers he stretched out his neck without speaking further. But when the executioner struck off his head, milk spurted upon the soldier's clothing. And when they saw it, the soldier and all who stood by were amazed, and glorified God who had given Paul such glory. And they went off and reported to Caesar what had happened.

6.   When he heard it, he marveled greatly and was at a loss. Then Paul came about the ninth hour, when many philosophers and the centurion were standing with Caesar, and he stood before them all and said:[4] "Caesar, here I am—Paul, God's soldier. I am not dead, but alive in my God. But for thee, unhappy man, there shall be many evils and great punishment, because thou didst unjustly shed the blood of the righteous, and that not many days hence!" (Acts 1:5) And when he had said this Paul departed from him. But when Nero heard (it) he was greatly troubled, and commanded the prisoners to be set free, including Patroclus and Barsabas and his companions.

7.   As Paul directed, Longus and Cestus went at dawn and with fear approached Paul's tomb. But as they drew near they saw two men praying, and Paul between them, so that at the sight of this unexpected wonder they were astounded, while Titus and Luke were seized with human fear when they saw Longus and Cestus coming towards them, and turned to flight. But they followed after them, saying: "We are not pursuing you to kill you, as you imagine, ye blessed men of God, but for life, that you may give it to us as Paul promised us, whom we saw but now standing between you and praying." And when Titus and Luke heard this from them, with great joy they gave them the seal in the Lord, glorifying the God and Father of our Lord Jesus Christ, unto whom be the glory for ever and ever. Amen (cf. 1 Tim 1:17, etc.).

Appendix II

Events Contemporaneous with the Life of Saint Paul

19 August 14	Death of the emperor Augustus.
	Emperor Tiberius.
26–36	Pontius Pilate prefect of Judea.
33–34	Tiberius joins the tetrarchy of Philip to the province of Syria.
36	Pilate recalled to Rome.
37	Death of Tiberius.
	Emperor Caligula. He gives to Herod Agrippa I—who becomes king—the tetrarchies of Philip and Lysanias.
	King Aretas takes control of Damascus.
39	Herod Agrippa I receives from Caligula the tetrarchies of Galilee and Perea.
41	Assassination of Caligula.
	Emperor Claudius. By receiving from him Judea and Samaria, Agrippa I reconstitutes the ancient domain of Herod the Great.
44	Death of Herod Agrippa I.
49	Claudius expels the Jews from Rome.
50	Herod Agrippa II obtains the principality of Chalcis and the title of king. Gallio proconsul in Corinth.

52   Felix procurator of Judea.

53   Herod Agrippa II exchanges Chalcis against the ancient
                tetrarchies of Philip and Lysanias.

54   Assassination of Claudius.

                Emperor Nero.

60   Festus procurator in Judea.

64   Burning of Rome.

68   Death of Nero.

70   Siege of Jerusalem by Titus.

                Burning of the Temple.

Appendix III

Sources

Along the way, I have indicated the complementary character of the Letters and Acts. I had recourse to the method introduced since 1950 by J. Knox, according to which in the case of a difference between Paul and Luke, the text of the apostle—the actor—naturally wins over the account of the chronicler. The reader must understand that these two associated sources represent an exception almost unique in antiquity. That Paul, speaking to communities, appears regularly in long autobiographical passages—by way of example or not—is a privilege with which very few personages of that time have blessed their descendants. Another signal opportunity: a contemporary, Luke, whom we know is intent on verifying with witnesses the accuracy of the events he narrates and of the discourses he quotes, is devoted to Paul, accompanies him on many of his travels, and leaves us a document of incomparable value. On the Acts of the Apostles, I will refer to the scholarly preface of Jean-Robert Armogathe in the translation of Hugues Oltramare (1998 and 2001) and the enlightening study of Etienne Trocmé: *Le "Livre des Actes" et l'Histoire* (1957).

The name Etienne Trocme leads me to underline what I owe to the staff of the *Monde de la Bible* to which he belonged and whose work constantly enriches the specific phenomena by making use of an expanded documentation, namely archaeological. The recent collection of works of some thirty specialists for the composition of the text *Origines du christianisme* (Paris, 2000), must be considered as the mirror of actual knowledge on this great subject, in particular on Saint Paul; it will be referred to in the notes by the initials *O.C.*

Among authors of the past, I will stop at Flavius Josephus. Totally unknown to the Christian world, the writer of *The Antiquities of the Jews,* of *The Wars of the Jews,* and of his own autobiography gives us invaluable information about the context within which this story, along with the characters that move within it, unfolds.

In addition, I referred most often to recent works, with the exception of classics like the famous *Saint Paul* by Ernest Renan (1869) or research studies.

The number of titles dedicated to Saint Paul in every language is immense. The following is a selection of books still in print and available through Pauline Books & Media centers (see addresses at the back of this book).

Works on Saint Paul

Becker, Jurgen. *Paul Apostle to the Gentiles.* Translated by O. C. Dean, Jr. Louisville: Westminster John Knox Press, 1993.

Beker, Johan Christiaan. *Paul the Apostle: The Triumph of God in Life and Thought.* Minneapolis: Augsburg Fortress Publishers, 1980.

Bornkamm, Gunther. *Paul.* Minneapolis: Augsburg Fortress Publishers, 1995.

Daniel-Rops, Henri. *Daily Life in Palestine at the Time of Christ.* Phoenix Press, 2002.

Dunn, James D. G. *The Theology of Paul the Apostle.* Grand Rapids: Eerdmans Publishing Company, 1997.

Josephus, Flavius. Translated by Willliam Whiston. *The New Complete Works of Josephus.* Kregel Academic and Professional, 1998.

Gager, John G. *Reinventing Paul.* New York: Oxford University Press, 2002.

Jeremias, Joachim. *Jerusalem in the Time of Jesus.* Minneapolis: Augsburg Fortress Publishers, 1979.

Murphy-O'Connor, Jerome. *Paul: His Story.* New York: Oxford University Press, 2005.

———, *Paul the Letter-Writer: His World, His Options, His Skills.* Collegeville: Michael Glazier Books, 1995.

Ridderbos, Herman. *Paul: An Outline of His Theology.* Grand Rapids: Eerdmans Publishing Company, 1997.

Sanders, E. P. *Paul and Palestinian Judaism.* Minneapolis: Augsburg Fortress Publishers, 1977.

Stendahl, Krister. *Paul Among Jews and Gentiles.* Minneapolis: Augsburg Fortress Publishers, 1977.

Sources Chapter by Chapter

Chapter 1: No Mean City

For the description of Tarsus, consult the *Strabo* of R. Baladie, 1978. On the birth of Paul in Tarsus, Michel Trimaille: *Que sait-on de Paul au-jour-d'hui?* (*O.C.*). On the Roman citizenship of Paul, Jean-Robert Armogathe: *op.cit.;* A.-N. Sherwin White: *Roman Citizenship,* 1973; on the wrath that Cassius poured out on Tarsus: H.-D. Saffrey, *op.cit.* The quote from Flavius Josephus on the pride of the Jews in *The Wars of the Jews,* II, 398. On the Diaspora, J. Juster: *Les Juifs dans l'Empire romain,* 1914; Schalom Ben-Chorin: *Paul, un regard juif sur l'apôtre des gentils,* translated by Paul Kessler, 1999; A. Paul: *Le monde des juifs à l'heure de Jésus* 1981; A. Momogliano: *Sagesses babrbares, les limites de l'hellenisation,* 1984; Folker Siegert: *Les judaismes au 1er siècle,* and Joseph Mélèze-Modrzejewski: *Un judaisme d'expression grecque* (*O.C.*). On the religions of Tarsus, Giuseppe Riccioti: *op.cit.;* on the Septuagint, Marguerite Harl and Cecile Dogniez: *O.C.;* on Jewish sects, Flavius Josephus: *Antiquités,* XIII, X, 5.

Chapter 2: The Cornerstone

On the general context, A. Hamman: *La vie quotidienne des premiers chrétiens* [*The Daily Life of the First Christians*], 1971; on the mode of travel, Jean-Marie Andre and Marie-Françoise Baslez: *Voyager dans l'Antiquité* [*Traveling in Antiquity*], 1993; H.-V. Morton: *Sur les pas de saint Paul* [*In the Footsteps of Saint Paul*], 1948; on Gamaliel and his time, Marcel Simon, *O.C.*, and J. B. Neusner: *From Politics to Piety: the Emergence of Pharisaic Judaism,* New York, 1979; on education, A. Lemaire: *Les écoles et la formation de la Bible dans l'ancien Israël* [*Schools and the Formation of the Bible in Ancient Israel*], 1981, on Roman authority in Jerusalem, J.-P. Lemonon: *Pilate et gouvernement de la Judée* [*Pilate and the Government of Judea*], 1981; the thesis of Andre Chouraqui on rabbi Paul in *O.C.* according to F. Amiot: *Les idées maîtresses de saint Paul* [*The Main Ideas of Saint Paul*], 1959 and Giuseppe Riccioti: *op. cit.*

Chapter 3: The Road to Damascus

On the Christian community in Damascus, Michel Quesnel *O.C.;* on the apparition of Jesus on the road to Damascus, the major work of Jurgen Becker tranlsated from the German by Joseph Hoffmann, 1995, and also Schalom Ben-Chorin: *op.cit.;* the explanation of the vision in Alfred Loisy: *La carrière de l'apôtre Paul* [*The Career of the Apostle Paul*] *Revue d'histoire et de littérature religieuse* [*Review of History and Religious Literature*] 1920), and Daniel-Rops: *The Church of Apostles and Martyrs,* 1948; on Paul's immersion in Judaism, Leo Baeck: *The Faith of Paul*, 1961; on the Jewish presence in Damascus, B. Lifshitz: *Donateurs et fondateurs dans les synagogues juives* [*Donors and Founders in the Jewish synagogues*], 1967.

Chapter 4: Fifteen Days to Know Jesus

On ancient writing, Michel Quesnel: *Histoire des Evangiles* [*The History of the Gospels*], 1987; on the *Papyrus Chester Beatty*, Edouard Cothenet: *Petite vie de saint Paul* [*A Short Life of Saint Paul*], 1995; on the description of Antioch, Ernest Renan: *Les Apotres* [*The Apostles*], 1866; on the Antiochene milieu, G. Downey: *A History of Antioch in Syria*, 1961 and R.-E. Brown and J.-P. Meyer: *Antioch and Rome*, 1988; on Barnabas, *Salamine de Chypre* [*Salamine of Cyprus*], XIII, who collects local traditions.

Chapter 5: Where Saul Becomes Paul

On the sojourn in Cyprus, Father Jean-Luc Vesco: *En Méditerranée avec l'apôtre Paul* [*In the Mediterranean with the Apostle Paul*], 1972; *Paul l'envoyé du Christ. Premier Voyage* [*Paul the Envoy of Christ: First Journey*], Notebook 5 of *Monde de la Bible* July 1978; T.-B. Mitford: *Roman Cyrus*, 1980; on Sergius Paulus, H. Halfman: *Die Senatorem aus dem östilichen Teil des Imperium Romanum* [*The Senators of the Eastern Part of the Roman Empire*], 1979.

Chapter 6: On the Attack from Anatolia

On the route of Paul: Notebook 5 of *Monde de la Bible* July 1978; on Pisidian Antioch, Michel Hubaut: *Sur les traces de saint Paul* [*In the Footsteps of Saint Paul*], 1995, according to H.-D. Saffrey: *op. cit.*, and Schalom Ben-Chorin: *op.cit.;* on the routes, Victor W. von Hagen: *Les voies romaines* [*Roman Roads*], 1967, and R. Chevallier: *Les voies romaines*, 1972.

Chapter 7: Under the Sign of Circumcision

On the apostle James, Pierre-Antoine Bernheim: *Jacques frère de Jésus* [*James Brother of Jesus*], 1996; on the pagans in the synagogues, Flavius Josephus: *Guerre des juifs* (VII, 45); on Luke, Edouard Delebecque: *Les Actes des Apôtres* [*The Acts of the Apostles*], 1982; the preface of Jean-Robert Armogathe for the edition of the New Testament translated by Hughes Oltramare: *Les Actes des Apôtres*, 1998.

Chapter 8: Beyond the Aegean

On the crossings of Paul, R. Richard: *Navigations de saint Paul* [*The Sea Voyages of Saint Paul*] Etudes, 1927; on the second and third journeys of Paul:

Notebook 6 of *Monde de la Bible,* October 1978; Henri Metzger: *The Routes of Saint Paul's Journeys in the Greek Orient,* 1954; on the sojourns in Philippi, Msgr. Jean Rodin, in *Les saints de tous les jours* [*Everyday Saints*], vol. 6, 1958; on the sojourn in Athens, A.-J. Festujiere: *L'enfant d'Agrigente* [*The Child of Agrigenta*], 1950.

Chapter 9: Corinth

On the sojourns in Corinth, Lucien Cerfaux: *L'Eglise des Corinthiens* [*The Church of the Corinthians*], 1946, and J. Murphy O'Connor: *Corinthe au temps de saint Paul d'après les texts et l'archéologie* [Corinth at the Time of Saint Paul According to the Texts and Archaeology], 1986. We are indebted to Strabo for an invaluable depiction of the environment of Corinth: similarly for Cenchrae as evoked by Apuleius: *Métamorphoses.* Cf. Paul de Surgy and Maurice Carrez: *Les Epîtres de Paul* [*The Epistles of Paul*], 1996–1997. On the collection, D. Georgi: *Die Geschichte des Kollekte des Paulus für Jerusalem* [*The Story of the Collection of Paul for Jerusalem*], 1965.

Chapter 10: Sufferings and Struggles in Ephesus

On Paul's route, cf. J. Rouge: *Recherches sur l'organisation du commerce maritime en Méditerranée sour l'Empire romain* [*Investigations on the Organization of Maritime Commerce on the Mediterranean under the Roman Empire*], 1966, and J. Berard: *Les itinéraries de saint Paul en Asie Mineure* [*The Itineraries of Saint Paul in Asia Minor*], 1935; on the mountain routes mentioned in Acts, cf. Strabo XIV, 2, 29; on Paul's stay in Ephesus, H.-D. Saffrey: *Paul à Ephèse, patrie d'Artemis* [*Paul in Ephesus, the Homeland of Artemis*], in *Monde de la Bible* 57, 1989.

Chapter 11: The Road to Jerusalem

On the comings and goings of Paul, N. Ugede: *Saint Paul et la Grèce* [*Saint Paul and Greece*], 1982; J. Murphy O'Connor, *op. cit.;* on the Epistle to the Romans, the studies are numerous but one always returns to Pere Lagrange. Marie-Françoise Baslez, *op. cit.,* indicates that the date of its editing can be specified "according to two points of reference" that situate the characters that can be identified as a certain Herodion who left Rome in 53 and Narcissus who committed suicide in 54. Cf. also J. W.-C. Wand: *Ce que saint Paul a vraiment dit* [*What Saint Paul Really Said*], French translation, 1970; no one can ignore the importance of *Commentaire de l'Epître aux Romains* [*The Commentary on the Epistle to the Romans*] published by Martin Luther (Works, vol. 11, 1983).

Chapter 12: The Man in Chains

On the Fortress Antonia, a Hasmonean structure reconstructed by Herod, cf. B. Rapske: *The Book of Acts and Paul in Roman Custody,* 1994. We read in Flavius Josephus (*La Guerre des Juifs,* V, 243): "At the place where [the Antonia] joined the porticoes of the Temple were the stairs from which the guards descended, for a Roman cohort was permanently quartered there." We could not omit consulting the work of Daniel-Rops, particularly his chapter on Jerusalem: *Daily Life in Palestine at the Time of Jesus,* 1961, as well as the major study of Joachim Jeremias: *Jérusalem au temps de Jésus* [*Jerusalem at the Time of Jesus*], French translation, 1967; on the administration of Felix, cf. Flavius Josephus, *Antiquités judaïques* XX, 8 and 9; he also mentions the bandit Eleazar sent to Rome for judgment: *La Guerre des Juifs,* III, 253; on the Mediterranean journey, cf. Paul Dreyfus, *op. cit.;* J. Rouge: *Recherches sur l'organisation du commerce maritime en Méditerranée sous l'Empire romain,* 1966, J.-M. Andre and M.-F. Baslez: *op. cit.;* on the sojourn in Malta, Nicolas Monsarrat: *The Kappillan of Malta,* 1973.

Chapter 13: Paul and Nero

Beginning with that of Suetonius, biographies of Nero are numerous; that of Georges Roux (1962) retains all of its value; on Rome, the book of Jerome Carcopino, a masterpiece of historiography, has aged but little: *La vie quotidienne à Rome à l'apogée de l'Empire* [*Daily Life in Rome at the Apogee of the Empire*], 1939; on the Jews of Rome, cf. Flavius Josephus: *Antiquités judaiques,* XVIII, 81–84 and Charles Perrot: *La diaspora juive de Rome* [*The Jewish Diaspora of Rome*] (*O.C.*); on the burning of Rome, cf. Tacitus' famous text: *Annales;* on the last days of Paul, François Brossier: *La fin de Paul à Rome* [*The End of Paul in Rome*] (*O.C.*).

NOTES

Chapter 1: No Mean City

1. He "approved of their killing" (Acts 8:1). Cf. *Sources,* p. 242.

2. Cf. the *Sources* at the end of the book.

3. H.-D. Saffrey. The titles of the works of authors cited in the notes are included in the *Sources* beginning on p. 242.

4. *Pro Flacco* 28.

5. Giuseppi Riccioti.

6. Saul had at least one married sister and perhaps a brother whom he called Rufus, but who, in the context of the letters, seems rather to have been an adopted brother.

7. Marguerite Harl and Cecile Dogniez.

8. In Hebrew "to eat bread" is equivalent to "to have a meal."

9. "It is good to study the Law while at the same time attending to a profession" (Mishna Avot).

10. From there comes the *cilices*—hair shirts—that certain mystics wore against the flesh to mortify it.

Chapter 2: The Cornerstone

1. Quoted by Jean-Marie André and Marie-Françoise Baslez.

2. A remnant of it remains today: the "wailing wall."

3. Marcel Simon.

4. *La Bible. Ecrits intertestamentaires* (1987).

5. J-B Neusner.

6. Statement attributed to Johanan ben Zakkai in praise of Eliezar, his disciple.

7. The gift of tongues—*glossalalia*—enabled one, it was believed, to communicate in a language that escaped those not initiated in it.

8. Friday, April 7, 30, if we accept the chronology of the Synoptic Gospels.

9. Introduction by Pierre Geoltrain to the collection, *Origines du christianisme* (2000).

10. The term "Christian" will not appear until several years later in Antioch. It is used here to accommodate the reader.

11. The Jews, under Roman occupation, did not have the authority to impose the death penalty.

12. Translation of *The Acts of Paul* by Wilhelm Schneemelcher and Rodolphe Kasser in *New Testament Apocrypha. Volume Two: Writings Relating to the Apostles; Apocalypses and Related Subjects* (Revised Edition), edited by Wilhelm Schneemelcher; English translation by R. McL. Wilson (Louisville: Westminster John Knox Press, 2003), 239.

13. An ancient form of priest.

14. *The Acts of Paul,* 239.

15. The "large letters" refer to the line that Paul personally added at the end of certain of his letters that were dictated to a scribe.

16. The word is not found in the Acts of the Apostles.

Chapter 3: The Road to Damascus

1. This refers no doubt to the city of Sebaste built by Herod the Great.

2. Michel Quesnel.

3. The term "the Way" designated in this case the members of the community of Christ's faithful.

4. Professor of New Testament exegesis at Kiel.

5. Schalom Ben-Chorin.

6. Since 258, Saint Paul has been honored on June 29, at the same time as Saint Peter.

7. A fragrant herb from India from which a sought-after perfume was extracted.

Chapter 4: Fifteen Days to Know Jesus

1. Chester Beatty Library.

2. Cf. the convincing argument of Jurgen Becker. His monumental scientific work cannot but arouse admiration and gratitude on my part.

3. A member of the tribe of Levi, dedicated to the service of the Temple.

4. Literally, "son of consolation."

5. Jean-Robert Armogathe.

6. Jewish tradition has retained five to ten heavens. Seven is the most popular number. Paradise is generally located in the third heaven.

Chapter 5: Saul Becomes Paul

1. Charged by the imperial government with an archaeological mission in Syria, Renan visited neighboring Palestine in April–May 1861 and took from it

his own vision of Jesus, "an incomparable man, so great that I do not want to contradict those who, struck by the exceptional character of his work, call him God."

2. I insist here on saluting the memory of Renan, who, having left his study and library, ventured into those regions where Europeans hardly dared to go except for commercial reasons. I see in him the precursor of modern historians avid to draw out the truth by contemplation of sites.

3. Not to be confused with the Greek island of Salamis, which saw the defeat of Xerxes by the Athenian fleet.

4. Cf. T.-B. Mitford and H. Halfman.

5. Joseph Holzner.

6. Kepha is the common Aramaic noun for "rock." It was first translated into Greek as Petros, which was in turn rendered in Latin as Petrus.

7. The name Asia Minor only dates from the tenth century.

Chapter 6: On the Attack from Anatolia

1. Michel Hubaut.

2. Victor W. von Hagen.

3. We can also add that there are, in the garden of the museum of archaeology, a number of large tombs—of stone or marble—whose wealth is naturally flaunted according to the importance of the deceased.

4. Simon Legasse.

Chapter 7: Under the Sign of Circumcision

1. This is what he himself refers to in his Letter to the Galatians 2:4.

2. Luke presents this letter as a document from an archive, very unusual in Acts.

3. The word must be taken to mean "the good news of salvation in Jesus Christ." There was never a Gospel of Paul comparable to those of Mark, Matthew, Luke, and John.

4. Peter's presence in Antioch for a considerable period of time is attested by local tradition and also evoked by a cave two miles from the city center, toward the Syrian border. It contains evidence of the early presence of Christians and is called the "grotto of Saint Peter."

5. Pierre-Antoine Beruheim.

6. In all of Paul's Letters this is the only time when he himself quotes the words of the speech he made.

7. On this itinerary, cf. Michel Hubaut and also Paul Dreyfus, both experts on the travels of Saint Paul.

Chapter 8: Beyond the Aegean

1. Jean Colson.

2. These identifications are made in Rom 16:20–21, as well as in Acts 17 and 20. Cf. Marie-Françoise Baslez.

3. Archaeological research has identified the river in question to the west of the city as the river Gangites.

4. Epigraphy attests to it.

5. The contents of the tomb were transported to Thessaloniki and are considered today to be the most precious treasures of the museum of archaeology.

6. The word can be rendered "parrot" or "black crow"—*spermologos*—a term that designated the regulars at the agora who discussed everything and nothing.

7. The singular used here is entirely of Luke's devising. Several inscriptions of this kind are known, but they read, "To the unknown gods." It is true that the singular used in this passage settles things considerably.

8. The exact text of Aratos reads: "We get from him our origins." The modified version is similar to Genesis.

Chapter 9: Corinth

1. Nero personally supported the project to break through the isthmus and even came to break ground with a golden mattock, but nothing came of it. Herod Atticus also attempted to complete the project, but he did not succeed. The canal at Corinth was not completed until 1893.

2. Dieter Hildebrandt.

3. Psalm 24:1 (LXX 23:1).

Chapter 10: Sufferings and Struggles in Ephesus

1. Timothy's presence is considered probable according to Jurgen Becker. In fact Paul found himself with him in Antioch. As far as Silas is concerned, he disappeared for good from this story.

2. This journey to Jerusalem pointed out by Luke alone has raised numerous discussions. Some, like Simon Legasse, guess that Luke imagined it out of his concern to keep Paul under the aegis of the mother church. In the Letter to the Galatians, Paul enumerates his visits to Jerusalem without referring to this one.

3. Because of the expression "house of Caesar," it was long believed that the letter dated from the later time of Paul's imprisonment in Rome. This point of view has been abandoned today for a logical reason. In the letter addressed to Philemon, Paul announced to Philemon that he hoped to be freed and that, because of that fact, he would see him soon at his home in Philippi. Rome is excluded because three months by sea were needed to go from the capital of the Empire to Philippi, which was no more than a five day's walk from Ephesus.

4. At the Council held in Ephesus in 431, the Virgin Mary was given the title "Mother of God."

5. Renan meticulously recovered all of these names.

6. Genesis 2:21–23.

7. Cf. Genesis.

8. Jean-Robert Armogathe.

9. Genesis 12:3.

10. Deuteronomy 21:23.

11. Jesus spoke similar words (Mk 12:31 and par.), presenting them as "the greatest commandment"; they are drawn from Leviticus 19:18.

Chapter 11: The Road to Damascus

1. Acts 19:21

2. The Judaizers.

3. Introduction to the Epistle to the Romans (TOB).

4. I cannot recommend highly enough the introduction to the Epistle to the Romans by the staff of the TOB—*Traduction oecumenique de la Bible.* As we know, this great work was born of one will: to present a French translation of the Bible common to all the different Christian faiths. In the spirit of its compilers, the Epistle to the Romans was considered as the test, because they were convinced that "the ecumenical translation of the Bible would not run up against insurmountable obstacles if the Epistle to the Romans could be presented in a version acceptable to all." According to the happy formula of the pastor Boegner, "the text of our divisions" had to become "the text of our encounter."

5. J. Murphy O'Connor.

6. The use of the word "the Jews" in the Scriptures designates the Jews who did not become Christians.

7. Other translations have been suggested: "enchained by the Spirit," which would mean that the Holy Spirit was pushing him, or again, "enchained in the Spirit."

8. Pierre-Antoine Bernheim.

Chapter 12: The Man in Chains

1. This is the only time in the New Testament that Christians are called Nazarenes, like Jesus.

2. Paul Dreyfus.

3. Among the graffiti that adorned the walls of a former tavern, excavations have uncovered the image of a crucified man.

Chapter 13: Paul and Nero

1. Georges Roux.

2. Jerome Carcopino.

3. *Legatio ad Caium*, 155.

4. *Antiquities* XVII, 134.

5. *Ars amatoria* I, 76.

6. Might we admit the possibility of a trip to Spain during the two years of Paul's captivity in Rome? Those who affirm it recall the Epistle to the Romans, in which Paul announced that after visiting Rome he planned to evangelize Spain. The plan did not anticipate that he would have arrived there—as would have been the case—in prisoner's chains. Others refer to the Letter of Clement

of Rome, which evokes Paul occupied with teaching justice "and reaching the limits of the West": could that have meant Spain? These calculations do not hold water. How can we suppose that the Roman authorities, who since Paul's incarceration at Caesarea had taken so many precautions to keep him in their power, would have let him leave to evangelize Spain? We would have to imagine Paul, under permanent surveillance by a guard, embarking for Spain armed with the authorization of the prefect of the praetorium and, his mission accomplished, coming back of his own accord to be decapitated. And this is not likely.

7. *The Acts of Paul,* translated by Wilhelm Schneemelcher and Rodolphe Kasser in *New Testament Apocrypha. Volume 2: Writings Relating to the Apostles; Apocalypses and Related Subjects* (Revised Edition), edited by Wilhelm Schneemelcher; English translation by R. McL. Wilson (Louisville: Westminster John Knox Press, 2003), 260.

8. The words "my nation" designate the people of Israel. We find this variant in the Western version of Acts: "But only to save my soul from death."

9. "Hindrances" here must be taken figuratively.

10. TOB refers to *Traduction oecumenique de la Bible,* the French translation of the Bible undertaken jointly by Catholic, Protestant, and Orthodox churches. It appeared in its final form in 1987.

11. *The Letter of the Church of Rome to the Church of Corinth, Commonly Called Clement's First Letter.*

12. *Ecclesiastical History,* II, XXV, 5.

13. *The Acts of Paul,* 262.

14. Translation from the papyrus of Hamburg. Cf. Marie-Françoise Baslez.

15. Pierre Geoltrain.

16. Saint Justin.

17. Jean-Marie Lustiger.

18. Justin was the author of the *Dialogue of Trypho,* a polemic with a Jew. He was canonized.

19. The adverb "alone" would cause rivers of ink to flow because it was not in Saint Paul. Luther would be embattled for years to show that adding the word was necessary for the thought to be understood in German.

20. F. Amiot.

21. E. Trocmé.

Appendix I: The Martyrdom of St. Paul

1. The *Hamburg Papyrus* begins again here.

2. Here an addition in the *Hamburg Papyrus* from the *Hamburg Papyrus,* p. 2. 24ff.

3. Addition in the *Hamburg Papyrus,* which, however, is poorly preserved.

4. Addition in the *Hamburg Papyrus:* "through the voice of the Holy Spirit.

INDEXES

Index of Names

Index of Places

BOOKS & MEDIA

The Daughters of St. Paul operate book and media centers at the following addresses. Visit, call or write the one nearest you today, or find us on the World Wide Web, www.pauline.org.

CALIFORNIA
3908 Sepulveda Blvd, Culver City, CA 90230 — 310-397-8676
5945 Balboa Avenue, San Diego, CA 92111 — 858-565-9181
2640 Broadway Street, Redwood City, CA 94063 — 650-369-4230

FLORIDA
145 S.W. 107th Avenue, Miami, FL 33174 — 305-559-6715

HAWAII
1143 Bishop Street, Honolulu, HI 96813 — 808-521-2731
Neighbor Islands call: — 866-521-2731

ILLINOIS
172 North Michigan Avenue, Chicago, IL 60601 — 312-346-4228

LOUISIANA
4403 Veterans Memorial Blvd, Metairie, LA 70006 — 504-887-7631

MASSACHUSETTS
885 Providence Hwy, Dedham, MA 02026 — 781-326-5385

MISSOURI
9804 Watson Road, St. Louis, MO 63126 — 314-965-3512

NEW JERSEY
561 U.S. Route 1, Wick Plaza, Edison, NJ 08817 — 732-572-1200

NEW YORK
150 East 52nd Street, New York, NY 10022 — 212-754-1110

PENNSYLVANIA
9171-A Roosevelt Blvd, Philadelphia, PA 19114 — 215-676-9494

SOUTH CAROLINA
243 King Street, Charleston, SC 29401 — 843-577-0175

TENNESSEE
4811 Poplar Avenue, Memphis, TN 38117 — 901-761-2987

TEXAS
114 Main Plaza, San Antonio, TX 78205 — 210-224-8101

VIRGINIA
1025 King Street, Alexandria, VA 22314 — 703-549-3806

CANADA
3022 Dufferin Street, Toronto, ON M6B 3T5 — 416-781-9131

¡También somos su fuente para libros,
videos y música en español!